Professional
Automated
Trading

Founded in 1807, John Wiley & Sons is the oldest independent publishing company in the United States. With offices in North America, Europe, Australia and Asia, Wiley is globally committed to developing and marketing print and electronic products and services for our customers' professional and personal knowledge and understanding.

The Wiley Finance series contains books written specifically for finance and investment professionals as well as sophisticated individual investors and their financial advisors. Book topics range from portfolio management to e-commerce, risk management, financial engineering, valuation and financial instrument analysis, as well as much more.

For a list of available titles, visit our Web site at www.WileyFinance.com.

Professional Automated Trading

Theory and Practice

EUGENE A. DURENARD

WILEY

Contents

Preface

*P*rofessional Automated Trading, Theory and Practice: comes from several years of research and practice of successful implementation of automated systematic trading strategies in the context of proprietary trading at a few major financial institutions and my own firm.

On one hand, trading is a science that is based on a variety of techniques coming from mathematics, physics, psychology, biology, and various computer science techniques. On the other hand it is an art of knowing and respecting the market and equally importantly of knowing oneself. But foremost it is a business that hinges on a carefully understood discipline and process of seeking reward under risk.

This book presents some of the science and some of the process involved in building a scalable diversified systematic trading business. The art is mostly left to the reader: You are encouraged to find your own way of crystallizing your intuition about the external world and translating it into trading models and risk management that fit best your psychology, capital, and business constraints.

The aim is to provide a set of tools to build a robust systematic trading business and is mostly directed toward proprietary trading groups, quantitative hedge funds, proprietary desks, and market-making businesses at investment banks, and asset management companies, as well as ambitious individual traders seeking to manage their own wealth on such principles.

The book is divided into an introductory section and four parts, each coming with a specific sub-goal. The introductory chapter aims at comparing the systematic and discretionary trading disciplines from several angles. They are discussed in the philosophical, business, and psychological contexts. It is an important analysis as it shows that the two disciplines are equally valid as far as their raison d'être and business efficiency are concerned. Hence it is argued that the choice between the two hinges on the psychological makeup of the trader. An overview of various types of systematic market players and specific techniques are presented in the historical context.

The book's central idea is to frame systematic trading in the framework of autonomous adaptive agents. This framework comes from recent studies in robotics and artificial life systems. It opens the avenue to implement concepts of adaptation, evolution, and learning of trading agents. It also aims at bridging the gap between systematic and discretionary trading by making those robotic trading agents acquire some animal-like traits. It is very much research in progress and a fascinating area with a lot of future potential.

Part One introduces the basic conceptual and programmatic framework for the design of trading strategies as trading agents. The representation of the agent's core decision making by way of reactive finite-state machines is introduced. The framework also allows the trading agents to communicate and signal to each other either in a parallel or sequential computational cycle.

The discussion continues with a set of broad types of automatic decision-making models that perform in various market regimes. In particular basic trend-following, breakout, mean-reversion, acceleration, and conditional market-making strategies are discussed.

As diversification of markets and models is most important for success, a fair amount of emphasis is put on designing tools that enable efficient treatment of portfolios. The concept of an aggregate agent is introduced for this purpose.

Detailed implementations of back- and forward-testing engines are presented and pitfalls associated with curve-fitting and statistical insignificance are discussed.

The goal of Part Two is to give the reader insights into building robust trading systems that can gracefully withstand changes of regime. The agent-based representation of strategies is a handy and natural framework for making progress toward this goal.

Trading strategies can be seen as filters that help discover implicit market regimes and changes of regime. When the market regime changes, strategies that were compatible with the old regime may lose performance whereas other strategies may start performing better with the arrival of the next regime. In order to quantify strategy performance and exploit its variability, absolute and relative fitness measures are introduced.

One avenue to adaptation comes from studying the persistence of performance of parametric sets of nonadaptive strategies. It is realized via the implementation of an automatic choice mechanism that switches between a set of nonadaptive strategies. The book introduces swarm systems that are aggregate agents that embed various types of switching mechanisms.

The discussion encompasses the robustness and effectiveness of the choice mechanisms underlying the swarm systems. Measures of efficiency are introduced and ideas from reinforcement learning are used to train the parameters of the choice algorithms.

This paradigm for adaptation can be explained in the following terms. The collection of nonadaptive strategies is a set of potential behaviors of the aggregate adaptive agent. The adaptive agent runs all those potential behaviors in parallel in a simulation mode. It is endowed with criteria to choose a subset of behaviors that is expected to produce a positive performance over the next foreseeable future. This is the behavior that the agent implements in real trading. As time unfolds, the agent learns from experience to choose its behavior more effectively. Effectiveness means that as the market goes through various cycles of regime changes, the performance during those change periods does not degrade.

From this it is evident, because history tends to repeat itself, that it is wise to endow the swarm system with a large enough set of potential behaviors that have proved to be effective at some periods of the past. However a degree of innovation is also needed, akin to the exploration versus exploitation in reinforcement learning. This aspect is touched upon and constitutes an active area of my research at present.

Part Three focuses on the important aspect of trading costs and slippage. It starts with the analysis of the intra-day bid-offer and volume seasonality in major markets, then explores the volume-price response functions. It discusses several algorithmic execution strategies designed to help reduce market impact once a decision to trade had been made.

Part Four presents the implementation of a scalable and efficient low-latency trading architecture that is able to support a set of signals generated by a swarm of adaptive models. The complexity of dealing with real-time swarm systems leads to design the whole trading architecture on the basis of feedbacks between a set of distributed concurrent components.

The discussion encompasses design patterns for data and state persistence, the advantages of designing different components in different appropriately chosen languages, and a domain model that allows seamless communications between these components via message-passing algorithms.

Efficiency constraints on data representation and complexity for internal and external communications and various protocols are touched upon. Details of the order management system (OMS) with its architecture of a recursive controller are given. The OMS is further optimized by allowing order aggregation.

Solving the inverse problem of dis-aggregation at the middle-office level an infrastructure able to support a "dark pool" is discussed.

A variety of real-time human interface controllers that are necessary to complete various feedbacks in the system are presented. In particular the real-time risk, P & L, position managers, and the model controllers are discussed.

As the whole architecture itself is designed to be robust and resilient to various bottleneck or disconnect issues, emphasis is on advice to architect the system in a way that ensures fast self-recovery and minimal downtime.

Robustness and continuity also need to be achieved at the level of releases and patches. Solutions are suggested from standpoints of software and hardware.

Finishing with hardware, the state of my own practical research is discussed. It applies techniques from parallel processing on one hand and designer chips on the other hand to further improve the efficiency of the original design in certain appropriate situations.

The theoretical Parts One to Three can be read independently of the practical Part Four yet there is a definite logical thread running through them. Many designs in Part Four were introduced to specifically address the concepts introduced in Parts One to Three in concrete implementations that I and my teams performed in practice.

This book aims to provide a methodology to set up a framework for practical research and selection of trading models and to provide tools for their implementation in a real-time low-latency environment. Thus it requires readers to have some knowledge of certain mathematical techniques (calculus, statistics, optimization, transition graphs, and basic operations research), certain functional and object-oriented programming techniques (mostly LISP and Java), and certain programming design patterns (mostly dealing with concurrency and multithreading). Most modern concepts coming from research in evolutionary computing, robotics, and artificial life are introduced in an intuitive manner with ample references to relevant literature.

As one sees from this overview this book is first of all a synthesis of many concepts coming from various domains of knowledge. As an academic environment, I always feel the importance to institute a creative environment with little legacy or a priori dogmas that allow for the confluence of various ideas to bear fruit.

I hope that this book will provide an inspiration to creatively compete in the fascinating world of automated trading of free markets. In the same sense that trading is a means-ends process that maximizes the reward-to-risk ratio, the design of the architecture of the trading technology is a means-ends process that maximizes the throughput-to-downtime ratio. I aim to demonstrate that the two concepts are intimately, linked in the modern world.

I am dedicating this book to my parents Alexis and Larissa, who encouraged me to start it and to my soulmate Caroline who has supported me throughout the process of writing it.

I would like to thank the whole team at Wiley, and in particular Bill Falloon, Meg Freeborn, Tiffany Charbonier and Vincent Nordhaus for all their help and guidance during the writing and editing process.

CHAPTER 1

Introduction to Systematic Trading

S ystematic trading is a particular discipline of trading, which is one of the oldest human activities. Trading and the associated arena set by the marketplace coevolved in time to become one of the dominant industries on the planet. At each stage of their development, new efficiencies were introduced.

Starting as barter where goods were exchanged "on sight," the first major evolutionary step was the introduction of a numeraire (be it gold or fiat money) that literally allowed comparison between apples and oranges. It also allowed the storage of value in a compact way. Then the first organized exchanges in Flanders and Holland introduced several key concepts: first and foremost the concept of the exchange as a risk disintermediator, then the concept of standardization so important in comparing bulk commodities, and finally the technique of open outcry—the famous Dutch Auction at the basis of the modern exchange mechanism. Despite the fact that the concept of interest (via grain loans) was introduced by the Egyptians, the effective leverage in the marketplace only came with the growth of the stock markets and commodity futures markets in the United States in the early twentieth century. Also at that point the nascent global banking system spurred the creation of the money market where short-term loans are traded in a standardized fashion and help to transfer leverage between counterparties. An important factor in the stabilization of the market process was the introduction of floor specialists or market-makers who ensured orderly matching of buyers and sellers. With the advent of increasing computing power, the co-evolution of the marketplace and the trading associated with it has accelerated further. Not only has the banking system evolved into a global network of compensating agents where money can be transferred at the speed of light, but the whole flow of information has become available to a much larger group. The marketplace and trading have become truly global and gradually more electronic. This evolution has taken its toll on the open outcry system and on specialists, with some of them being gradually crowded out by robotic market-making computer programs and the increasing importance of semi-private matching engines like dark pools and electronic commerce networks (ECNs).

And this is where we are right now, a world some would say of information overflow, of competition for microseconds, of over-leverage and over-speculation. Each evolutionary stage comes with its share of positives and negatives. A new organism has to keep searching for its boundaries independently of its forebears and try to learn from its rewards and mistakes so as to set the stage for its own progress.

This book focuses on a subset of trading techniques that applies to a subset of the marketplace. It explores the systematic automated trading of liquid instruments such as foreign exchange, futures, and equities. It is an activity on the edge of the evolutionary path that also tries to find its current boundaries, technologically and conceptually.

This introductory chapter sets the philosophical context of trading and puts on equal footing the seemingly contradictory approaches of systematic and discretionary trading. They are compared as business activities by presenting a cost-benefit analysis of each, concluding with the viability and similarity of both. The psychological implications of choosing one path over the other is analyzed and it is argued that it is the defining criterion from a rational trader's perspective. The chapter concludes by putting the theoretical Parts One to Three and the practical Part Four of the book into the historic context and showing how the evolution of systematic trading is intimately related to the progress in technology and science.

1.1   DEFINITION OF SYSTEMATIC TRADING

The majority of successful traders design their trading strategy and trading discipline in the most objective way possible but cannot be qualified as systematic, because many of their decisions are based on their perceived state of the world, the state of their mind, and other factors that cannot be computationally quantified. The type of trading that is relying on noncomputable processes will be qualified as discretionary in this book.

As opposed to the discretionary, the qualifier *systematic* encompasses the following two concepts:

1. The existence of a rules-driven trading strategy that is based on objectively reproducible (computable) inputs.
2. The application of that strategy with discipline and outside of the human emotional context.

Systematic trading implies the construction of a mathematical model of a certain behavior of the market. This model is then encompassed in a decision-making algorithm that outputs continuously the allocation of exposure to such a model in the context of the trader's other models' behavior, total risk allocation, and other objective and reproducible inputs. The continuous running of such an algorithm is oftentimes best left to a robot.

Before making further comparisons let us now explore the two trading approaches in a broader philosophical context of the perceived behavior of the market and its participants.

1.2 PHILOSOPHY OF TRADING

The philosophy of trading derives from a set of beliefs about the workings of the human mind, the behavior of crowds of reward-seeking individuals, and the resulting greed-fear dynamics in the market. Trading is a process, a strategy, a state of mind. It is the mechanism by which a market participant survives and thrives in the marketplace that itself is composed of such participants and constrained by political and regulatory fads and fashions.

Choosing a trading style is as much about knowing and understanding the workings of the market as it is knowing and understanding oneself. The nonemotional self-analysis of behavior under stresses of risk, reward, and discipline are part of the personal effort any trader has to evolve through, most often by trial and error. I will defer comments on this self-analysis to later and will now focus on the more objective and observable part related to the market.

1.2.1 Lessons from the Market

Let us first see what conclusions we can derive from observing the market as a whole and the behavior of its participants. The most relevant observations can be summarized as follows:

- *Macroeconomic information unfolds gradually, therefore prices do not discount future events immediately.* Why is it the case that at the peak of the business cycle asset prices do not discount its next through and vice versa? Because no one knows when the next through is coming despite the seeming regularity of business cycles. Things always look so optimistic on the top and so pessimistic at the bottom. This is why we observe long-term trends in all asset prices and yields.

- *The leverage in the market yields a locally unstable system because individuals have finite capital and are playing the game so as to survive the next round.* This instability is increased by the asymmetry between game-theoretic behaviors of accumulation and divestment of risky positions. When you accumulate a position you have all the incentive in the world to tell all your friends, and it is a self-fulfilling virtuous circle as people push prices in "your" direction, thus increasing your profit. This is the epitome of a cooperative game. On the other hand, when you divest, you have no incentive to tell anyone as they may exit before you, pushing prices away from you. This is a classic Prisoner's Dilemma game where it is rational to defect, as it is not seen as a repeated game. This is why we observe a great deal of asymmetry between up and down moves in prices of most assets, as well as price breakouts and violent trend reversals.

- *There is a segmentation of market participants by their risk-taking ability, their objectives, and their time frames.* Real-money investors have a different attitude to drawdowns than highly leveraged hedge funds. Pension fund managers rotate investments quarterly whereas automated market-makers can switch the sign of their inventory in a quarter of a second. In general, though, each segment reacts in a similar way to price movements on their particular scale of sampling. This explains the self-similarity of several patterns at different price and time scales.

- *The market as a whole has a consensus-building tendency, which implies learning at certain timescales.* This is why some strategy classes or positions have diminishing returns. When people hear of a good money-making idea, they herd into it until it loses its money-making appeal.

- *The market as a whole has a fair amount of participant turnover, which implies un-learning at certain longer timescales.* A new generation of market participants very rarely learns the lessons of the previous generation. If it were not the case why are we going through booms and busts with the suspicious regularity commensurate to a trading career lifespan of 15 to 20 years?

- *There is no short-term relationship between price and value.* To paraphrase Oscar Wilde, a trader is a person who knows the price of everything but the value of nothing.

1.2.2 Mechanism vs. Organism

The above observations do not reflect teachings of the economic orthodoxy based on the concept of general equilibrium, which is a fairly static view of the economic landscape. They become more naturally accepted when one realizes that the market itself is a collection of living beings and that macro-economics is an emergent property of the society we live in. The society, akin to an organism, evolves and so does the market with it. The complexity of the macroeconomy and of the market is greater than what is implied by overly mechanistic or, even worse, static models.

In thinking about the market from this rather lofty perspective, one is naturally drawn into the debate of mechanism versus organism, the now classic debate between biology and physics. The strict mechanistic view of economics, where the course of events is determined via an equilibrium con-cept resulting from the interaction of a crowd of rational agents, has clearly not yielded many robust predictions or even ex post explanations of real-ized events in the last 100 years of its existence. Thus despite the elaborate concepts and complicated mathematics, this poor track record causes me to reject the mechanistic view of the world that this prism provides.

The purely organistic view of the market is probably a far fetch from reality as well. First of all, the conceptual definition of an *organism* is not even yet well understood, other than being a pattern in time of organized and linked elements where functional relationships between its constituents are delocalized and therefore cannot be reduced to the concept of a mecha-nism (that is, a set of independent parts only linked by localized constraints). There are clearly delocalized relationships in the market, and stresses in one dimension (whether geographic location, asset class, regulatory change, etc.) quickly propagate to other areas. This is in fact one of the sources of vari-ability in correlations between different asset classes as well as participants' behaviors. On the other hand, on average these correlation and behavioral relationships are quite stable. Also, unlike in a pure organism, the removal or death of a "market organ" would not necessarily imply the breakdown of the organism (i.e., market) as a whole. For example, the various sovereign debt defaults and write-downs in the past did not yield the death of the global bond market.

1.2.3 The Edge of Complexity

So, intuitively the market is not as simple as Newton equations nor is it as complicated as an elephant or a mouse. Its complexity lies somewhere in between. It has pockets of coherence and of randomness intertwined in time. A bit like a school of silverside fish that in normal circumstances has an amorphic structure but at the sight of a barracuda spontaneously polarizes into beautiful geometric patterns.

The good thing is that the market is the most observable and open human activity, translated into a series of orders, trades, and price changes—numbers at the end of the day that can be analyzed ad nauseam. The numeric analysis of time series of prices also yields a similar conclusion. The prices or returns do not behave as Gaussian processes or white noise but have distributional properties of mild chaotic systems, or as Mandelbrot puts it, turbulence. They are nonstationary, have fat tails, clustering of volatility that is due to clustering of autocorrelation, and are non-Markovian. A very good overview of the real world properties of price time series is given in *Theorie des Risques Financiers* by Bouchard and Potters.

1.2.4 Is Systematic Trading Reductionistic?

As per the definition above, systematic trading is essentially a computable model of the market. Via its algorithmic nature it can appear to be a more reductionistic approach than discretionary trading. A model reduces the dimensionality of the problem by extracting the "signal" from the "noise" in a mathematical way. A robotic application of the algorithm may appear overly simplistic.

On the other hand, discretionary traders often inhibit their decision making by strong beliefs ("fight a trend") or do not have the physical ability to focus enough attention on many market situations thus potentially leaving several opportunities on the table. So discretionary trading also involves an important reduction in dimensionality but this reduction is happening differently for different people and times.

1.2.5 Reaction vs. Proaction

A common criticism of systematic trading is that it is based on backward-looking indicators. While it is true that many indicators are filters whose calculation is based on past data, it is not true that they do not have predictive power. It is also true that many systematic model types have explicitly predictive features, like some mean-reversion and market-making models.

At the same time one cannot say that discretionary trading or investing strategies are based solely on the concept or attempts of prediction. Many expectational models of value, for example the arbitrage pricing theory or the capital asset pricing model, are based on backward-looking calculations of covariances and momentum measures. Despite the fact that those models try to "predict" reversion to some normal behavior, the predictive model is normally backward-looking. As Niels Bohr liked to say, it is very difficult to predict, especially the future.

1.2.6 Arbitrage?

Many times I've heard people arguing that the alpha in systematic strategies should not exist because everyone would arbitrage them away, knowing the approximate models people use. The same could be argued for all the discretionary strategies as most of the approaches are well known as well. Thus the market should cease trading and remain stuck in the utopian equilibrium state. Yet none of this happens in reality and the question is why? Probably exactly because of the fact that people do not believe that other people's strategies will work. So as much as it is seemingly simple to arbitrage price discrepancies away, it is less simple to arbitrage strategies away. Having said that, the market system in itself is cyclical and, as mentioned above, strategies get arbitraged away temporarily, until the arbitrageurs blow up all at the same time because of their own sheer concentration of risk and the cycle restarts with new entrants picking up the very valuable mispriced pieces.

1.2.7 Two Viable Paths

Viewing trading and the market from this level yields a positivist view on the different ways to profit from it. The discretionary traders see in it enough complexity to justify their approach of nonmechanizable intuition, insight, and chutzpah. The systematic traders see in it enough regularity to justify their approach of nonemotional pattern matching, discipline, and robotic abidance to model signals.

Which approach is right then becomes a matter of personal taste, as the edge of complexity the market presents us with does not allow for a rational decision between the two. In fact both approaches are right, but not necessarily all the time and not for everyone. Of course the Holy Grail is to be able to combine the two—to become an übertrader who is as disciplined as a robot in its mastery of human intuition.

This book of course does not offer the Holy Grail to trading; intuition and insight are quite slippery concepts and highly personal. There is no one way. But this work is not interested either in focusing on the same old mechanistic techniques that appeared at numerous occasions in books on systematic trading. It aims at moving further afield toward the edge of complexity, by giving enough structure, process, and discipline to manage a set of smarter, adaptive, and complex strategies.

1.3 THE BUSINESS OF TRADING

If, as was derived in the last section, there is no a priori rational way to choose between discretionary and systematic trading paths, one should then aim at objectively comparing the two approaches as business propositions. Seeing it this way will lead naturally to a choice based on the trader's own psychology; that is, which of the two business propositions is the most compatible with the inner trust of his own ability to sustain and stand behind that business activity over time.

The goal of a business is to produce a dividend to its stakeholder. Any sustainable business is built on four pillars:

1. *Capital:* provides the necessary initial critical mass to launch the business and sustain it through ups and downs
2. *Product:* the edge of the business, the innovation relative the rest of the competition
3. *Factory:* the process by which the products are manufactured, which is an integral part of the edge itself
4. *Marketing:* the means by which information about the product reaches the outside world and helps replenish the capital, thus closing the loop

Both discretionary and systematic trading businesses should be seen in the context of those necessary contexts. Of course trading is not per se manufacturing of anything other than P & L. So the product is the trader's edge or algorithm and the factory is the continuous application of such trading activity in the market. Marketing is the ability to raise more capital or assets under management based on performance, regulatory environment, or good looks. Here the *trader* can mean an individual, a group, or a corporate body.

So let us do a comparison between systematic and discretionary trading, keeping in mind the above concepts.

1.3.1 Profitability and Track Record

Before one even starts looking at the individual pillars of business, can one say anything about the long-term profitability of the two trading styles? This is an important question as it may provide a natural a priori choice: If one type of business is dominantly more profitable than the other then why bother with the laggard?

Interestingly it is a hard question to answer as the only objective data that exists in the public domain is on hedge fund and mutual fund performance. Any of the profitability data of bank proprietary desks is very hard to come by as it is not usually disclosed in annual reports. Also the mutual funds should be excluded on the basis of the fact that their trading style is mostly passive and index-tracking. This leaves us with comparing discretionary to systematic hedge funds.

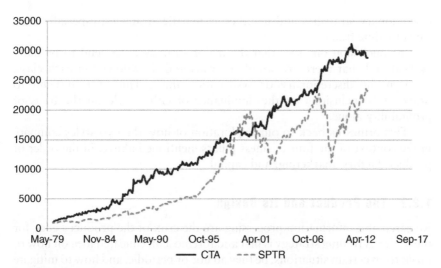

FIGURE 1.1 HFR CTA Index versus SP500 Total Return Index

In both camps there is a wide variety of underlying strategies. In the discretionary camp the strategies are long-short equity, credit, fixed-income relative value, global macro, special situations, and so on. On the systematic side the strategies are commodity trading advisors (CTAs), statistical arbitrage, high-frequency conditional market-makers, and so on. What is the right comparison: absolute return, assets under management (AUM)–weighted return, return on shareholders equity? Because private partnership is the dominant corporate structure for hedge funds, the return on shareholders equity is not a statistically significant comparison as far as publicly available data is concerned. Hence one has no choice but to compare strategy returns. As on average the fee structure is similar in both camps, one may as well compare net returns to investors.

Figure 1.1 shows the comparative total return on the Hedge Fund Research CTA Index and the total return on the SP500 stock index. Table 1.1 shows the comparative statistics of major Hedge Fund Research strategy indices from 1996 to 2013.

Some of the earliest hedge funds were purely systematic and have survived until now despite the well-known attrition in the hedge fund industry as a whole. Many commodity trading advisors and managed account firms have been involved in the systematic trading business for at least 40 years. Their track record represents an interesting testament to the robustness of the systematic approach, from the performance and process perspective. Also systematic strategies have in general low correlation to discretionary strategies and to other systematic strategies, especially classified by time frame.

In conclusion one sees that the major strategy types tend to be quite cyclical and that there are sizable up-runs and drawdowns in each class, be it in the discretionary or systematic camps. Thus it is difficult to draw any conclusions on the dominance of either style on the basis of profitability alone.

This brings us back to our exploration of how the two styles compare in the context of the four business pillars mentioned above, in the order of product, factory, marketing, and capital.

1.3.2 The Product and Its Design

Research and information processing are the crux of the product's edge for the trader. A trading strategy is first and foremost an educated idea on how to profit from certain situations, be they ad hoc or periodic, and how to mitigate losses from unexpected events. It requires an ability to gather, process, and research a large quantity of information.

Information   In the discretionary world, this information is categorized into the following seven areas and the trader forms an intuiton based on this set in order to pull the trigger:

1. Macroeconomic
2. Political
3. Asset-class specific
4. Idiosyncratic to a company
5. Specific to a security (share, bond, etc.)
6. Price and transactional
7. Flow and holdings

The majority of the time in the systematic world, the information required is limited to the price and transactional and in rarer occasions on the holdings and flows (such as the Commitment of Traders report in the futures markets). Most of the systematic models base their decision making on the extraction of repeatable patterns from publicly available data on prices and executions. The statistical significance of such patterns is derived from simulation (the action of back- and forward-testing).

Both activities are clearly information-intensive but this intensity manifests itself in quite different dimensions. The discretionary style requires processing of a broad scope of nonnumerical data, and traders read and rely on a range of broker and analyst research along with continuous news and political analysis. A lot of useful information is also seen in the flow and holdings that are obtained via brokers, that is, who are the transacting participants and how much. This in itself implies that discretionary trading is difficult to do solo and often requires teams of people to digest all the information flow. Interestingly, some firms have started creating numerical sentiment indices based on textual and voice news flows, a technique used initially by intelligence agencies to discover subtle changes in political rhetoric.

For the systematic style, the dimensionality of the information is much lower; the models are in general only interested in price or tick data but they require a continuous feed and automated processing of this data at high speeds, especially in the current context of the ECNs. This means that from a technological perspective, especially for high-frequency business, the required connectivity and throughput needs to be large. This in general has cost implications.

Most systematic models also require prior and continuous recalibration, thus large databases of historical data need to be kept for research purposes.

Research Information is useless if it cannot be interpreted in context, be it intuitive or model based. To be able to form such an educated view, some research needs to be performed on the relevant data.

In the discretionary context, most useful research falls into (1) political and regulatory analysis, (2) macroeconomic analysis, (3) asset-specific research, or (4) quantitative research. Many investment banks and institutions have large departments focused on macroeconomic analysis and asset-specific research. Discretionary traders or teams have access to such research via prime brokerage relationships and those costs are implicitly absorbed into trading and clearing fees. A few smaller private firms run by former bank or government institutions officials provide political and regulatory analysis and macroeconomic analysis for fees and also use their former contacts to introduce clients to current central bankers, finance ministers, and other officials. Such relationships are invaluable for certain strategies such as global macro, where fund managers constantly try to read between the lines for changes of moods or rhetoric in order to form their own expectations on upcoming policy moves. Thus a lot of research that is valuable for discretionary trading is already out there. It needs to be gathered, filtered, read, and distilled to be presented to the portfolio managers. Large discretionary hedge funds hire in-house economists and analysts to do such work but many operate just using publicly available and broker research.

There is a subset of discretionary strategies that is driven by quantitative modeling. Fixed-income relative value, long-short equity, and volatility strategies are such areas, for example. Each require a fair amount of advanced mathematical techniques, pricing tools, and risk management tools. Although there is commercially available software with standard libraries for pricing options, interpolating yield curves, or handling large-scale covariance analysis, the vast majority of quantitative discretionary operations employ in-house quants to write a series of models and pricing tools as well as to maintain the relevant data and daily process. This has clear cost implications on such businesses.

The systematic approach is entirely research-driven and in a very direct sense research innovation is the backbone of the business. The principal areas of research fall into the following four categories:

1. *Individual Models.* The goal is to produce a set of diversified robust trading agents that exploit various repeatable price and trade patterns. Various techniques of back- and forward-testing are employed for this goal. It is the key area for the success of the whole business. It is the focus of Part One.
2. *Adaptation of Model Portfolios.* The goal is to produce an automated allocation rule for a portfolio of models by studying the persistence of behavioral regimes of individual models. It is an important area for integrated risk management in the high-frequency trading domain. Part Two is dedicated to some of my findings in the matter.
3. *Trading Costs Minimization.* The goal is to minimize market impact from model execution by slicing the trades according to various execution algorithms that derive mostly from liquidity distributional analysis. This is explored in Part Three.
4. *Trading Process Optimization.* The goal is to optimize the trading process from the perspective of computational efficiency as well as to ensure fast recoverability from downtime. It is a vast area to which the practical Part Four is dedicated. It encompasses the design of low-latency order management systems and their coupling with various model engines, domain models for state persistence and recovery, distribution of computational tasks among components, and so on.

These four categories are closely intertwined in automated systematic trading and demonstrating this concretely is an important feature of this book.

1.3.3 The Trading Factory

Process Designing and implementing a disciplined trading process on the basis of either computable or subjective signals is key to the success of the business of trading. The process presupposes an infrastructure and a technology optimized for the production of the trading widget. It is not enough to have a good widget idea; one also has to be able to manufacture it efficiently. Of course, having a great factory producing widgets that no one wants is a waste of time and money. But as much as great trade ideas or strategies are necessary, they are not sufficient if not implemented correctly. The underlying processes of discretionary and systematic businesses present many similarities but also major differences, as we will show now.

In the discretionary world, choosing the winning set of human traders is key. The traders have to have at least the following four features, with the last three criteria being essentially a strong self-discipline:

1. *Profitability:* Ability to generate revenues in different market conditions
2. *Predator Mentality:* Proactive trade idea generation stemming from continuous information processing accompanied by aggressive sizing into good opportunities
3. *Ego Management:* Proactive risk management and survival skills
4. *Clear Head:* Knowing when not to overstay one's welcome in the market and take time off when the picture is not clear

Several successful traders have published honest and objective self-analyses of their occasional failings in instituting such discipline, courage, or focus and drew lessons for the benefit of the whole trading community. Of course longer-term survival let alone profitability hinges on the discipline of applying the trading process as per the last three criteria.

As mentioned in the previous section, the systematic business is research-driven. The principal goal of that research is to produce a portfolio of profitable models. It implies that the continuous fostering of innovative research is a key element to the process and to the success of the business. Finding a set of robust models in the systematic world is equivalent to hiring a desk of good traders in the discretionary world.

The systematic approach a priori formalizes a lot of the individual trader's discipline as models are run continuously, have embedded stop-losses and profit targets, and can be scheduled to be turned on or off during certain periods. The trading process is thus run as an algorithm. The key four features for success are similar in nature to those mentioned above:

1. *Profitability:* A diversified set of models that are profitable in various market conditions
2. *Continuous Monitoring:* The models are continuously processing data and output either position or order changes, thus opportunities are exploited to the maximum, 24 hours a day and across many markets
3. *Dynamic Risk Management:* Portfolios of models have an embedded dynamic sizing algorithm that controls the exposure as a function of the performance of each model and the portfolio as a whole

4. *Model Fitness:* A higher-level feedback mechanism compares a portfolio of possible models and dynamically chooses a subset to trade on the basis of a fitness measure, thus models are demoted and promoted dynamically from a prior set of potential candidates

The systematic trading process is much more involved than the discretionary one as by its nature it is automated. The increased complexity comes from the fact that many things that are second nature to humans are actually hard to implement in software (for example, automatic recovery mechanisms from data disconnects or loss). It is a technology-driven process as the technology implements the factory element. Thus from the technology perspective, the systematic business requires an investment into software and hardware much larger than for the discretionary business. We focus in Part Four on the analysis of the various key elements one needs to master to put such a process in place.

Cooperation   We have come to another important aspect of the nature of communication and cooperation within the two businesses. In a discretionary hedge fund, especially in areas like global macro, there is a tendency to encourage trade diversification by discouraging communication between various traders. This is a noncooperative game scenario and some funds push it even further by encouraging traders to compete for the biggest risk allocation from the same pot thus creating potential friction, jealousy, and mutual dislike between people.

Interestingly, on the systematic side such selection is done implicitly by the higher-order model feedback mechanism. So the noncooperative game is left to the machine and one does not hear models screaming or squealing when they get demoted. The research process, though, has to be a cooperative game where cooperation between team members serves the exact purpose of creating a diversified portfolio of models. Efficient systematic research has to be run on the examplar of academic institutions where people are given enough leeway to innovate and learn from communication with each other, and are driven by the common good of cooperative success.

There is another important cooperative game going on in the systematic trading business. It is the natural synergy between the research, development, technology, infrastructure, and monitoring teams. Research needs an optimized implementation that in turn needs efficient technology run on a robust infrastructure that is being monitored continuously. All areas need research to come up with money-making models to produce cash and sustain the whole food chain. The success of some large systematic funds is corroborated by my own knowledge of the way such cooperation had been instituted within them.

1.3.4 Marketing and Distribution

The differences in the products and processes discussed above imply differences in the approach to marketing and branding of discretionary and systematic strategies. One could say that the brand of a discretionary trading business falls more into the craft category, whereas the brand of a systematic trading business falls more into an industry category. The last remark could be justified from our analysis of the process, not the product. Both product design processes are crafts, coming from accumulated intuition of traders on one hand and researchers on the other. From a marketing perspective, the element of skill is crucial in both worlds.

One could argue that it is somewhat easier for a newcomer to launch a systematic fund rather than a discretionary fund. The crucial point that comes in all capital raising discussions is the ability to produce a credible track record. It is difficult for discretionary traders to have a track record unless they have traded before, which is of course possible only if they traded their own money or could take their track record from a previous firm (a very tricky exercise in itself). Thus the majority of discretionary traders start in market-making and other sell-side careers then graduate to a proprietary trader status. Only then can they start to build their independent track record.

The situation is quite different in systematic trading as there is a reasonable degree of acceptance among allocators of back-tested and paper-traded track records. This of course supposes that the simulated net asset value (NAV) contains a realistic (or, even better, pessimistic) assessment of transaction costs, scalability, and sustainability of the market access and the trading process in general. The discussion then focuses on how this track record was generated and whether there was a risk of over-fitting and using future information in the process of building the models.

Once the fund has been launched, let us compare the hypothetical clues to answer the four main types of questions clients would usually ask while doing their due-diligence assessment:

1. *Can your profitability be sustained?* In the discretionary world, everything hinges on the ability of the head trader to keep performing, whereas in the systematic world, it is all about the quality and innovation of the head of research.
2. *Is your market risk management robust?* In the systematic world, risk management is embedded in the model and portfolio processes and can be explained very clearly. In the discretionary world, it is usually harder to formalize and a fair amount of due-diligence time goes into drilling the head trader on the reaction to various past and hypothetical

situations, as well as on the discipline with which the trading team abides by the constraints imposed on them by the risk management team.

3. *What is your operational risk?* In the discretionary world, one source of operational risk is the key man risk. Once the head trader gets run over by the proverbial bus so goes the fund generally. In the systematic world, once the automated process has been put in place the focus is on its sustainability and resilience. One has to show that the process has live disaster-recovery sites and can be rerouted or delocalized if need be to protect from data loss and market disconnects. The aspects of accumulated data recovery as well as people relocation in case of premises incapacitation are the same in both worlds.

4. *What is your capacity?* This of course depends on the time frame of trading given the liquidity of products traded. In the systematic world, one could argue that it is easier to estimate the impact of increased trading volume on transaction costs because most products are exchange traded or have excellent price and volume transparency.

In conclusion, I believe that it is somewhat easier to start a systematic fund but it requires a similar marketing effort as for a discretionary business.

1.3.5 Capital, Costs, and Critical Mass

Enlightened by the comparison of the three functional parts of the business, we now come to the crucial questions of necessary initial capital and of running capital for operations. Of course we need to compare the two businesses pari passu as far as size and revenue goals are concerned. We use the example of hedge funds because they are stand-alone entities where all costs and revenues can be objectively estimated.

How much is needed to start the business? In 2010, the realistic critical mass of initial capital needed to start a hedge fund business is north of $50 million and better at $100 million. The main reason is the structure of allocators—funds of hedge funds, asset managers, and family offices. Most of them will rarely look at a target with AUM below $50 million because they do not want to participate more than 10 percent in any fund. This helps them to reduce the risk of concentration of other clients in the fund if, of course, the other clients are also invested less than 10 percent each. As they get lesser fees than hedge funds themselves, an investment of less than $5 million is not worth the costs and time of due-diligence process.

It is actually not a bad thing for the fund itself as it forces it to be diversified in its client base, so that losing one client will not put the fund in jeopardy. But then the question comes down to the classic chicken-and-egg: How would one start a fund in this difficult environment? One needs to find a set of seed investors, hopefully all at the same time, a lot of performance luck, and a lot of marketing effort! This is the same across various strategies and the systematic business is no different from the discretionary in this respect. Thus the barriers of entry are quite high for either type of stand-alone trading business.

How much is needed to maintain the operations? As the seeders invariably take a cut of the economics, the resulting revenue is probably not the usual 2 percent management:20 percent performance fees structure but closer to 1 percent:15 percent. Assuming raising $50 million of AUM the first year, the realistic management fee revenue is around $500,000.

Certain types of trading styles can be perfectly run on minimal infrastructure consisting of the head trader (Chief Investment Officer), a middle-office person (Chief Operating Officer and Chief Risk Officer), and a marketing and client relationship person who can also hold the title of Chief Compliance Officer. Those four functions combined into three people tick the minimally accepted boxes as far as institutional allocators are concerned in their goal toward reducing operational and key-man risks. Other functions can be outsourced, in particular many back-office functions of control, fund administration, IT support, and legal support. The costs of renting a furnished office space plus utilities of course varies but be it offshore or onshore, it comes roughly to at least $50,000 per year. The IT and legal support costs, communications (phone and Bloomberg feed), and directors' and officers' insurance also come to at least $50,000 a year but may be larger. Adding travel and entertainment costs puts the total pre-salaries expenses at around $150,000 conservatively. The salary expenses then pretty much take up the rest of the fees, with usually $150,000 to the COO, $150,000 to the marketing person, and the rest to the head trader, who probably is the sole partner working for the upside call option. The business can survive one or two years on this without making extra trading revenue but if it does not, clients will usually pull the capital anyway. So the $50 million is indeed the low end, the necessary but not always sufficient critical initial mass.

There are several styles on the discretionary and systematic sides that are doable under the above setup. Those styles usually do not require either a large amount of assets to trade nor a high frequency of trading. Styles that would be difficult to fit in this minimal mold are, for example, equity statistical arbitrage, high-frequency systematic trading, global emerging markets strategies, and global credit strategies. These require more people trading more markets or a more complicated technology that needs to be overseen and run by more people.

For example, the high-frequency systematic business requires at least a team of two full-time researchers and two full-time technologists in addition to the minimal model above. From my personal experience in building such a business, this is required in order to ensure operational stability in a 24-hour operation. That automatically increases the costs by roughly $500,000 the first year and means that a realistic stand-alone critical mass for such a business becomes $100 million AUM. The statistical arbitrage style has very similar features. Of course, one could buy an off-the-shelf integrated solution that provides in the same package a financial information exchange (FIX) engine, connectivity setups, a complex event processor, databasing, and an ability to program in your models. Is this really cheaper than developing all the infrastructure in-house? Those packages are actually priced not far from the salary of two technologists. One still needs a technologist to maintain the system and a researcher for innovation, so the off-the-shelf solutions are not dissimilar in costs to building everything in-house.

Cost of Capital and Leverage   Another important consideration is the cost of running trading positions. Here the answer tends to be more clearly in favor of systematic strategies simply because they tend to use very liquid low-margin and exchange-traded products. The leverage in the most liquid products can be up to 50-to-1 even taking into account the extra margining imposed by prime brokers. On the contrary, many discretionary strategies exploit risk concessions that arise from liquidity premiums and those strategies essentially benefit from providing liquidity to the market. Some products, such as emerging market credit instruments and insurance-linked securities, have no leverage at all and one has to pay the full price to participate in them. So in general CTAs and other systematic trading strategies are quite long cash on which they can earn a premium whereas credit and arbitrage funds mostly borrow cash which sometimes can be costly.

How much is locally too much?   This means how much capital could be allocated to a single strategy style above, which the efficiency starts decreasing because of trading costs? In general scalability is directly proportional to the liquidity of the market traded and inversely proportional to the frequency of trading. Many discretionary strategies actually extract alpha by buying risk concession in illiquid instruments and hence have limited scalability. Systematic high-frequency price-taking strategies have limited scalability because they aggress the market and move it in the process. It is difficult to draw general conclusions and we will discuss this specifically for strategies on stocks, futures, and foreign exchange (FX) markets in Part Three.

How much is globally too much?   This means how much global commitment to the same class of strategies yields a decrease of efficiency for everyone involved? There is no hard answer to this but the study of damage from various strategy bubbles—the 1997 crash of carry trades, the subsequent crash of LTCM, the 2006 crash of Amaranth, the 2007 crash of statistical arbitrage, the 2008 crash of long carry in credit—all point out that this number is growing. The monetary inflation and quantitative easing only add to the fire. The next bubble is probably going to be bigger than the sum of the previous ones.

* * *

In conclusion, the systematic business has an advantage on the discretionary from the lower capital usage, but can have a disadvantage of higher up-front costs if one wants to compete at the cutting edge of technology and research.

1.4 PSYCHOLOGY AND EMOTIONS

The previous section aimed at showing that from an objective business perspective the systematic and discretionary trading activities have a lot in common. They all hinge on finding and maintaining efficient trading agents and instituting the adequate discipline for the trading process. Also the costs to start and maintain the businesses are comparable at comparable scales of revenue. Another section argued that longer-term profitabilities are on average the same. From a more conceptual and philosophic perspective based on our analysis of the market complexity, the two approaches are equally viable.

Thus we come to a subjective and personal point: What is the style of trading that is compatible with one's psychological makeup? In this section we try to suggest what trader psychologies best fit the two trading styles. My personal choice was made a long time ago in favor of systematic trading.

1.4.1 Ups and Downs

As simple as it sounds, the crucial psychological skill is the ability to deal with losses and gains. The volatility of the profits on the trading book is a natural feature of the trading process. The psychological ability to unemotionally deal with the upside and the downside volatility is the crucial aspect of the maintenance of the trading process.

The systematic approach embeds a sophisticated money management strategy. Not only does each model have its own sizing, stop-loss, and profit-taking rules, but the portfolio of models itself is managed on the basis of global sizing rules that allow it to deal with variability in correlations between the individual model returns. Also, automatic selection rules based on the fitness of each model can be introduced. Model-specific rules are explored in Part One and portfolio and fitness rules in Part Two. Part Three explores the important issue of slippage that must be taken into account to produce realistic downside expectations during periods of stress.

The discretionary approach does not formalize explicitly any such money management rules. Traders take a view on how much they can allow themselves to lose on a particular position and have expectations of how much they can gain. The risk manager is then responsible for making sure that the exposures do not breach certain levels of value at risk (VAR) or some other measure based on historical covariances.

The unformalized approach presents positives and negatives. On the negative side, there is no automated stop-loss. Often traders hang on to their positions because they "know" they are right. It is then only a matter of time before either the management or the traders themselves throw in the towel, and the damage is a multiple of what could have been had a hard stop-loss been respected. Also, because all the VAR calculations are backward-looking and have a large lag, sudden correlational shocks cannot be dealt with in a timely fashion. On the positive side, the trader's human judgment and intuition can sometimes save the position from a stop-loss forced in by silly market behavior stemming from overreaction to some irrelevant news or rumors. Just as important is the ability to recognize an outsized opportunity relative to historic data and stick with the position for much longer than by respecting an a priori computed profit-taking level.

1.4.2 Peer Pressure and the Blame Game

Emotions always are in overdrive in situations of stress. Choosing the systematic approach exposes the participant to the criticism from his discretionary peers that the approach is formalized in a finite set of rules. When you lose money, your models must be wrong or too simplistic. On the other hand, choosing the discretionary approach, which is opaque to a formal analysis, yields equally strong criticisms from the systematic peers. When you lose money, you must have a lack of discipline or focus or are a macho, fighting obvious patterns and thinking you are smarter than the market.

The ensuing soul-searching comes down to a question: What aspect of your psyche do you trust more, the computational or the intuitive, the right or the left side of the brain?

1.4.3 Trust: Continuity of Quality

On what basis does one trust a trading process? Intuitively, we trust based on two traits:

1. *Quality:* the ability to deliver and survive in different stress scenarios
2. *Continuity:* the ability to "wake up every morning and bite the ass off a bear," as John Gutfreund allegedly said on the Salomon Brothers trading floor

On the systematic front, the quality aspect comes down to being able to organize and deliver solid, innovative research in profitable strategies. The continuity comes down to being able to automate the application of those strategies in a dynamic and adaptive portfolio context. So the trust comes down to the ability to deliver an efficient research and development (R&D) process. This book's goal is to provide a very solid base for such a delivery.

On the discretionary front, quality is about the trader's instinct and discipline. Continuity is about knowing how to choose quality traders and organizing a reward/punishment structure that retains the best over time. Quality nevertheless is a dominant feature as the complexity of the process is lower relative to the systematic world.

Thus from a psychological perspective the discretionary process is more individualistic. As we noted above, it does not have to be a cooperative game at the level of a group of traders as it arguably helps to diversify ideas and risk. On the systematic side, the process has to be cooperative, first between researchers themselves, then between different groups—research, technology, infrastructure, and monitoring.

1.4.4 Learning from Each Other

Given that we are all competent business people and can organize an efficient money-making factory, the question then boils down to which we enjoy more, the thrill of the unexpected just before the non-farm payrolls come out or the quiet humming of our servers crunching terabytes of tick data? It is basically an affinity to mathematical abstraction versus to human language.

With different psychological makeups compatible with systematic and discretionary trading styles, this section suggests what actual elements one style of trading can learn from the other.

The primary intuition about patterns that can be systematically exploited comes from the discretionary side. It is ultimately the analysis of participants' emotions toward making or losing money that gives clues as to what patterns are exploitable at different price and time scales. Another most important point of adaptation comes from observing human and animal behavior toward problem solving and Part Two of this book explores several avenues to systematize it in a broader context. Thus the behavior of the discretionary traders is really useful to understand for the systematic researchers.

At the same time the inherent discipline toward money management and the robotic trading process naturally present in the systematic trading are useful role models for the discipline of discretionary traders. Also, the knowledge of systematic models is useful for discretionary traders for predicting stress, trend reversal, and breakout levels.

Thus the two trading disciplines can be seen as a coevolving set. In fact the whole thing did not start as such because the marketplace was initially dominated by discretionary traders. But especially since the coming of the technological mega-trend and computerization of major markets, the landscape is changing by the day with more and more automated systematic trading strategies coming online and in some markets even starting to dominate the traded volume at the expense of discretionary participants.

The question is, who is going to learn faster? The humans with their zillions of neurons and synapses or the cloud-based parallel supercomputers? We are definitely living in very exciting times where the arms race of cold war weaponry has been crowded out by the arms race of trading bots!

1.5 FROM CANDLESTICKS IN KYOTO TO FPGAs IN CHICAGO

Understanding systematic trading in a historical context is interesting and important as it sheds light on the natural progress from the very beginnings of data and pattern representation to the modern highly parallel adaptive processes connected directly to exchanges and crunching data in microseconds. An overview of this history is given here that shows its constant coupling with the developments in the relevant scientific and technological spheres.

Systematic trading as a style has been in existence since the advent of organized financial markets and the associated record keeping of prices and transactions data, long before the introduction of computers and even of the ticker tape. Its origins can be traced to the sixteenth century rice traders in Japan who introduced tools to represent price activity in a visual way that lead to the discovery of certain patterns, often bestowed with poetic names.

Data representation is a very important part of an effective analysis of a situation. It quite often is achieved through the concept of compression, or in other words the removal of irrelevant details. Of course the whole concept of relevance is tightly linked to the goal of the analysis, in other words to the extraction of the signal from the noise. Part One starts by covering various ways data can be usefully represented for systematic trading and explaining which features are retained and which features are compressed away.

The field was then taken to the next level by Charles Dow in the early 1900s in the study of the U.S. stock markets. Driven by the fast expansion of industry and transportation in the United Sates in the late nineteenth century, the New York Stock Exchange (NYSE) had aquired a prime position as the center for organized exchange of risk and price discovery, a position it still holds. Charles Dow introduced various indicators based on industry and transportation sub-indices, moving averages, and various other filters, and was the first to formalize certain trading rules coming from the relationships between those indicators. Several people refined those trading rules, resulting in flamboyant trading careers for the likes of Jesse Livermore and W. D. Gann.

We continue Part One by discussing the concept of an indicator and various examples of them. Indicators are filters that presuppose a choice of the data represenation methodology and are the building blocks of the underlying signals to the systematic trading models.

Risk management rules were formalized from the observations of widths of trends and extensions of common price patterns. Interestingly, the origins of the money management rules most commonly used in modern system- atic trading come from a different crowd than the community of buy-side speculators and asset managers. Namely, the increasing importance in the mid-twentieth century of the highly leveraged futures markets in agricul- tural products in Chicago attracted a large crowd of pit traders who were mostly scalpers and market-makers, trading hundreds of times per day for a couple of ticks here and there. By the sheer frequency of their trading they had to adopt very strict money management rules to survive till the end of each trading day. Those tricks of the floor trader have been formalized into numerical rules on stop-loss and profit-taking based on the volatility and the liquidity of the market and applied with almost robotic discipline of their implementation.

The design of the indicators is the first step toward building a mecha- nized strategy. They provide the signals on which the triggers to enter or exit positions are based. Most of the indicators are filters that have an inherent lag and may expose the strategy to the risk of being too slow to react to low probability market moves. Thus a money management overlay is warranted in the majority of cases to build a better trading strategy but at the expense of increasing its complexity and potentially its brittleness.

The advent of increasingly cheap computing has created an avenue to test such more complex strategies. A whole cottage industry of trad- ing systems, indicators, and methods resulted from this in the 1980s and 1990s. After discussing several strategy types, Part One focuses on some key implementation aspects of the design and testing of trading systems using the full capabilities of modern computing techniques. In particular, a unified representation of strategies as finite-state machines is introduced and scalable back-testing and forward-testing engines are built on that basis.

Starting in the 1960s, new conceptual developments in areas of control and adaptation gradually coevolved with the uptrend in technology and culminated in what was labeled in 1990 as artificial life. Initially, the real defining driving force was the more ambitious endeavor of artificial intelligence (AI) started in the 1950s by John McCarthy, continuing the intellectual lineage of Alan Turing and John von Neumann. But after an initial jump in the progress toward building intelligent machines able to emulate and surpass humans, a plateau was reached in the late 1980s. The main approach at that point was mainly top-down, trying to automatically create a semantic or visual analysis of the surrounding world. It of course brought a lot of benefits to the progress in pattern recognition, computer vision, and graphics as well as attempts at ontological analysis that ultimately links us now to the semantic web. But the ultimate goal of programmed intelligence was still quite far off, so the whole field found itself in a stasis.

A defining moment in progress came from Rodney Brooks at MIT in the early 1990s. He essentially turned the top-down approach upside-down and designed very efficient robots based on a new concept of control. His bottom-up concept of control is based on a subsumption architecture that receives signals from a set of concurrent sensors, ranks the signals' importance, makes the decision, and sends it to the actuators. The control architecture is itself evolved through trial and error via a genetic algorithm or a reinforcement learning scheme that embeds a concept of fitness of the robot's behavior. This approach is distributed and reactive in nature rather than monolithic and proactive. Brooks demonstrated much better results than the original top-down approach on several important examples. It has yielded progress in many other fields, the most important ones in my mind being the distributed agents systems, swarm computing, and of course the optimization of software design patterns and operating systems to tackle parallel processing, multithreading, and the associated concurrency problems.

Despite the fact that the new approach has not solved the old problem of artificial intelligence, it refocused the research community on tackling other no-less-interesting problems and the field was coined articial life (AL) by Chris Langton in 1990. With a much better understanding of evolutionary computing techniques such as genetic algorithms, genetic programming, and reinforcement learning, a whole new door was opened to breed and play with lifelike creatures that evolve through adaptation and learning and provide a test bed for both Darwinian and Lamarkian ideas. One of the main observations from that exercise is the natural emergence of complexity incarnated into a higher organizational order, an effect already observed through the study of nonlinear dynamic systems a couple of decades before.

At the same time that these great theoretical advances in adaptation were happening, the global financial markets were going through their own technological revolution. Many exchanges, starting with Eurex, were moving gradually into electronic market access and automated matching engines. The trend accelerated when the competition to major exchanges came from new electronic commerce networks (ECNs) in the late 1990s with competing liquidity at faster access times and lower prices. Exchanges at the end of the day are money-making institutions that thrive on high volume of transactions. So the initial trickle of business away from traditional open outcry in the pits to the screens accelerated faster than some exchanges could predict and sometimes handle. Added to this, technology enabled several cost-saving exercises for large institutions in the form of dark pools that are explored in Part Four.

This innovation has increased the share of systematic trading in three ways, all taking advantage of this technological trend:

1. A new breed of systematic trading strategies appeared mostly in the higher-frequency domain, driven as much by the then existing players as by the cohort of locals leaving the pits for the screens.
2. Major sell-side institutions have implemented automated market-making engines and introduced several new algorithmic execution techniques, replacing many locals.
3. Many hedge funds and bank proprietary desks have increased their share of electronically executed systematic risk taking as the barriers to entry have been decreasing thanks to the advent of electronic connectivity providers and price aggregators.

It is difficult to estimate what exact proportion of global electronic volume is originated by systematic strategies but some anecdotal evidence suggests that certain specific markets have already passed the 50 percent mark thanks to the dominance of automated market-makers.

Of course, like any other fad, this technological trend is feeding on itself. According to Ray Kurzweil, we have not seen anything yet as it is feeding in a super-exponential fashion! While the singularity is a few years away, we still need to adapt, but at an increasingly faster pace.

Part Four focuses on the design of an infrastructure that supports efficient low-latency systematic trading with modern electronic exchanges and ECNs. That infrastructure parallels the architecture of such exchanges and also contains an internal matching engine for competing model orders, that is, a mini dark pool. The increasing dominance of fast electronic transactions came in hand with many new technological advances in hardware and software. Namely, we discuss how the following six innovations, among others, naturally fit into the design of our integrated low-latency trading infrastructure:

1. Multithreading and concurrency design patterns that allow the emulation of parallel processing
2. Distributed in-memory caching that solves several state persistence and fast recovery issues
3. Message-passing design patterns that are the basis for a distributed concurrent components architecture and help reduce latency
4. Web server technology that allows remote control of components
5. Universal communication protocols that ensure smooth data passing between counterparties, such as the FIX protocol
6. FPGAs (Field Programmable Gate Arrays, which are programmable chips) and GPUs (Graphics Processing Units, which are highly parallel graphics chips) that help optimize certain algorithms

While the fields of electronic finance and artificial life are both experiencing strong independent growth, one cannot exactly yet call them co-evolving entities. The fundamental goal of this book is to suggest avenues to bridge that gap. Philosophically, given that the discretionary world is driven by humans, why not endow our systematic machines with better learning and adaptive skills? The artificial life paradigm is giving us a first genuine step in that direction. It does not yet give us automated foresight, the holy grail of artificial intelligence. We will need to wait for that one a bit longer.

Part Two provides several concrete examples where artificial life techniques can be profitably applied to finance by building robust adaptive systematic trading strategies. Adaptation is studied both from the viewpoint of endowing an individual with more complexity (akin to the subsumption architecture discussed), as well as from an automated choice of individuals from a population (akin to a genetic algorithm). Appropriate concepts of strategy fitness are introduced. Higher-frequency systematic strategies present the best test-bed for such concepts because they quickly generate large and statistically significant trade samples.

Of course implementing concretely such concepts requires nontrivial machinery, and the design of an integrated low-latency trading architecture in Part Four is tuned to the task of processing parallel swarms of adaptive strategies.

Coming back to Earth from musings into the ever-bright future, let us comment on the less positive features that the electronic trading dominance has left the world with. As mentioned above, the traditional pits with open outcry had almost disappeared by the early 2000s. This fundamental evolution of access and reaction to information has changed some of the long-established features of how the market operates. While increasing efficiency locally it has also introduced a share of global instability. The resulting dynamic is becoming more akin to an arms race where firms compete for speed of data access and delivery for exchanges and clients.

The main change in some markets is that specialists, that is, appointed market-makers, have lost a lot of ground to a set of human and automated agents doing noncommittal conditional market-making and who are not held to provide a two-way orderly market. Automated conditional market-makers provide two-way or one-way liquidity as they see fit and can switch off automatically in situations of stress, leaving the bulk of the flow to more traditional specialists who cannot normally deal with it.

Such structural change is most likely the main cause behind shocking self-fulfilling events like the Flash Crash of May 6, 2010, that spurred a lot of soul-searching as much from the Securities and Exchange Commission (SEC) as from the algorithmic firms community. After initial talk of fat finger or other malfunction, none of the subsequent analysis of transactions and operation logs have managed to pinpoint such kind of cause. It is most probably the automated conditional market-making engines that pulled bids when they saw an increasing selling flow from automated portfolio hedgers and other stop-loss algorithms. It is therefore very difficult to argue that the nature and cause of the Flash Crash was that different from the 1987 meltdown. Yet the recoil from the bottom was indeed different because it happened much faster. That fast recovery was probably helped by a set of automated high-frequency momentum strategies that went long, a feature that was much less present in 1987.

Of course such events will not go without consequences on regulation and self-regulation of the markets. It is well known that some participants do flood the markets with masses of orders outside of the immediate trading range in order to tilt the market-making engines of others and sometimes to slow down the whole system. Also the affair of flash orders that create a false sense of liquidity but cannot be reached by most participants due to their access latency is still being investigated and debated.

The modern Goulds, Drews, and Fisks shall also be found out either by people or by algorithms; it is just a matter of time and evolution. Every new organism has to test its boundaries to adapt and survive. In the current fashion of detox by regulation that started during the hangover from the credit bubble, one will probably see a formal response to high-frequency market abuse soon. The main difficulty will be, as with any other regulation, to ensure fairness without hampering efficiency.

The self-fulfilling nature of the technological uptrend of the marketplace with its associated growth of the automated systematic strategies lets us wonder whether it is a bubble ready to burst. As we commented at the beginning, any sector of the market (as well as of human activities more generally) is quite naturally prone to a boom-bust cycle, and this one should be no exception!

Currently this market arena presents high hurdles for entry and in consequence there is a fragmented technological landscape giving privileged access to only a few. There is still a large scope for competition that will invariably drive further increases in efficiency. This points to the fact that we are not yet at crunchpoint; the trend is still up, thus it is still rational to participate!

It is now time to move on to the heart of the matter and start exploring in Part One data representation, indicators, basic model types, and techniques to test them.

One

Strategy Design
and Testing

P art One sets the stage and the basic concepts for the rest of the book. It argues that the classic techniques of investing and strategy building are not fully adequate to tackle the real complexity of the market. The market is seen as a complex adaptive system that has subtle feedbacks at different time and price scales.

To make progress in that complex world new methods have to come into play. Robots operate in the complex "real" world and trading systems operate in the complex market. The direct analogy between robotics and trading is striking indeed. It is also the analogy that bears all the fruits when adaptive behavior is discussed in Part Two.

The progress is set in motion by framing the whole systematic trading activity in the language of autonomous adaptive agents. The individual trading systems are represented by agents that react to informational events. Those events can be any external events like price and order book changes as well as communications between agents. This approach yields naturally a high degree of parallelism and the ability to create complex agents from simple ones by means of communication and signalling.

In the automated systematic trading arena one of the most desired and important features is the recoverability from data disconnects and other faults. This recoverability is facilitated by formalizing the concept of state of the system and by exhausting the possible state transitions that the system may undergo. The trading system must always know what state it is in to continue operating. The automated trading agents are hence endowed with control systems represented by finite state machines (FSM).

This part discusses details of the programmatic framework for this new paradigm. I chose to present the code in LISP rather than in pseudocode because it is as easy to understand and can be directly implemented rather than rewritten. LISP is one of the most advanced and important computer languages; it has been in active operation since the late 1950s in the academic and defense communities and is making its way back into the commercial world. It is a functional language that has also a more powerful object orientation than the specifically designed "OO" languages and ranks second in speed to C++ and faster than Java.

This part continues with several methods of data representation. This is a first and elementary step to filter signal from noise. It focuses on the desired share of time dimension versus price extent in the construction of indicators and tradable patterns.

The different data representations form the basis to explore a set of classic and novel trading strategies. Those strategies include price-taking and price-making techniques, and objective criteria for their applicability in real trading are formulated. These basic trading strategies are presented in the context of the agent-based paradigm by their finite-state machine representations.

Those nonadaptive techniques served well and will probably continue to do so for certain domains of applicability, namely for long and medium term trading. Structural reasons stemming from the way authorities manage the macroeconomy tend to create tradable long-term trends of which the amplitude and duration reflects those of the business cycles. Calendar-driven data releases and asset auctions tend to create other tradable medium-term oscillation patterns. Periodic shortages and overproduction in the commodity sectors also tend to create repeatable trend and acceleration patterns.

Those trend, oscillation, and acceleration patterns present reasonably stable statistics and have been successfully exploited by commodity trading advisors (CTAs) over the last 40 years. As mentioned in the introductory chapter, CTAs, as a strategy class, have one of the longest track records among all hedge funds.

With the coming of electronic markets, market making has evolved into an important activity with the participation and sometimes dominance of conditional liquidity providers. A framework for market making is presented that allows the development of conditional liquidity provision in the agent-based context.

The discussion then moves on to the next level of complexity, namely optimal portfolio construction of multiple strategies on one asset as well as the optimization of portfolios of models on a variety of assets. "Idealized" equity curves are introduced to help formulate criteria of maximizing expected return-to-drawdown ratios.

Part One finishes by exploring the framework for simulation and estimation techniques. It introduces forward-testing and shows how to simulate data by resampling of observed histories as well as with a priori defined distributional and autocorrelational constraints. Those techniques tend to be overlooked in many books but they deserve much more attention as they provide stress-testing and parameter estimation techniques complementary to the more classic back-testing. The forward-testing will also prove to be useful for computing the efficiency of dynamic model choice algorithms in Part Two.

CHAPTER 2

A New Socioeconomic Paradigm

2.1 FINANCIAL THEORY VS. MARKET REALITY

Financial theory has been for a long time based on a top-down approach dominated by sweeping assumptions on rationality of agents, equal access to information, completeness of markets, and a coherent formation of expectations across the marketplace. Those assumptions are, in fact, a set of constraints that yield the theory to predict static equilibria and the associated price formation in the markets.

That approach, however, has had a particularly disappointing track record of explaining market behavior, especially the many nonlinearities observed at various time scales, from the longer term large scale crashes to the intraday whippy price dynamics of individual securities. Basically there have been numerous unsuccessful attempts to marry the classical theory to everyday practice, so to speak.

In the following subsections some plausible behavioral causes for the existence (and sometimes ubiquity) of market nonlinearities are suggested. Some classic failures are discussed as a prelude and motivation to dedicate energy to the study of adaptation, learning, and survivability of trading systems. To paraphrase the title of the famous book by Sornette (2003), the hunt is under way for causes as to "Why Markets Crash So Often."

2.1.1 Adaptive Reactions vs. Rigid Anticipations

To illustrate the above, a glance at history is warranted as a first step. Starting from the basics, the Figures 2.1, 2.2, and 2.3 show the lack of stationarity of return, volatility, and cross-correlation of three fundamental price indices—the stocks (S&P index), bonds (U.S. 10-year total return index), and commodities (the CRB index)—over the last 40 years.

The market dynamics are even wilder when considered on an intraday basis. The intraday price and volatility distributions have more pronounced

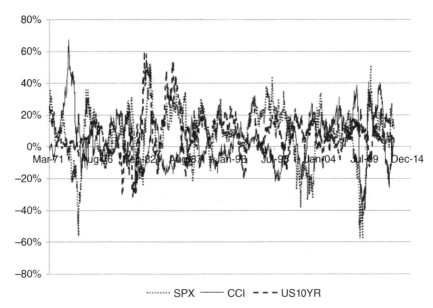

FIGURE 2.1   Rolling 1-Year Returns on SP, 10Y Bonds, and CRB

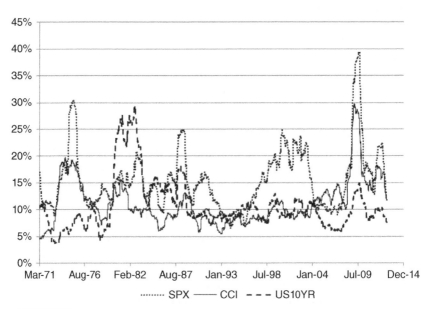

FIGURE 2.2   Rolling 1-Year Volatilities on SP, 10Y Bonds, and CRB

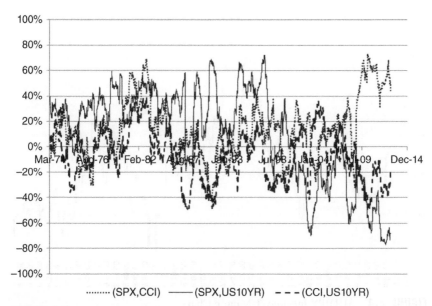

········ (SPX,CCI) ——— (SPX,US10YR) − − − (CCI,US10YR)

FIGURE 2.3   Rolling 1-Year Correlations on SP, 10Y Bonds, and CRB

fat tails, and lack stationarity even more than when sampled daily. Figures 2.4 and 2.5 provide a sample of different price behaviors both in clock time and in event time.

Figure 2.6 in log-log scale shows the fat tails and a power-law fit of the absolute returns of the S&P index sampled at time scales from ticks to years.

Overuse of mean-variance optimization on static return and covariance assumptions has brought to near-banckruptcy several large pension systems across the world (specifically several municipal and state pensions in the United States). As seen above, the market returns, variances, and correlations are quite unstable, and, most important, are not stable on a time frame that is commensurate with the average timing of pensions payouts. Hence the overreliance on static efficient frontier optimizations have generated genuine train wrecks that are very difficult to rectify now.

On the other hand, as pointed out in Chapter 1, systematic commodity trading advisors have had, so far, the longest successful track record in the history of money management. Most of their success comes from reacting to the market fast enough, rather than trying to predict and extrapolate it. This may mean that although markets are complex, some behavioral patterns can be exploited systematically.

FIGURE 2.4   AUDJPY Intraday 1-Minute Chart

FIGURE 2.5   USU1 Intraday Tick Chart

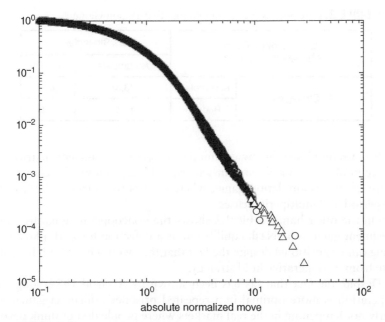

FIGURE 2.6 S&P Absolute Return Distribution: Log-Log Scale

2.1.2 Accumulation vs. Divestment Games

One basic root cause of the market complex dynamics lies in the asymmetric behavior of agents under accumulation and divestment from risk, and sudden switching of behavior from a cooperative to a noncooperative game.

Accumulation provides oftentimes stabilizing forces to the market. Namely, learning and/or copying of perceived successful strategies by a herd of participants may, in certain cases, smooth out the price process by reducing volatility and discrepancies between related assets. Successful relative-value strategies have a similar stabilizing effect, with pure arbitrage, when found, being the extreme lucky case. This herd-like game of accumulation is cooperative, because it makes sense to openly attract more people to the trade, in order to generate paper profits on your own book.

But accumulation of risk most often ends in tears. When the price discrepancies come to be arbitraged away or when the price gets over-stretched relative to value, the game changes to the classic defection in a one-period prisoner's dilemma game. The divestment game is noncooperative, because early entrant participants have no incentive to broadcast to the rest of the market that they are intending to sell out their positions. If they do, someone else will go first and widen the prices against their current paper profits.

TABLE 2.1 Cooperative Accumulation Two-Person Game

Accumulation Game (*A's payoff, B's payoff*)		B's Strategies	
		Accumulate	Reduce
A's Strategies	Accumulate	(3,3)	(4,2)
	Reduce	(2,4)	(1,1)

It is useful to see this by examining the classic two-agent matrices for the accumulation and divestment games. Table 2.1 shows the cooperative nature of the accumulation game, where it pays to cooperate both in the one-period and multiperiod cases.

On the other hand, Table 2.2 shows the noncooperative nature of the divestment game. The Nash equilibrium is a defection for both players (by selling out of positions) despite the fact that they would have both benefited more from a cooperative hold strategy.

Despite the fact that (as has been shown by Axelrod 1984) long-term cooperation is more optimal in a repeated prisoner's dilemma game, it is clearly not happening in the real markets where people do not think beyond the next minute in situations of stress.

2.1.3 Phase Transitions under Leverage

Most of the market is highly leveraged, and the above game change gets magnified into large behavioral asymmetry toward gains versus losses that further increases the nonlinearity of the price process. If and when word comes out that large players are getting out, the market can spin out of control pretty brutally with a liquidity air pocket followed by forced stop-outs, often exacerbating the disconnect between price and value.

As we mentioned before, the market participants are quite segmented, and each cohort is sensitive to a distinct time and price scale. Thus a small

TABLE 2.2 Noncooperative Divestment Two-Person Game

Get-Me-Out! Game (*A's payoff, B's payoff*)		B's Strategies	
		Stay	Get Out
A's Strategies	Stay	(3,3)	(1,4)
	Get Out	(4,1)	(2,2)

FIGURE 2.7 Silver Spot Daily

shock can create a cascade of events that gets magnified into a genuine phase transition, often referred to mildly as a risk-on to risk-off switch.

That behavior is also the major source of trends in the market, and explains part of the asymmetry observed in the dynamics of the uptrends and downtrends in asset markets. By *assets* one means securities that are usually held primarily for long-only investments (like stocks, bonds, and commodities), as well as auxiliary assets like commodity-linked and high-yielding currencies. Examples of this asymmetry are given for Silver and Nikkei in Figures 2.7 and 2.8.

Market crashes are the extreme incarnations of the above. The world has seen major global crashes of the leveraged market many times: tulips (Holland 1637), the combined South Sea, Mississippi and paper money bubbles (United Kingdom and France 1720), the Florida Real Estate Bubble (1926), Great Crash of 1929, Crash of 1987, emerging market currencies (Asian Crisis in 1997), yield curve forwards and volatility (LTCM and Russia in 1998), Nasdaq in 2001, natural gas forwards (Amaranth in 2007), credit and mortgages (Bear Stearns, Lehman, et al. 2007–2008), Flash Crash 2010.

Every time different(ish) assets, every time people saying, "It's different this time," and every time a different trigger. Yet the same game theory and

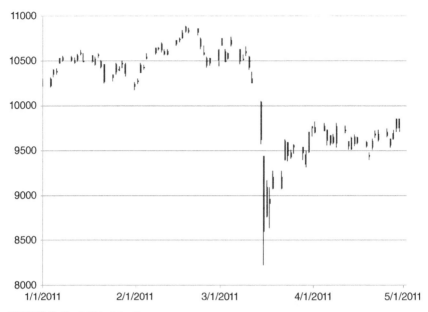

FIGURE 2.8   Nikkei Daily

the same physics of phase transitions. I do not doubt such events will occur again, despite any efforts at new regulation.

Of course, these examples are extreme in their global scale, reach, and consequences on the world economy and politics. But as shown in the price graphs above, mini-crashes or milder nonlinearity are happening at smaller scales with higher frequency, and are partly responsible for the intraday fat tails alluded to above. This behavior is also one of the sources of non-stationarity of distributions and correlations of returns.

2.1.4   Derivatives: New Risks Do Not Project onto Old Hedges

It is also important to add that yet another, but related, source of nonlinearity in the market comes from derivatives, usually nonlinear contracts written on underlying primary traded instruments.

First of all, in the classic theory of no-arbitrage pricing of derivatives, contracts with negative convexity require increasingly higher hedge activity as prices move away for any reason, putting further pressure on prices to move away in the same direction. This reflexive behavior is not present in the theory.

Second, and most important, this classic theory does not hold most of the time, and mathematically speaking it holds with probability zero.

The main reason is that, for any non-Gaussian price distribution, there is mathematically no way to project the derivative back to the underlying; that is, the risk-neutral measure that would do the projection trick does not exist. This means that derivatives are genuinely *novel* assets (or rather liabilities), that cannot be hedged-out via continuous trading in the underlying, as per the delta-hedging mechanism that the classical theory portends to provide. Derivatives create new dimensions in the risk space that are orthogonal to the underlying (in the sense of covariance or any similar measure of entanglement).

By this token, derivatives yield an incomplete market because in general they are sold to end-holders who do not trade in them, and therefore do not provide a continous and viable price-discovery mechanism. In situations of stress, the actual convexity of those instruments becomes higher than expected (i.e., classically estimated), because of lack of viable critical mass of market-makers for that orthogonal risk. This yields sometimes an even higher tension on the underlying market due to a more desperate hedging activity. Recurring examples of such nonlinearities have been seen arising from hedging mortgages, credit derivatives, equity put options during crashes, libor-square products, quantos, and so on.

The obvious solution to this problem is to create exchanges for the derivatives, the same way they exist for the primary instruments like stocks and futures. Let the market discover the price in function of supply and demand, rather than via an approximate model. The leading example is the Chicago Board Options Exchange (CBOE) for equity options. It is interesting that the originators of the Black-Scholes formula initially lost a lot of money trying to arbitrage their model option price to the CBOE market. They had to recognize that the market was the ultimate pricer of the implied volatility on options, and their approach had no predictive power as to that fundamental source of risk for options, which, as mentioned, is orthogonal to the risk of the underlying stock. To be completely clear on this subject, it is the variability in implied volatility that the market is discovering, via the clearing of the supply and demand for implied volatility.

2.1.5 Socio-Political Dynamics and Feedbacks

Looking at the realpolitik of the world, how can one forget the feedbacks that the socioeconomic dynamics of our society force onto the financial markets? There are periodic shocks supplied to the markets by events in different parts of the world as well as political actions from governments.

In particular, wars and revolutions are nonlinear. If they were not, they probably would be tamed way before they got out of hand! This also points to the poor predictive power by most people and societies, and the associated atavism of linear extrapolation. Many of those have been seen before, many will probably be seen in the future. They will probably be expected but with their timing not predictable. Very little of those feedbacks are tackled in the classical macroeconomic texts, yet they are an important source of fat tails in market returns and societal changes.

In the root of all revolutions resides the concept of critical mass. It could be the relative size of a political party of movement, legitimate or not. Or it could be the adoption of a new technology that crowds out the old one, à la Shumpeter. Or it could be a viral spread of a religion. In any case, the revolutionary phase transition happens in a time frame which is scales of magnitude lower than the time it took to build the old regime. This dynamic has been seen in the rise and fall of many societies, like the Romans, as well as the rise and fall of the use of horses as a means of transportation. In any event, the socio-political scene exhibits from time to time phase transitions that affect the marketplace.

Symmetrically, one should also be mindful of the scope of the positive and negative feedbacks of the riches or rags that financial markets periodically bestow on the real economy, the society, and people's behavior. A recent case in point being the boom and bust dynamics seen in the United States. Initially the paper profits of the stock market provided extra spending power to a certain section of the population, and those people rightly invested in real estate. A larger crowd followed, leveraging themselves into real estate as prices of homes were rising, with banks providing the bulk of the cheap credit. When leverage reached 20-1 and the expectations of ever-rising prices dampened, suddenly there were a lot of people who found themselves holding negative equity (meaning more real debts than expected revenues). Debts were not paid, homes foreclosed, and prices fell further. The banking system went into a collapse and dragged the rest of the economy with it, with equities falling more than 50 percent at some point. Then came soul-searching, finger-pointing, and sacrificial-goating, followed by real consequences of the regulatory fallout on the financial markets and larger tax burdens on the society as a whole.

Thus, markets and societies are intertwined into a complex coevolving set and cannot be seen or understood separately. This Popperian analysis of market and social revolutions is, in my hope, a stepping stone for a long-overdue revolution of the classical financial theory.

2.2 THE MARKET IS A COMPLEX ADAPTIVE SYSTEM

A change of paradigm to challenge the classical theory is clearly needed, and the beginnings of it have already emerged. The goal of the new paradigm is to be able to rationalize and anticipate a large range of observed market phenomena. For the purpose of this book, the main goal is to be able to formulate an approach to survive and thrive in the marketplace.

As the famous AI expert Herbert Simon said, social sciences are the "hard sciences." By this he meant that the underlying degree of complexity is far greater than that of, for example, physics. In physics it happens to be the case that a large set of phenomena in the inanimate universe is representable and predictable by a small, albeit tricky, set of equations. Physics is still living the "dream of the final theory," as Steven Weinberg put it.

Biology, ecology, and the sciences of societal organization, on the contrary, are much harder to mathematize, and even to come up with a set of concepts that reflect the observed reality. As noticed in the Introduction, the very concept of *organism* is not yet fully understood in biology, neither on theoretical nor practical grounds.

2.2.1 Emergence

The unifying theme behind these hard sciences is the trend toward the emergence and organization of higher order structures from a large set of simpler interacting elements. That emergence is not fully predictable even though the systems from which it emerges are deterministic (nonrandom). The emergence is based on a set of positive and negative feedbacks that, at some point, end up creating coherent meso-scale structures of lower-order elements, and defining the patterns of behavior and interaction of those meso-scale structures. Think in terms of the emergence of fashions in a society, organization of an ant colony, hurricanes in the Atlantic, trends in the market.

One promising approach was initiated at the Santa Fe Institute in the early 1990s and has been, since then, studied across several institutions throughout the world. It is based on the investigation of the market as a complex adaptive system. Let me first introduce the concept and phenomenology behind it. To paraphrase Holland a Complex adaptive system is a dynamic system with the following four features:

1. *Parallelism.* It is composed of many elements that interact locally between each other in parallel and are not driven by a central or coherent mechanism. In particular, only local rules of interactions are known.
2. *Emergence and Self-Similarity.* Larger-scale patterns (parts) emerge from those distributed interactions of elements. The whole system may exhibit self-similarity, and parts themselves may interact to create patterns at a yet larger scale. Hence, a variety of patterns exist on intermediate scales (between the scale of the elements and the system as a whole).

The system is characterized by its behavior on such meso-scales, and the feedbacks that larger-scale parts provide to the smaller-scale parts.

3. *Adaptation.* The dynamics at each scale are characterized by their own ecology, with parts evolving and adapting to their environment, constrained by other parts on the same or larger scales.

4. *Anticipation.* The system may have anticipatory features where, over time, expected responses of some parts are learned by other parts, in order to adapt better.

This concept is abstract, so let me rephrase it in a more suggestive manner, looking at the market. To start with, the preceding section suggested that the observed complexity of the markets reflects mainly the complexity of its participants and of their interactions:

1. *Parallelism.* The market is composed of many participants trading various assets. They are either humans or trading robots that are based on strategies written by humans. They trade with each other in parallel and are not driven by a central or coherent decision-making mechanism (even though the mechanics of trading may be facilitated by exchanges).

2. *Emergence and Self-Similarity.* The market participants organize themselves into specialized firms, pools, and societies in order to have more staying power. Those larger-scale coherent organizations have proportionally larger impacts on asset demand and supply, thus yielding the emergence of larger-scale price patterns.

3. *Adaptation.* Individuals, firms, and governments compete for market access, price, and value, and adapt for survival in their own space. Oligopolies and cooperative behavior emerge at certain scales only to be offset by competition at other scales.

4. *Anticipation.* Each participant tries to anticipate the behavior or reponse of a larger participant, in order to either exploit or survive the price action. That behavior is sometimes mimetic, providing a positive feedback and price accelerations, and sometimes contrarian, yielding a dampening of amplitude of price moves.

2.2.2 Intelligence Is Not Always Necessary

Conceptually, one could say that the predecessor of models of complex adaptive systems is the Ising spin-glass model, which has been used by physicists to study phase transitions. Such models allow for a unified but simplified framework to study and understand several nonlinearities observed in the markets. Importantly, it shows that those nonlinearities are a generic feature of a system that exhibits a minimal degree of complexity. This is one of the reasons why the emergent field of study based on such models had been called econo-physics.

In relation to the comments on socio-political feedbacks above, many nontrivial dynamics can be modeled as emergent properties of interactions between simple agents. By gradually increasing the complexity of agents from a minimum, more subtle dynamic properties emerge. These increasingly complex social interactions provide a solid basis to study the organization of societies as seen in Epstein and Axtell, 1996.

Zero-intelligence models of agent behavior explain market microstructure much better than sophisticated models with utility-maximizing agents [see Farmer, Patelli, and Zovko, 2005].

2.2.3 The Need to Adapt

In my opinion, the main conceptual lesson from the complex adaptive systems theory, as pertaining to the market, is that trying to predict the future by imposing normative views is a futile exercise. As Niels Bohr said, predicting is difficult, especially the future. And he had no excuse—he was a physicist!

Seeing the market through this new prism, however, does not mean that all hope is lost. Prediction is still a valid exercise, but only when established in a more realistic framework that respects the nature of the complexity of the markets. Part of this complexity, as discussed above, is coming from the adaptation patterns of participants.

Adaptation is the essence of life, as without adaptation there is little chance for survival. Understanding and exploiting adaptation patterns of other agents is an adaptation strategy in itself.

2.3 ORIGINS OF ROBOTICS AND ARTIFICIAL LIFE

It is probably fair to say that the nineteenth century was the launchpad for the era of machines that is epitomized by the incredible acceleration of global growth and progress in the twentieth century. Machines are now underpinning our civilization, from thermostats in our houses to space probes reaching the edge of our solar system. Machines are systems that can be split into identifiable parts that are machines in their own right. They can be very complicated, like the space shuttle, but ultimately composed of simpler identifiable parts that have specific functions.

The end of the twentieth century saw immense progress in a class of machines that are designed to compute (process numeric data). Those machines arose in the 1940s from the necessity of simulating complicated equations related to warfare, but soon became universal numerical simulators. These computers were based on the theories of universal computation, proposed originally by Turing and then developed by Church, to be implemented by Von Neumann. The original and still current design of such a universal digital computer is called the Von Neumann architecture.

The confluence of computers and ideas from control theory gave rise to cybernetics, the science of control systems with feedbacks introduced by Wiener. Cybernetics is one of the building blocks of modern robotics. Robotics is the science of intelligent mechanisms, machines that could interact with humans and behave on par with them.

Beginning in the 1950s, serious attempts at understanding cognition and intelligence led to the field of artificial intelligence. Thanks to the work of Simon, Newell, McCarthy, and Minsky, among others, great progress has been made in developing general problem solver algorithms, reinforcement learning, and symbolic knowledge representation systems, which has led to the development of the LISP and Prolog languages. In parallel, the work of Pitts, McCulloch, and Rumelhart explored models of the neural connections and gave rise to progress in supervised learning, pattern recognition, and computer vision. Despite this immense progress, however, AI has hit a bit of a roadblock and "true artificial" intelligence remains elusive at the time of writing this book.

The end of the twentieth century also saw substantial progress in life sciences. Part of this achievement came from a much deeper mathematical understanding of some features of biological systems and the ability to model those features with computers.

Biology has eluded mathematization for a long time because of its inherent complexity. An organism is not a machine because it cannot be subdivided into independently functioning organs. The degree of interconnectedness in an organism is immense, and the whole is definitely much bigger than the sum of its parts.

Mathematics originally came to biology via the study of population dynamics as well as the study of biophysics. The breakthrough came when mathematical and computer models started being applied to the study of genetics and evolution.

Evolutionary theories came originally from ideas of Lamark and Darwin by observing the adaptations of animals to their environments. A crucial breakthrough in the understanding of evolutionary processes came from genetics, originating in the work of Mendel. The structure of DNA, intuited by Heisenberg and discovered by Watson and Crick, spurred the rapid progress in biochemistry and medicine, and pointed to the dominant influence of the genotype on the development and survival success of an organism. It also brought to light the immense complexity gap that exists between the organism's genotype (i.e., its DNA encoding) and its potential phenotype (i.e., the final structure of the organism itself).

Moore's law of super-exponential increase in computing power per unit of silicon has mirrored the explosion of cheap computing, which led to the study of more and more complex phenomena within realistic time frames. Complex phenomena such as deterministic chaos and strange attractors, first intuited by Poincaré, Julia, and Lorentz, could be studied in the digital lab, and then displayed as art on the wall like the colorful fractals of Mandelbrot.

Computers started being utilized to model complex genetic phenomena and this gave rise to a whole class of evolutionary algorithms that could be used for general optimization tasks. Those algorithms, initially developed by Holland, Koza, and others, use the basic principles of reproduction, mutation, and selection of the fittest to evolve solutions to various problems. Those problems usually involve finding optimal phenotypes by the brute force of Darwinian evolution.

In parallel to the study of the general-purpose evolutionary algorithms, a new strand of thought has emerged called artificial life, spurred by research conducted by Langdton and others at the Santa Fe Institute. This science is about understanding life as it could be rather than what it is as currently observed on planet Earth. However elusive the concept of life itself, progress is being made in understanding and modeling proto-life, digital organisms that coevolve with their environment. It is a science of adaptive autonomous agents, a paradigm that this book proposes for the research and development of systematic trading strategies. It is also a science of emergent complexity of interactions and behaviors.

While artificial intelligence has been stalled, artificial life has made substantial progress. This progress is concretely seen in modern robotics with several individuals successfully operating on Earth and Mars. From the outset, artificial intelligence had a top-down approach where systems were designed with a central control mechanism that aggregated all the sensor data, made sense of it, and emitted signals to the actuators in order to influence the external world. That central control system had to build elaborate internal models of the external world to be able to plan the course of its actions. This approach proved to be very brittle to unpredicted changes in the external environment. At the end of the 1980s, Brooks introduced a bottom-up approach based on a concurrent set of basic behaviors that subsumed each other in certain circumstances. The robot would continuously run lower-level functions while higher-level functions would take precedence when needed. Efficient subsumption architectures could then be evolved with genetic programming techniques in order to discover flexible but robust distributed control systems. Those ideas led me to the design of the swarm systems introduced in the second part of this book.

In a way, one can say that the understanding of biology and the understanding of computers continue to coevolve. The modeling of the evolution of learning systems (or systems with learning) as well as recent progress in epigenetic phenomena is pointing strongly to the reacceptance of Lamarkian ideas and some distancing away from the prevailing reductionist Darwinian dogma. At the same time, the still unsolved problem of protein folding that the Von Neumann architecture struggles with continues to encourage fast progress in fundamentally new computing paradigms like systemic computing.

The complexity of the markets discussed in this chapter naturally led me to look beyond the physical paradigm purported in economic and financial theory to date. The fascinating ideas coming from the sciences of complexity and artificial life are in my mind the right building blocks for the modern discourse of socioeconomic and financial reality in the years to come. This book is my attempt to set this trend.

CHAPTER 3

Analogies between Systematic Trading and Robotics

This chapter introduces the central concept that underpins the book, namely the direct analogy between robotics and systematic automated trading strategies. This approach proves fruitful for an efficient understanding of the field, and opens the door to a much wider scope of research and development in finance that is naturally suggested by progress in the fields of complexity, self-organization, artificial life, and artificial intelligence. Part Two of the book concentrates on that bridge and suggests some future avenues.

3.1 MODELS AND ROBOTS

Similar to robots thrown into the real world, trading strategies need to survive the complexity of real markets. It is exactly the success of modern developments in robotics and artificial life that have inspired me to apply a variety of such techniques to systematic trading. In this chapter, the groundwork is set for the approach to building trading strategies that exhibit the features of adaptive autonomous agents (AAA). Part One of the book focuses on the autonomous feature and Part Two on the adaptive feature.

An AAA is a physical or software decision-making process that is composed of the following three elements.

1. *Sensors:* Any device that receives information from the external world.
   Robot: cameras, microphones, positioning devices, speed devices, etc.

Trading strategy: various indicators as well as performance measures of a range of simulated strategies.

2. *Actuators:* Any device by which the agent outputs information and acts on the external world. Robot: wheels, arms, guns, etc. Trading strategy: order management system that ensures current desired market position and emits current desired passive or aggressive orders

3. *Adaptive Control System:* A goal-oriented decision-making system that reads sensors and activates actuators. Robot: feedback and subsumption architecture that achieves optimal foraging behavior under constraint of power utilization and minimal damage to machinery. Trading strategy: feedback and subsumption architecture that achieves optimal profit under constraints of capital utilization and minimal drawdown.

In the above list, *device* is used instead of *mechanism* to draw a further and deeeper analogy with living organisms, which are the most sophisticated AAAs known.

The control system is of course of central importance: It is the brain of the AAA that achieves the required convergence from the current to the desired state. It is a goal-oriented system, in the sense that it has a final task in mind. It tries to achieve that task by balancing between short-term setbacks and long-term rewards, and closes the feedback loop between the real world and the *internal world* of the AAA. By *internal world* is meant the implicit or explicit representation of the real world that the AAA achieves via the input of sensor data into its control system.

3.2 THE TRADING ROBOT

Let us set the stage by introducing a direct parallel between a robot and a trading strategy by describing the flow of information from an observation to an action.

First of all, the trading robot has *sensors* that observe ticks, prices, bars, or any other compressed or uncompressed market event data. It then assembles this data into a representation that is usually a set of *indicators* that are computed via a *preprocessor*.

The indicators act as the first semantic layer of the robot—they filter and pre-interpret the data that is hitting the raw sensors. They can be, as a simple example, moving averages of the data observed. They are passed, along with the current state of the robot, to the *control system* that is its decision-making mechanism.

The control system makes the decision as to the position and orders to have in the market. The decison is enacted into the outside world by *actuators* that are typically a set of order management systems (OMS) that interface between the trading robot and the electronic commerce networks (ECNs) such as exchanges, dark pools, over-the-counter electronic markets, and so on.

The OMS sends the trade orders into the ECNs and manages the outputs from the ECNs. Once the trade is done, the OMS feeds that information back into the decision-making system of the robot.

Finally a *postprocessor* mechanism gathers the relevant data to compute the new state of the robot and makes it ready to observe the next event.

Figure 3.1 illustrates the information flow.

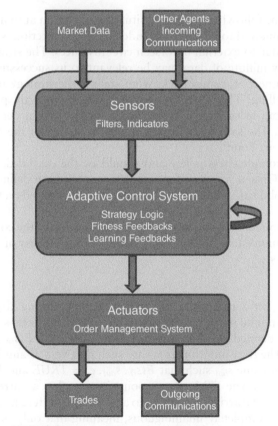

FIGURE 3.1 Block Diagram of Trading Strategy as an AAA

3.3 FINITE-STATE-MACHINE REPRESENTATION OF THE CONTROL SYSTEM

As per the discussion above, once the incoming data has been preprocessed and the relevant indicators calculated, the onus of the decision making falls onto the control system. Once that decision is made, an order is (or is not) generated and passed to the actuator that manages the interface with the external world.

What are the desirable features of a control system? Of course, the first and foremost is its ability to make money! Besides that, the principal feature is *completeness*, meaning a clear mechanism that enables the control system at every point in time to know what the current step should be. This, in itself, helps ensure *recoverability* from faults and hence reduces *operational brittleness*.

Assume the following real-world situation, where an automated trading strategy is connected to an ECN but suddenly the connection is lost for several minutes due to external unforseen circumstances. The strategy is short term, so every minute of data may be relevant to its successful operation. When the connection comes back, what state is the strategy in? Should it be buying? Selling? The control system should be built on the principle that whenever a gap in time or data occurs, it should have a defined plan to proceed with. The same actually holds for the design of the OMS and is discussed in Part Four.

Built-in completeness is key and should be the *central* design pattern for an AAA. Once a structure for completeness has been defined, the AAA stands on a solid basis, and then efforts can be concentrated on the quest for profitability.

This section focuses on the efficient representation of the control system by way of a finite-state machine that ensures completeness of its decision-making process.

Definition 1. Let S be a finite set of symbols representing abstract states, E a possibly infinite set of outside observable events. A finite-state machine $FSM(S, F)$ is defined by its complete set of transitions $F(s_{in}, s_{out}, e)$ with $s_{in}, s_{out} \in S$. The transition functions are such that $\forall e \in E$ and $\forall s_{in} \in S$ and there exists only one s_{out} such that $F(s_{in}, s_{out}, e) = TRUE$ and $F(s_{in}, s, e) = FALSE, \forall s \neq s_{out}$. The FSM, at any point in time, has a current state s_{in}. When a new event e arrives it changes to a potentially different state s_{out}, and that change is completely unambiguous, meaning that only one transition function is true and all others false. The set of transition functions can be represented by an $N * N$-matrix where $N = Card(S)$ is the number of states.

To illustrate how an FSM representation is implemented for a trading strategy, a simple example is discussed here. A set of more complicated real-world trading strategies is presented in the next chapter.

Consider a simple trend-following trading strategy that is always in the market. The strategy is long 1 unit when the price is above a simple moving average of length L, and short when it is below.

Initially, before any position is opened, at least L price update events $P(e_i)$ need to be received to calculate the simple moving average

$$SMA(L, i) = \frac{1}{L} \sum_{j=1}^{L} P(e_{i-j})$$

During that initial time the position of the strategy is zero.

One needs to preprocess the incoming data before presenting it to the FSM. Let $E = \{e\}$ the set of incoming market update events received since inception and $\Pi = \{P(e)\}$ the set of calculated prices. Here the price calculation function $P(e)$ returns the relevant price update depending on the nature of the event received. For example if e is an order book update that does not change the best bid and the best offer then it would be ignored, and the price calculation function would not return a value. On the other hand, trades or changes in the mid-price would be processed and added to Π.

Hence, a necessary and sufficient set of states for this strategy is

$$S = \{INIT, LONG, SHORT\}$$

Define the indicators $COUNTER$ and MA that are calculated on each new addition P to the set of price updates Π as follows:

$$COUNTER = Card(\Pi)$$
$$MA = SMA(L, COUNTER - 1) \text{ when } COUNTER > L$$

When an event e is received that yields a price update P, the indicators are recalculated—this is the function of the preprocessor explained above. They are then passed to the strategy's FSM as parameters. The FSM's transitions are explained here and the corresponding matrix representation is shown in Figure 3.2. In that matrix, the initial states are in the columns and the final states are in the rows. For clarity, this particular style of representing the FSMs has been adopted throughout.

The FSM starts in the $INIT$ state. It continues in that state until L price updates are gathered. At the next price update P the $COUNTER$

$$F(INIT, INIT, P) = (COUNTER <= L)$$
$$F(INIT, LONG, P) = (AND(COUNTER > L)(P > MA))$$
$$F(INIT, SHORT, P) = (AND(COUNTER > L)(P <= MA))$$
$$F(LONG, INIT, P) = NIL$$
$$F(LONG, LONG, P) = (P > MA)$$
$$F(LONG, SHORT, P) = (P <= MA)$$
$$F(SHORT, INIT, P) = NIL$$
$$F(SHORT, LONG, P) = (P > MA)$$
$$F(SHORT, SHORT, P) = (P <= MA)$$

FIGURE 3.2   FSM Matrix for the Moving-Average Model

indicator becomes $L + 1$. The preprocessor calculates the MA on the previous L price updates (not including this one) and passes the result to the transition matrix. Only the $F(INIT, *, P)$ row is considered by the processor and it consecutively starts computing the three Boolean functions.

The first one, $F(INIT, INIT, P)$ is false because $COUNT > L$. Hence either $F(INIT, LONG, P) = TRUE$ and $F(INIT, SHORT, P) = FALSE$ or vice versa. Notice the complementarity in the strict and nonstrict inequalities that ensure a nonoverlapping partition of the real line $R = \{P > MA\} \cup \{P <= MA\}$. This, in plain English, means that there is no chance for the FSM to fall through the cracks and find itself in an undefined state. This also means that at each price update there is no possibility for the FSM to simultaneously want to transition to two or more different states. There is one and only one transition possible (that of course may be to the same current state). Hence, depending on P, the FSM transitions to either the $LONG$ or the $SHORT$ state. Assume here that the strategy transitions to the $LONG$ state.

At this point, the final job of the control system is to emit a signal to the actuator to execute the buy trade. The OMS takes control and sends an order to the ECN. Once the trade execution confirmation comes back from the ECN, the OMS passes back control to the sensor, which is allowed to open its eye again for the next price update.

The actual details of the process of interacting with the ECN are far more involved and are covered in a later part. The OMS has to embed a finite-state machine of its own design to deal with complications arising from situations of partial fills, disconnects, and the like. Here and in Part Two the idea is to focus on the strategy's core decision making *assuming* that all trade executions are performed without such complications.

When that next price update comes, the process is restarted and the strategy will either remain $LONG$ or switch to the $SHORT$ state. If that is the case, the OMS will have to execute a sale of 2 units.

There are at least two recovery mechanisms possible in the case of a disconnect or any other operational problem that keeps the strategy off-line for a while:

1. The preprocessor takes the next available price P and computes the $COUNTER$ and MA indicators as if nothing happened, thus ignoring the gap.
2. The preprocessor queries a historic external database to fill as much missing data possible, thus repopulating the E and Π sets. Once done, it would use them and the next available P to compute the indicators.

Whichever way the recovery from fault is handled by the preprocessor, the FSM just takes its input and performs its decision-making work. In sum, the FSM embeds the core logic behind the trading strategy and disentangles it from any upstream and downstream operational issues. The FSM is the main element to focus on when researching and designing potentially profitable strategies.

Seeing trading strategies in the AAA context makes the representation of their brains as finite-state machines all the more natural. It puts them into a framework where a direct analogy with robotics can be exploited. It also emphasizes the event-driven nature of trading strategies as opposed to calendar-time driven.

In Part One various simple strategies will be exhibited via their FSMs. The control mechanism there is simply a position size decision-making matrix, based on the current state and the relationship between an indicator and the current price. The sensors observe the current price and the indicators are computed on a history of observed prices and other data. The actuators are not explicit; they will be covered in Part Four when an order management system and its connectivity to the electronic marketplace are described.

The representation of the strategy's core logic by way of a finite-state machine fosters a necessary degree of *discipline* for the design process. The goal is not to complicate that process but to ensure the strategy's stability and recoverability. These essential features are key for reducing the operational and management costs over time, let alone market-related losses. The less time spent on disentangling recovery problems, the more time spent on research and development of profitable strategies.

In order to put the above theory into practice, the next chapter jumps straight into a programmatic implementation of agent-based trading strategies.

CHAPTER 4

Implementation of Strategies as Distributed Agents

T he clear analogy between a trading strategy and a robot opens the way to think further and visualize a set of trading agents coexisting at any point in time in the computing environment. The trading agents consume events, update their states, and communicate internally and with the external world.

For each trading agent an efficient top-level code can be designed on the basis of Figure 4.1. Although additional code is given in the Appendix, this section provides the detailed explanation of its most important features, and focuses on the top-level implementation of the chain:

$$Event \rightarrow Sensor \rightarrow Preprocessor \rightarrow \cdots$$
$$\cdots \rightarrow Control\ System \rightarrow Postprocessor$$

4.1 TRADING AGENT

The core class for a trading agent is **AGENT**:

```
(defclass AGENT ()
  ((name
    :accessor name
    :initarg :name)
(timestamps
 :accessor timestamps
 :initform NIL)
(revalprices
 :accessor revalprices
 :initform NIL)
(orders
 :accessor orders
 :initform NIL)
```

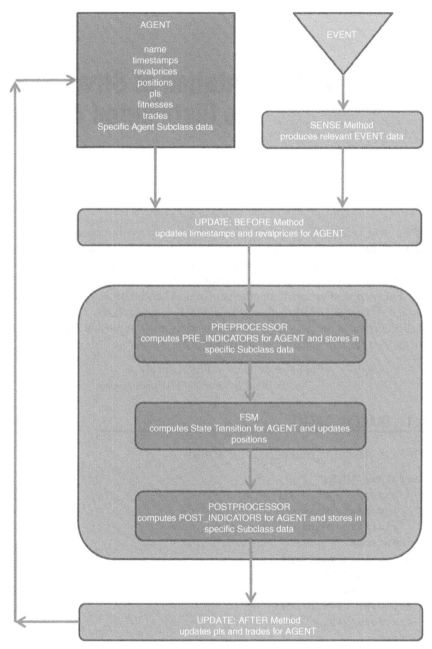

FIGURE 4.1   Top-Level Agent Architecture

```
(positions
 :accessor positions
 :initform NIL)
(pls
 :accessor pls
 :initform NIL)
(fitnesses
 :accessor fitnesses
 :initform NIL)
(trades
 :accessor trades
 :initform NIL)
(tradestats
 :accessor tradestats
 :initform NIL)
(incomingmessages
 :accessor incomingmessages
 :initform NIL)
(outgoingmessages
 :accessor outgoingmessages
 :initform NIL)
(recipientslist
 :accessor recipientslist
 :initarg :recipientslist
 :initform NIL)))
```

This class is just a data repository for each individual agent. At inception, when the class is created, the only input field required is the agent's name:

```
(defparameter *a* (make-instance 'AGENT
                         :name "MyFirstAgent"))
```

The data lists appearing in the agent class are divided in three main categories:

1. Data received from market update events: **timestamps** and **reval-prices**
2. Data calculated through trading activity: **orders, positions, pls, fitnesses, trades,** and **tradestats**
3. Data pertaining to communication with other agents: **incomingmessages, outgoingmessages,** and **recipients**, the latter being the list of agents that are declared as receivers of the agent's potential communications.

4.2 EVENTS

Events can be of different sources and have different natures. They all have the commonality that they carry information and that this information had been timestamped by some universal clock when emitted. The **EVENT** class reflects that abstract generality and contains slots for a timestamp and a value that can be anything:

```
(defclass EVENT ()
  ((timestamp
    :initarg :timestamp
    :accessor timestamp)
   (value
    :initarg :value
    :accessor value)))
```

It is specialized for market update events by the subclass **MARKETUPDATE** that contains the name or identifier of the security:

```
(defclass MARKETUPDATE (EVENT)
  ((security
    :initarg :security
    :accessor security)))
```

This class has child classes **PRC** for a single quote, **TICK**, **BOOK**, and **BAR** that are all discussed in Chapter 6, "Data Representation Techniques." The generic function **price** has methods defined to extract the price information from each type of market update object. This function also optionally contains the slippage in the context of a simulation environment as discussed later.

This section focuses on explaining the mechanics of the consumption by agents of market update events. More general events that contain the communication between agents is covered in the next section.

4.3 CONSUMING EVENTS

The top-level function that implements the reaction of an agent to an event is **consume**:

```
(defun consume (a e)
  (when (observe a e)
    (update a e)))
```

The **observe** generic function is the primary sensor of the agent and acts as a filter. The agent is only interested in certain events, for example market price updates for a particular security or communications from a particular other agent. Hence events that do not meet the "observable" criterion are simply not sensed by the agent. The example below of communicating agents will show how this method can be implemented. The most generic method of *observe* is simply all eyes open:

```
(defmethod observe ((a AGENT) (e EVENT))
  T)
```

Only relevant events are passed to **update**, which is the central and most important method, reponsible for the bulk of the logic of event processing.

4.4 UPDATING AGENTS

This section explains the *update* method for market update events. The next section handles inter-agent communication events for which similar methods apply. The method *update* is composed of three parts, the **:before**, **:main**, and **:after** methods that correspond to the preprocessing, main calculation, and postprocessing stages.

As soon as the agent starts listening to market update events, the timestamps and prices of the events received are recorded and stored in the **timestamps** and **revalprices** lists. These lists are kept in reverse-chronological order because their handling is greatly simplified by the use of the **push** and **pop** LISP functions and yields more efficient methods to compute indicators, especially when using recursion. When the above generic function is called it first calls the **:before** method:

```
(defmethod update :before ((a AGENT) (e MARKETUPDATE))
  (when (null (timestamps a))
    (push 0 (pls a))
    (push 0 (fitnesses a)))
  (push (timestamp e) (timestamps a))
  (push (price e) (revalprices a))
  (preprocess a e)
  (format T ":BEFORE completed for agent ~A and event ~A~%" a e))
```

At the initial phase when the agent is receiving its first market update the **pls** and **fitnesses** are initialized to zero. Those lists have the same length as the **timestamps** and **revalprices**.

Once this basic housekeeping has been done, the method calls the pre-processor that is specific to the agent and has to be defined separately. The preprocessor is responsible for computing indicators to pass to the agent's control system.

The agent's control system is also defined separately and constitutes the specific **main** method of the **update** generic function. Before those details are discussed, let us first complete the logical loop. Assume that instead of a robot, a human trader is sitting and watching the price updates. The trader decides on whether to trade and its **main** update method would simply be an input request of the following sort

```
(defmethod update ((a AGENT) (e MARKETUPDATE))
  (format T "Enter New Position for T= ~A and P= ~A ~%"
          (timestamp e) (price e))
  (let ((newposition (read)))
    (push newposition (positions a)))))
```

that simply records the trader's new desired position in the market (no error checking is performed—this is just an example).

Once the **positions** is updated, the control system has done its job. Now the process needs to complete in order to be open to receiving a new event. The **:after** method of the **update** generic function takes care of that:

```
(defmethod update :after ((a AGENT) (e MARKETUPDATE))
  (let* ((L (length (timestamps a)))
         (lastposition (first (positions a)))
         (prevposition (if (< L 2) 0 (second (positions a))))
         (tradequantity (- lastposition prevposition))
         (lastprice (first (revalprices a)))
         (prevprice (if (< L 2) 0 (second (revalprices a))))
         (pl (if (< L 2)
                 0
                 (* prevposition (- lastprice prevprice)))))
    (push pl (pls a))
    (unless (zerop tradequantity)
      (push (make-TRADE :timestamp (timestamp e)
                        :price (+ (price e)
                                  (slippage a e tradequantity))
                        :quantity tradequantity)
            (trades a))
      (push (compute-tradestats (trades a)) (tradestats a)))
    (postprocess a e)
    (format T ":AFTER completed for agent ~A and event~A~%"
            a e)))
```

This method starts by computing the incremental PL on this price update and appends it to the `pls` list. Here it is clear that the reverse-chronological representation is optimal as only the `first` and `second` elements of a list are traversed, which bears a low computational overhead.

The resulting trade from the change in position is computed and stored as a structure in the `trades` list, only if the resulting trade quantity is nonzero. In that case, the function `compute-tradestats` is also invoked to compute trade-by-trade statistics (pecent profitable, win-to-loss ratio, etc.) and the resulting structure is appended to the `tradestats` list. The `slippage` generic function is by default 0 but could be set to simulate frictional trading costs. The details of slippage and trade statistics calculations are discussed later in this part.

Finally the specific postprocessor to the agent is called. It may calculate another set of indicators that can only be defined once the position has changed. It also may or may not include a specific fitness calculation and update the `fitnesses` list. The concept of fitness will be relevant to Part Two and will be revisited there.

4.5 DEFINING FSM AGENTS

Having explained the top-level workings of the `update` method, it is now time to specialize the agent to contain a finite-state machine (FSM) representation of its control system. In the Common Lisp Object System it is a simple matter thanks to multiple class inheritance:

```
(defclass FSMAGENT (FSM AGENT)
  ((states
    :accessor states
    :initform NIL)))
```

The class **FSMAGENT** inherits all the slot definitions from **AGENT** and **FSM** and additionally will contain the history of its states that is updated for each event processed. Here the class **FSM** is defined to mirror the definition of the FSM given at the beginning of the chapter:

```
(defclass FSM ()
  ((currentstate
    :accessor currentstate
    :initarg :currentstate
    :initform NIL)
   (transitions
    :accessor transitions
    :initarg :transitions
    :initform NIL)))
```

One notices that only the **currentstate** and **transitions** are relevant. The finite set of N possible states is implicit in the complete list of $N * N$ transitions so it is redundant. The disciplined designs of the FSMs presented in this book ensure this completeness, hence the redundancy of the list of states. Each transition is represented as an instance of the **TRANSITION** class:

```
(defclass TRANSITION ()
  ((initialstate
    :accessor initialstate
    :initarg :initialstate)
   (finalstate
    :accessor finalstate
    :initarg :finalstate)
   (sensor
    :accessor sensor
    :initarg :sensor
    :initform #'(lambda (x) x))
   (predicate
    :accessor predicate
    :initarg :predicate
    :initform #'(lambda (x) NIL))
   (actuator
    :accessor actuator
    :initarg :actuator
    :initform #'(lambda (x) NIL))
   (effected
    :accessor effected
    :initform NIL)))
```

Before going into details as to how the FSM is initialized and maintained for a particular strategy class it is important to understand at the high level how the FSM is operated. First of all, the consumption of an event by a transition object is defined by the following **perform** method:

```
(defmethod perform ((tr TRANSITION) (e EVENT))
  (setf (effected tr) (funcall (predicate tr)
                               (funcall (sensor tr)
                                        e))))
```

This method first calls the transition's sensor function on the event (e.g., the **price** method discussed above). The output is passed to the transition's predicate that either returns T or NIL. NIL is equivalent to False in LISP whereas True can be represented by T or any non-NIL expression. This Boolean value is stored in the transition's **effected** field.

The consumption of an event by the whole FSM is performed by the **operatefsm** method:

```
(defmethod operatefsm ((fsm FSM) (e EVENT))
 (let* ((applicable-transitions
          (remove-if-not #'(lambda (x) (equal (initialstate x)
                                              (currentstate fsm)))
                         (transitions fsm)))
        (effected-transition
          (car (remove-if-not #'(lambda (x) (perform x e))
                              applicable-transitions))))
   (funcall (actuator effected-transition)
            (funcall (sensor effected-transition)
                     e))
   (setf (currentstate fsm) (finalstate effected-transition))
   (format T "Transition  $ ->  S~%"
           (initialstate effected-transition)
           (finalstate effected-transition)))))
```

This method works exactly as explained when the FSM concept was introduced initially. The **applicable-transitions** variable is initialized to the subset of potential transitions out of the FSM's current state. The **perform** method is applied to all these potential transitions and returns True or False. The transition for which it is True is stored in the **effected-transition** variable. The **effected-transition** is then made to perform some action (e.g., change of the agent's **position**) and for this task the transition's **actuator** function is called on the transition's sensor output. Finally the state of the FSM is changed to the final state of the effected transition.

To close the loop, here is finally the **main** method for the **update** generic function for the **FSMAGENT** case:

```
(defmethod update ((a FSMAGENT) (e MARKETUPDATE))
  (setfsm a)
  (format T "Set FSM completed for  ~S~%" (name a))
  (operatefsm a e)
  (format T "Operate FSM completed for ~S~%" (name a))
  (push (currentstate a) (states a))
  (format T ":MAIN completed for ~S and new state ~S added ~%"
          (name a) (currentstate a)))
```

This method overrides the manual main **update** method discussed for the hypothetical human agent. Remember that this **main** method is called after the **:before** method that contains all the preprocessing, and before the **:after** method that contains all the postprocesing. It initially resets the agent's FSM with the **setfsm** method that will be discussed below. This implicitly changes the FSM's parameters (indicators) given the observation of the event. It then runs the FSM decision matrix that implicity updates the agent's **positions** list. It appends the new state of the agent to the **states** list. Then it finally passes control to the **:after** method.

4.6 IMPLEMENTING A STRATEGY

The code discussed above implements the universal top-level process for consumption of events by FSM-endowed agents. To operate it concretely one needs to specialize the **FSMAGENT** class and the **setfsm** method to a particular trading strategy.

Here the simplistic trend-following strategy is explained in details. The next chapter discusses a series of real-world examples that are more complicated but the essentials of the code are the same as for the simple example here.

The strategy's class is defined as a subclass of *FSMAGENT*:

```
(defclass SIMPLEMODEL (FSMAGENT)
  ((L
    :accessor L
    :initarg :L)
   (COUNTER
    :accessor COUNTER
    :initform 0)
   (MA
    :accessor MA
    :initform 0)))
```

It contains the slot for the initially settable parameter **L** that is the length of the lookback period for the moving average calculation. The other slots are for the counter and moving average indicators that are computed by the process. To initialize a concrete class instance that has lookback value of 10 one would evaluate the following expression:

```
(defparameter *mod1* (make-instance
                      'SIMPLEMODEL
                      :L 10))
```

The instance of our class will be stored in the ***mod1*** global variable.

Before the agent is able to consume any events it needs some basic initialization. The **initialize** method sets the FSM's original state to **:INIT**. It also reflects the value of **L** in the internal name of the class, which is handy when one runs several instances at the same time and wants to output results in a practical format.

```
(defmethod initialize ((a SIMPLEMODEL))
   (with-slots (L states name) a
    (when (null states)
      (push :INIT states)
      (setf name (concatenate 'string
                      "SIMPLE_MODEL_"
                      (format NIL "A" L))))))
```

Assume for simplicity that the **SIMPLEMODEL** agent consumes all market update events that are passed to it. Thus no specific method on the **observe** generic function needs to be defined and hence it will always return True and will immediately pass control to the **update** method.

The preprocessor method, however, needs to be defined for the **SIMPLEMODEL** class:

```
(defmethod preprocess ((a SIMPLEMODEL) (e MARKETUPDATE))
   (with-slots (L COUNTER MA revalprices) a
      (setf COUNTER (length revalprices))
      (setf MA (avg-list (sub-list revalprices 0 (- L 1)))))))
```

It sets the counter to the length of the list of **revalprices** (which is the same as the length of the **timestamps** list). These lists are non-NIL because the preprocessor operates after the first event's price and timestamp had been added to them. The preprocessor computes the **MA** by invoking the **sub-list** function that returns the subset of the first **L** elements (or less if not available) of the **revalprices** list.

The **setfsm** method is the core of the strategy's decision making:

```
(defmethod setfsm ((a SIMPLEMODEL))
   (with-slots (L COUNTER MA states currentstate
                 revalprices transitions positions name) a
    (setf currentstate (first states))
    (setf transitions (list
                       (make-instance
                       'TRANSITION
                       :initialstate :INIT
```

```
:finalstate :INIT
:sensor #'price
:predicate #'(lambda (p)
              (<= COUNTER L))
:actuator #'(lambda (p)
             (push 0 positions)
             (format T
                "~S INIT->INIT ~%"
                name)))
(make-instance
 'TRANSITION
 :initialstate :INIT
 :finalstate :LONG
 :sensor #'price
 :predicate #'~S(lambda (p)
                 (and (> COUNTER L)
                      (> p MA)))
 :actuator #'(lambda (p)
              (push 1 positions)
              (format T
                 "~S INIT->LONG ~%"
                 name)))
(make-instance
 'TRANSITION
 :initialstate :INIT
 :finalstate :SHORT
 :sensor #'price
 :predicate #'(lambda (p)
               (and (> COUNTER L)
                    (<= p MA)))
 :actuator #'(lambda (p)
              (push -1 positions)
              (format T
                 "~S INIT->SHORT ~%"
                 name)))
(make-instance
 'TRANSITION
 :initialstate :LONG
 :finalstate :INIT
 :sensor #'price
 :predicate #'(lambda (p)
               NIL)
```

```
                         :actuator #'(lambda (p)
                                      NIL))
           (make-instance
           'TRANSITION
           :initialstate :LONG
           :finalstate :LONG
           :sensor #'price
           :predicate #'(lambda (p)
                           (> p MA))
           :actuator #'(lambda (p)
                           (push 1 positions)
                           (format T
                             "~S LONG->LONG ~%"
                             name)))
           (make-instance
           'TRANSITION
           :initialstate :LONG
           :finalstate :SHORT
           :sensor #'price
           :predicate #'(lambda (p)
                            (<= p MA))
           :actuator #'(lambda (p)
                            (push -1 positions)
                            (format T
                              "S LONG->SHORT ~%"
                              name)))
           (make-instance
           'TRANSITION
           :initialstate :SHORT
           :finalstate :INIT
           :sensor #'price
           :predicate #'(lambda (p)
                            NIL)
           :actuator #'(lambda (p)
                            NIL))
           (make-instance
           'TRANSITION
           :initialstate :SHORT
           :finalstate :LONG
           :sensor #'price
           :predicate #'(lambda (p)
                            (> p MA))
```

```
                    :actuator #'(lambda (p)
                                (push 1 positions)
                                (format T
                                    "~S SHORT->LONG ~%"
                                    name)))
                (make-instance
                'TRANSITION
                :initialstate :SHORT
                :finalstate :SHORT
                :sensor #'price
                :predicate #'(lambda (p)
                                (<= p MA))
                :actuator #'(lambda (p)
                                (push -1 positions)
                                (format T
                                    "~S SHORT->SHORT ~%"
                                    name))))))))
```

The **setfsm** method updates the FSM's state with the latest state of the agent (remember that the **states** list is in reverse chronological order like all the others). It then updates the **transitions** list with the parameters **COUNTER** and **MA** that have been computed and stored into the **SIMPLE-MODEL** class by the **preprocess** method above.

There are three states and nine possible transitions. However the $LONG \rightarrow INIT$ and $SHORT \rightarrow INIT$ transitions are not allowed and their predicate functions always return NIL (False). Hence, despite the fact that those transitions are declared for the sake of completeness, they will never happen in the course of the computation.

The sensor function for each transition is the **price** method on a **MARKETUPDATE** event. Each predicate would take that price as input if it is ever passed to it.

The actuator of a transition updates the **positions** list when that transition occurs, as per the **updatefsm** method explained above. So one and only one position update occurs when a market update event is processed. The actuator also prints which actual transition has occured.

Finally a postprocessor is not really needed here but one could just use it for outputting the agent's data at each event consumption:

```
(defmethod postprocess ((a SIMPLEMODEL) (e MARKETUPDATE))
(with-slots (name COUNTER MA states positions pls) a
  (format T "Event ~S ~S Consumed for Agent ~S :~%"
          (timestamp e) (price e) name)
```

```
(format T "Output: COUNTER= ~S MA= ~S State= ~S
         Position= ~S PL= ~S~%" COUNTER MA (first states)
         (first positions) (first pls)))))
```

This finishes the explanation of the structure of the basic code that implements the event consumption cycle of an FSM-driven agent.

To run the code and do a simulation of the simple model, suppose a list of market update events is created and called ***events***. That list contains the consecutive individual event classes in chronological order.

Then to run the ***mod1*** strategy on that list, one would simply invoke

```
(dolist (e *events*)
  (consume *mod1* e))
```

and watch the outputs from the existing **format** calls on the console.

Also, assume we define a list of 100 simple strategies of the kind by varying the **L**, storing the result into the ***agents*** list:

```
(defparameter *agents* NIL)

(for (i 10 110)
     (push (make-instance
             'SIMPLEMODEL
             :L i)
           *agents*))
```

Then running all the agents at once on the events list is easy:

```
(dolist (e *events*)
  (dolist (a *agents*)
    (consume (a e))))
```

Here we assume that for each **e**, the agents consume that event in a single thread (consecutively). However, it is easy to make each agent run the update process in a different concurrent thread and synchronize the results before the next event is consumed. This topic will be covered in Part Four.

CHAPTER 5

Inter-Agent Communications

The framework of handling market update events extends naturally to a more general class of communication events. Endowing trading agents with the ability to communicate with each other opens a whole new avenue in the design of trading strategies.

The subclass of communication events contains the reference to the originating entity (an agent) and the list of recipients for which that communication is addressed to:

```
(defclass COMM (EVENT)
  ((originator
    :accessor originator
    :initarg :originator)
   (recipients
    :accessor recipients
    :initarg :recipients)))
```

The message of the communication event would be contained in the subclass **value** field and it would also be timestamped like any other event.

5.1 HANDLING COMMUNICATION EVENTS

The agent should take into consideration all the communication events directed at it and ignore all the rest. If it is not one of the intended recipients, the event is not handled by the agent. Also, the agent does not talk to itself and, just in case, filters out all messages that it emits. Hence the *observe* method that implements that primary sensor is

```
(defmethod observe ((a AGENT) (e COMM))
  (and (member a (recipients e))
       (not (equal a (originator e)))))
```

In the most general case, the handling of the communication event by the **update** method goes by exactly the same design pattern as explained above for handling market events. No new top-level logic needs to be written but the **preprocess** and **postprocess** methods need to be implemented for a particular agent subclass. The FSM transitions need to handle communication events independently of market update events while maintaining logical completeness. Such a complete version is discussed in the context of handling some inter-market execution algorithms in Part Three.

Here a simpler example is given where one assumes that the handling of communication events only affects the parameters of the FSM but not the state of the agent. This reduced version already allows for testing an interesting range of strategies.

The events that are relevant to the agent are passed initially to the **update** preprocessing stage, that is, its **:before** method:

```
(defmethod update :before ((a AGENT) (e COMM))
  (push e (incomingmessages a))
  (preprocess a e)
  (format T ":BEFORE completed for agent ~A and COMM event
                                          ~A~%" a e))
```

The preprocessor interprets the meaning of the message that needs to be implemented for any particular agent subclass as is shown in the example later.

In this simplified implementation, the interpretation of the information contained in the message yields a change of internal parameters of the trading agent, but not an immediate change of its state. The state can only change when the next market update is consumed by the agent. Hence the **:main** update method for handling a communication event by an FSM agent is simply

```
(defmethod update ((a FSMAGENT) (e COMM))
  (setfsm a)
  (format T "Set FSM completed for ~S~%" a)
  (format T "MAIN method completed for ~S and COMM event
                                          ~S ~%" a e))
```

So the only thing that happens here is that the FSM of the agent is reset with the new parameters that the preprocessor has computed from the interpretation of the message. Finally some postprocessing may be done (e.g., saving the new agent's internal parameters in some external database for recovery from fault purposes):

```
(defmethod update :after ((a AGENT) (e COMM))
   (postprocess a e)
   (format T ":AFTER completed for agent ~A and COMM event
                                            ~A~%" a e))
```

In this simplified design pattern the **operatefsm** method is not called after the FSM had been reset to the new parameters. Hence the agent does not change its state when such a communication is handled. Quite a few situations can be dealt with in this way, in particular in the context of designing and simulating price-taking strategies (rather than strategies that use limit orders, like market-making). To perform a trade, the agent needs to wait for the next price or order book update and would act as soon as that information is received.

5.2 EMITTING MESSAGES AND RUNNING SIMULATIONS

The method that an agent uses to emit a message to its recipients is

```
(defmethod emit ((a AGENT) msg)
   (push (make-instance 'COMM
                         :originator a
                         :recipients (recipientslist a)
                         :timestamp (first (timestamps a))
                         :value msg)
         *events-queue*)
   (push (list (first (timestamps a)) msg)
         (outgoingmessages a)))
```

For simplicity, it uses the last timestamp available to the agent (timestamp of the last market update received) but this can obviously change to the system clock time in a real-time implementation. The *emit* method can be called from any point in the **update** chain (preprocessor, transitions, postprocessor).

The ***eventsqueue*** is a global list, seen by all the agents, that buffers all the events being broadcast. In a simulation environment it is initially populated by the history of market update events. When an agent emits a message, that message is placed at the top of the queue by the **push** function, so this will be the first message to go out unless other agents place their messages on top of this. Once all the agents are done placing their messages on the queue, the events are broadcast one by one.

Here it is important to note that the handling of a communication event by an agent precludes the possibility of the agent emitting another communication event. An agent can only emit a communication event when handling a market update event. This is done to avoid spamming the broadcast with inter-agent communication at the expense of handling market price events. With this in mind, a convergent simulation process is given by the following function:

```
(defun run-simulation (events)
  (dolist (a *agents*)
    (initialize a))
  (setf *events-queue* events)
  (while *events-queue*
    (let ((e (pop *events-queue*)))
      (dolist (a *agents*)
        (consume a e)))))
```

After all the agents have been initialized, the ***events-queue*** is set to the list of (initially market update) events to handle. The first element is popped from the queue and distributed for the consumption of all the agents. **(pop lst)** is a destructive operation that returns the **car** of the **lst** and resets **lst** to **(cdr lst)**.

During the consumption process loop on the ***agents*** list, any agent can emit one or more messages that are consecutively pushed onto the queue. These messages are handled one by one by all the agents in the next step, but as written above, no more communication events can be emitted at this stage. When all these communication events are processed, the next event will be a market update event and the whole process restarts until the ***events-queue*** gets depleted to the empty list **NIL**.

5.3 IMPLEMENTATION EXAMPLE

In this section, a concrete example of communicating agents built on the simplified design pattern is presented. Each agent trades one particular security and communicates to the other its state. The agents take each other's state into account so as to always be in a situation of opposite trading positions—either (Long,Short), (Short,Long), or (Flat,Flat). This simulates a trend-following pairs-trading model where only high conviction trades are allowed (with one security trading up while the other is trending down).

The strategy class can be defined as a subclass of **SIMPLEMODEL**:

```
(defclass SIMPLEMODELCOMM (SIMPLEMODEL)
  ((MKT
    :accessor MKT
    :initarg :MKT)
   (UNBLOCKSHORT
    :accessor UNBLOCKSHORT
    :initform -1)
   (UNBLOCKLONG
    :accessor UNBLOCKLONG
    :initform 1)))
```

The **MKT** field is the identifier of the security that a particular instance of the class is operating on. It is used to filter the market update events via the implementation of the **observe** method:

```
(defmethod observe ((a SIMPLEMODELCOMM) (e MARKETUPDATE))
  (equal (MKT a) (security e)))
```

Before the agent starts processing any events, it needs to be initialized. The **initialize** method emits a message communicating the agent's **:INIT** state. This "I'm alive" message will be automatically picked up by the other agent and vice versa.

```
(defmethod initialize ((a SIMPLEMODELCOMM))
  (with-slots (MKT L states name) a
    (when (null states)
      (push :INIT states)
      (setf name (concatenate 'string
                              "SIMPLE_MODEL_"
                              (format NIL "~A_~A" MKT L)))
      (emit a :INIT)))))
```

The **preprocess** generic function now has two distinct methods to handle the different event types. The market updates are handled by the same method as the superclass, but for clarity it is as follows:

```
(defmethod preprocess ((a SIMPLEMODELCOMM) (e MARKETUPDATE))
  (with-slots (L COUNTER MA revalprices) a
          (setf COUNTER (length revalprices))
          (setf MA (avg-list (sub-list revalprices 0 L)))))
```

The communication events from the other agent are handled by:

```
(defmethod preprocess ((a SIMPLEMODELCOMM) (e COMM))
  (with-slots (UNBLOCKSHORT UNBLOCKLONG) a
              (case (value e)
                    (:INIT (setf UNBLOCKSHORT 0)
                           (setf UNBLOCKLONG 0))
                    (:LONG (setf UNBLOCKSHORT -1)
                           (setf UNBLOCKLONG 0))
                    (:SHORT (setf UNBLOCKSHORT 0)
                            (setf UNBLOCKLONG 1)))))
```

This function performs the interpretation of the message received from the other agent. If the other agent is in the :INIT state, it blocks its own long and short positions. If the other agent is in the :LONG state, it blocks its own long positions. If the other agent is in the :SHORT state, it blocks its own short positions. This ensures that the agents are either both flat or have opposite sign positions at all times.

The setup of the FSM explicitly takes these **UNBLOCKLONG** and **UNBLOCKSHORT** values to alter the market exposure of the agent:

```
(defmethod setfsm ((a SIMPLEMODELCOMM))
  (with-slots (L COUNTER MA UNBLOCKLONG UNBLOCKSHORT states
               currentstate revalprices transitions positions name) a
    (setf currentstate (first states))
    (setf transitions (list
                        (make-instance
                         'TRANSITION
                         :initialstate :INIT
                         :finalstate :INIT
                         :sensor #'price
                         :predicate #'(lambda (p)
                                        (<= COUNTER L))
                         :actuator #'(lambda (p)
                                       (push 0 positions)
                                       (format T
                                               "~S INIT->INIT ~%"
                                               name)))
                        (make-instance
                         'TRANSITION
                         :initialstate :INIT
                         :finalstate :LONG
                         :sensor #'price
                         :predicate #'(lambda (p)
                                        (and (> COUNTER L)
                                             (> p MA)))
```

```
                        :actuator #'(lambda (p)
                                    (push UNBLOCKLONG positions)
                                    (emit a :LONG)
                                    (format T
                                            "~S INIT->LONG ~%"
                                            name)))
                  (make-instance
                   'TRANSITION
                   :initialstate :INIT
                   :finalstate :SHORT
                   :sensor #'price
                   :predicate #'(lambda (p)
                                (and (> COUNTER L)
                                     (<= p MA)))
                   :actuator #'(lambda (p)
                               (push UNBLOCKSHORT positions)
                               (emit a :SHORT)
                               (format T
                                       "~S INIT->SHORT ~%"
                                       name)))
                  (make-instance
                   'TRANSITION
                   :initialstate :LONG
                   :finalstate :INIT
                   :sensor #'price
                   :predicate #'(lambda (p)
                               NIL)
                   :actuator #'(lambda (p)
                               NIL))
                  (make-instance
                   'TRANSITION
                   :initialstate :LONG
                   :finalstate :LONG
                   :sensor #'price
                   :predicate #'(lambda (p)
                                (> p MA))
                   :actuator #'(lambda (p)
                               (push UNBLOCKLONG positions)
                               (format T
                                       "~S LONG->LONG ~%"
                                       name)))
                  (make-instance
                   'TRANSITION
                   :initialstate :LONG
                   :finalstate :SHORT
                   :sensor #'price
                   :predicate #'(lambda (p)
                                (<= p MA))
```

```
          :actuator #'(lambda (p)
                          (push UNBLOCKSHORT positions)
                          (emit a :SHORT)
                          (format T
                                  "~S LONG->SHORT ~%"
                                  name)))
  (make-instance
   'TRANSITION
   :initialstate :SHORT
   :finalstate :INIT
   :sensor #'price
   :predicate #'(lambda (p)
                   NIL)
   :actuator #'(lambda (p)
                   NIL))
  (make-instance
   'TRANSITION
   :initialstate :SHORT
   :finalstate :LONG
   :sensor #'price
   :predicate #'(lambda (p)
                   (> p MA))
   :actuator #'(lambda (p)
                   (push UNBLOCKLONG positions)
                   (emit a :LONG)
                   (format T
                           "~S SHORT->LONG ~%"
                           name)))
  (make-instance
   'TRANSITION
   :initialstate :SHORT
   :finalstate :SHORT
   :sensor #'price
   :predicate #'(lambda (p)
                   (<= p MA))
   :actuator #'(lambda (p)
                   (push UNBLOCKSHORT positions)
                   (format T
                           "~S SHORT->SHORT ~%"
                           name)))))))))
```

The agents **emit** their state only when their state changes. This is handled in the particular transition **actuator** functions. This communication is parsimonious (necessary and sufficient).

Finally, there is no need for a **postprocess** method on a communication event as the acknowledgment that the event has been processed is handled by the **update**'s **:after** method. The **postprocess** on a market update can be used (automatically) from the **SIMPLEMODEL** superclass.

The agents can be instantiated and their recipients lists set by evaluating the following set of expressions:

```
(defparameter *a1* (make-instance
                    'SIMPLEMODELCOMM
                    :MKT "AAPL"
                    :L 10))

(defparameter *a2* (make-instance
                    'SIMPLEMODELCOMM
                    :MKT "DELL"
                    :L 10))

(push *a2* (recipientslist *a1*))
(push *a1* (recipientslist *a2*))

(push *a2* *agents*)
(push *a1* *agents*)
```

Finally a simple simulation can be performed using the **run-simulation** function. For this one needs to create a data set with market update events

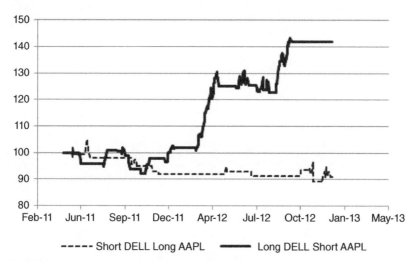

FIGURE 5.1 Communicating Agents Example

for the two securities. Figure 5.1 is an example of an output that shows the polar opposite market positions of the two agents.

In this simple example, each agent preserves its state independently of the other. The state is solely defined by the position of the price **P** relative to the **MA** and is independent of the agent's **position** in the market. This means that each agent is always in sync with its market but varies its position taking into account both agents' states.

CHAPTER 6

Data Representation Techniques

I n the Introduction, systematic trading was described as being an art, a
science, and a business. This book focuses primarily on the scientific and
business aspects. The scientific endeavor of systematic trading consists of
discovering persistent and predictable patterns in market activity and the
business aspect consists of efficiently exploiting them.

Any science starts with observational data—the raw materials of research on which concepts and theories are consequently built. However, not
all data is relevant at all times, and more often than not, data overload can
stall scientific progress, as one cannot see the forest for the trees when for-
mulating useful concepts. Hence part of the art of the researcher comes in
the form of an intuitive filter that helps decide what data to focus on. This
chapter introduces the data filter techniques relevant to systematic trading
and forms the basis for data analysis in the book.

6.1 DATA RELEVANCE AND FILTERING OF INFORMATION

The raw materials for systematic trading are (1) time series of transactions
(price and volume), (2) time series of orders (depth of book), and (3) time series of news (economic releases, idiosyncratic company news, world events).
Most of the models discussed in this book are based on the first two streams
of data, however the third one is also briefly discussed in this chapter.

The question of what data is relevant is ultimately a function of the
goal of the inquiry. In the world of systematic trading, this translates into
understanding the timescale, price scale, and type of pattern one is trying to
exploit. A data filter is usually formed of three components: (1) a sampling
technique, (2) a compression technique, and (3) a representation technique.

In this book, all the trading strategies are discussed and implemented
within the paradigm of distributed trading agents. In this paradigm, any

data consumed by the agent is represented by events that the agent observes and reacts to. This paradigm is the closest model to the real world and has the significant advantage that the concepts and code developed here apply equally well to real-time trading and to simulation environments. A comprehensive event-driven simulation environment is presented later in Part One.

Events fall into two classes, the **MARKETUPDATE** representing all external market data coming from exchanges and ECNs and the internal **COMM** events that carry inter-agent communications.

This chapter focuses on the market update events and the construction of more elaborate events from the sampling and compression of elementary ones. These elementary transaction and orders events fall into two categories:

1. A trade is performed and the price and volume information is communicated to the world.
2. The order book changes and the new state of the order book is communicated to the world.

Events are filtered by the trading agent via its observe method that not only can choose what securities prices to observe but in what format. Hence this method contains the sampling and compression techniques alluded to above.

6.2 PRICE AND ORDER BOOK UPDATES

Although introduced in the beginning, it is worth revisiting the object-oriented design of the main **EVENT** class.

Throughout Parts One to Three, it is assumed that the raw data that comes from the ECN (via either the FIX protocol or a more efficient ECN-specific protocol) is converted by a data adaptor to a class instance that is broadcast to the trading agents.

The top-level **EVENT** class contains a timestamp and a value (that can contain anything):

```
(defclass EVENT ()
  ((timestamp
    :initarg :timestamp
    :accessor timestamp)
  (value
    :initarg :value
    :accessor value)))
```

It is specialized for a market update event and contains an additional security identifier field:

```
(defclass MARKETUPDATE (EVENT)
  ((security
    :initarg :security
    :accessor security))))
```

6.2.1 Elementary Price Events

The most elementary market update events that can be observed from an ECN are single traded price updates and are represented by instances of the class **PRC**, a child class of **MARKETUPDATE**:

```
(defclass PRC (MARKETUPDATE)
  ((lastprice
    :accessor lastprice)
   (lastvolume
    :accessor lastvolume)))

(defmethod initialize-instance :after ((e PRC))
  (setf (lastprice e) (first (value e)))
  (when (second (value e))
    (setf (lastvolume e) (second (value e))))))
```

PRC's **value** field is a list with two elements that are the traded price and the volume traded at that price (if that information is available and NIL otherwise). These events basically represent the entries of the quote recap table, which is a feature available for all exchange-traded securities. The **initialize-instance :after** method populates the relevant fields that can be accessed by the agent. Here the use of the **initialize-instance :after** method may seem a bit superfluous but it is actually quite handy when the raw data is passed to the LISP class as a simple array from the ECN interface via a foreign-function implementation.

Figure 6.1 shows what a standard quote recap data time series looks like.

6.2.2 Order Book Data

The order book represents at a point in time the set of posted resting orders for a particular security at an exchange. It is basically two ordered lists of pairs: the bid side of the book is the collection of bid prices and respective sizes of aggregate buy orders at those prices; the offer side of the book is

Time	Size	Price
12:32:59	2	143.62
12:32:55	15	143.62
12:32:54	4	143.62
12:32:51	249	143.56
12:32:41	1	143.62
12:32:21	10	143.63
12:32:13	3	143.63
12:32:04	3	143.63

FIGURE 6.1 Quote Recap Data Example

the collection of ask prices with the respective size of aggregate offers to sell at those prices. The order book data was once the private information of stock specialists, but with the advent of the electronic markets, it became completely public and is displayed in real time on all trading applications (such as Trading Technologies or J-Trader).

Figure 6.2 is an illustration of a change in order book from one instant to another as well as the associated trade. Note that the trade size (in this case a buy at the best ask price) does correspond to the change in the best ask

Event 1		Event 2		Event 3	
Original book		Trade: Lift 50 lots at 143.58		Removed best offer for 20 lots	
143.62	120	143.62	120	143.62	120
143.61	89	143.61	89	143.61	89
143.6	388	143.6	388	143.6	388
143.59	430	143.59	430	143.59	430
143.58	76	143.58	26	143.58	6
143.57	489	143.57	489	143.57	489
143.56	236	143.56	236	143.56	236
143.55	184	143.55	184	143.55	184
143.54	303	143.54	303	143.54	303
143.53	95	143.53	95	143.53	95

FIGURE 6.2 Order Book Change Example

quantity. At the second instant the best ask quantity is reduced not because of a trade but because someone pulled an existing sell order (potentially in response to the trade that just happened). Here it is assumed that all the events come in the correctly time-stamped order from the ECN, but it has to be pointed out that in practice this is unfortunately not always the case, because of technological failings and latency issues that may occur at the exchange itself.

The state of the order book is represented by the **BOOK** class. The **value** field is a list of two lists l_b and l_a that contain lists of bids and bid sizes and asks and ask sizes. The **BOOK** class also has a specific method of initialization that sets up the best bids, offers, average bid, and offer prices and all associated sizes:

```
(defclass BOOK (MARKETUPDATE)
  ((mid
    :accessor mid)
   (bidbest
    :accessor bidbest)
   (bidbestsize
    :accessor bidbestsize)
   (bidtotsize
    :accessor bidtotsize)
   (bidavgprc
    :accessor bidavgprc)
   (askbest
    :accessor askbest)
   (askbestsize
    :accessor askbestsize)
   (asktotsize
    :accessor asktotsize)
   (askavgprc
    :accessor askavgprc)))

(defmethod initialize-instance :after ((e BOOK) &key)
  (let* ((v (value e))
         (lb (first v))
         (la (second v)))
    (setf lb (sort lb #'(lambda (x y) (> (first x) (first y)))))
    (setf la (sort la #'(lambda (x y) (< (first x) (first y)))))
    (setf (bidbest e) (first (first lb)))
    (setf (bidbestsize e) (second (first lb)))
    (setf (bidtotsize e) (sum-list (mapcar #'second
                            lb)))
```

```
(setf (bidavgprc e) (/ (sum-list (mapcar #'(lambda (x)
                                             (* (first x) (second x)))

                                  lb))
                        (bidtotsize e)))
(setf (askbest e) (first (first la)))
(setf (askbestsize e) (second (first la)))
(setf (asktotsize e) (sum-list (mapcar #'second
                                       la)))
(setf (askavgprc e) (/ (sum-list (mapcar #'(lambda (x)
                                             (* (first x) (second x)))
                                  la))
                        (bidtotsize e)))
(setf (mid e) (* 0.5 (+ (bidbest e)
                        (askbest e))))
(setf (value e) (list lb la))))
```

The list of bid-side and ask-side quotes contained in the **value** field of the class instance is processed automatically by the **initialize-instance :after** method and populates all the relevant fields that can be used by the agent's preprocessor and control system.

In practice, the ECN broadcasts the changes to the order book, not the book itself (unless specifically requested by the application). The **DELTA** class is designed to represent the change in the order book from one moment to the next. Those details are covered in Part Four and here one assumes that the trading system's interface to the ECN automatically converts these book updates into the instance of the **BOOK** class before broadcasting it to the agents.

6.2.3 Tick Data: The Finest Grain

The elementary market update events embodied in the **PRC** and **BOOK** events are colloquially called *ticks*. Tick data is the purest event data. The systematic trading activities for which tick data is *essential* are automated market-making and algorithmic trading. The strategies behind those activities use both the trade updates and the full book information to detect changes in supply and demand. Although a much more difficult task, one can also attempt to uncover hidden competing algorithms (like iceberg orders and others).

Collecting, processing, and storing tick data is a daunting task due to the sheer volume of information. An important tool in that matter is to use a networked cached memory that automatically saves chunks of data onto hardware without creating latency bottlenecks due to database read-writes.

Co-locating of trading servers on an ECN for ultrafast market and data access becomes essential for the efficient implementation of such activities because latency creates an unwanted sampling limitation. Indeed if the market access latency is L then the turnaround from receiving market data, processing it, and sending an order is limited from below by $2L$, and despite receiving all the event data, one is still limited in one's actions by latency-induced time-sampling. One should also be careful about the ECNs and brokers throttling data, where they do actually filter data at the outset and only send it by packets in order to not overload the network.

These practical matters are discussed in detail in Part Four of the book.

6.3 SAMPLING: CLOCK TIME VS. EVENT TIME

The two most important sampling techniques for financial data are time and event sampling. The difference between the commonly used clock time and the timescale derived from the occurence of elementary market events is explained here.

In time-interval sampling, one chooses a particular clock time interval of length T and observes a price at the end of each consecutive interval. For example, many traders build models using closing or last traded prices at the end of each trading day and hence react only to daily changes in prices. Longer-term models use last traded weekly or even monthly prices. Any intermediate data is simply omitted or ignored by those models. One can also sample intraday using sampling every T minutes or seconds.

The markets go periodically through bursts and troughs of activity, which are characterized by a varying volume of transactions in time. Time sampling is appropriate for longer term strategies on timescales where such varying activity is averaged out and is not deemed to influence decision making. However, a more event-driven approach is warranted for shorter term and intraday trading.

In event sampling, instead of sampling every T minutes, one samples every N^{th} event. This means that the sampling naturally accelerates and decelerates in clock time in step with the market activity. This difference between clock and event time is particularly relevant for short-term trading that needs to react quickly to changing market conditions as it usually exploits patterns stemming from such waves of activity.

The decision between clock and event sampling is the central decision for the relevant filtering technique when designing a model. The subsequent compression and representation techniques are then based on the same principles. To illustrate the point, Figure 6.3 shows two price graphs of the same intraday price action in clock and event time.

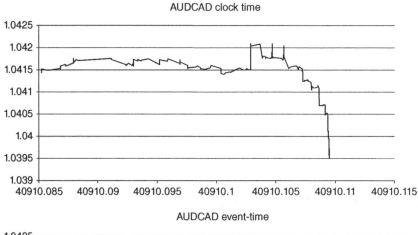

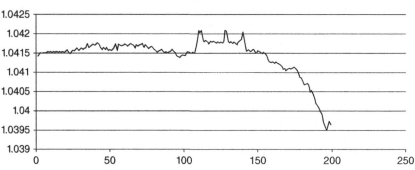

FIGURE 6.3 Price Action in Clock vs. Event Time

In the trading agent paradigm introduced in this book, there is no difference of implementation between models using event or clock time because clock-driven sampling is a subset of event-driven sampling. From a backtesting or forward-testing perspective, the processing of a stream of time-sampled or event-sampled prices is the same. The advantage of the design presented in the book is that it applies equally well for simulation and real-time trading environments.

6.4 COMPRESSION

6.4.1 Slicing Time into Bars and Candles

Some models use intermediate information between time or event sampled data. The most common compression technique is called a *bar* and carries information on the beginning (opening), the high, the low, and the last (closing) price in each time interval. The following figure shows the 10-minute time-bars and the 1,000-event tick-bars and highlights the difference between the sampling techniques. The *range* of the bar is the distance between the high and the low price.

Bursts of volatility in the market are usually synonymous and concurrent with bursts in event activity, namely trading and order book changes. These events seem to accelerate in clock time. Symmetrically, when the markets are in transitions between time zones or during holidays, the event frequency comes down and so does volatility. Sampling with constant clock time slices through such periods of higher or lower activity yields respectively higher or lower ranges.

A *candle* is a bar of which the "body," that is, the range between the opening and closing price, is either filled, when the closing price is below the opening, or empty, if the closing price is above the opening. This gives a tool for the trader to represent graphically serial correlation of moves (short term trends). Figures 6.4 and 6.5 show representative bar and candle charts.

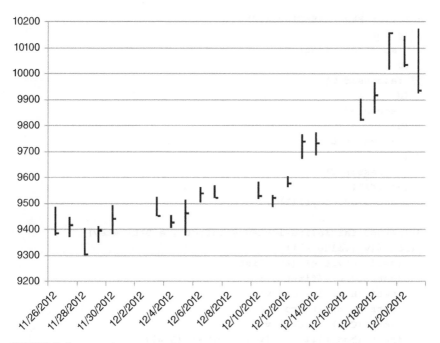

FIGURE 6.4 Bar Chart Example

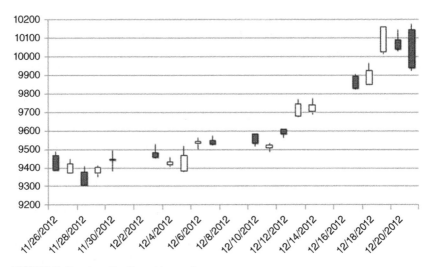

FIGURE 6.5 Candle Chart Example

The bars and candles are represented as instances of the class **BAR**:

```
(defclass BAR (MARKETUPDATE)
  ((pivot
    :accessor pivot)
   (O
    :accessor O)
   (H
    :accessor H)
   (L
    :accessor L)
   (C
    :accessor C)
   (bodyfill
    :accessor bodyfill)))

(defmethod initialize-instance :after ((e BAR) &key)
  (let ((v (value e)))
    (setf (pivot e) (avg-list v))
    (setf (O e) (first v))
    (setf (H e) (second v))
    (setf (L e) (third v))
    (setf (C e) (fourth v))
    (setf (bodyfill e) (if (>= (C e) (O e))
                           NIL
                         T)))))
```

The **value** field of the class is just the list of the opening, high, low, and closing prices. The **initialize-instance :after** method populates the readable fields and also determines the candle's body fill field. Hence this class contains the candle information as well if needed.

The class is further specialized into event-driven and time-driven sampling:

```
(defclass TICKBAR (BAR)
  ((numticks
    :accessor numticks
    :initarg :numticks)))

(defclass TIMEBAR (BAR)
  ((numtimeunits
    :accessor numtimeunits
    :initarg :numtimeunits)
   (timeunit
    :accessor timeunit
    :initarg :timeunit
    :initform :MINUTE)))
```

Bars and candles can be easily generated on the fly given a stream of real-time or database-read **PRC** events. The illustration of it is given here for **TICK-BAR**s and the methodology uses the very same concepts that underpin the agent-based paradigm introduced in the earlier chapters. Namely the **TICK-BARGENERATOR** will be an agent that consumes **PRC** events and broadcasts **TICKBAR**s to the top of the ***events-queue*** stack. The class is defined by:

```
(defclass TICKBARGENERATOR (FSMAGENT)
  ((MKT
    :accessor MKT
    :initarg :MKT)
   (N
    :accessor N
    :initarg :N)
   (COUNTER
    :accessor COUNTER
    :initform 0)
   (BUFFER
    :accessor BUFFER
    :initform NIL)
   (OP
    :accessor OP
    :initform NIL)
```

```
(HI
 :accessor HI
 :initform NIL)
(LO
 :accessor LO
 :initform NIL)
(CL
 :accessor CL
 :initform NIL)))
```

The original inputs are the security identifier **MKT** and the number of events **N** to build the bar from. For example one can define two bar generators for two different securities and event numbers:

```
(defparameter *b1* (make-instance
                    'TICKBARGENERATOR
                    :MKT "AAPL"
                    :N 5))

(defparameter *b2* (make-instance
                    'TICKBARGENERATOR
                    :MKT "MSFT"
                    :N 7))

(push *b2* *agents*)
(push *b1* *agents*)
(setf (recipientslist *a1*) *agents*)
(setf (recipientslist *a2*) *agents*)
```

As with any other FSM agent, one needs to define the filter, initialization, and preprocessor methods:

```
(defmethod observe ((a TICKBARGENERATOR) (e MARKETUPDATE))
   (and
    (equal (MKT a) (security e))
    (not (equal (type-of e) 'BAR))))

(defmethod initialize ((a TICKBARGENERATOR))
   (with-slots (MKT N states name) a
    (when (null states)
     (push :EMIT states)
     (setf name (concatenate 'string
                            "TICKBARGENERATOR_"
                            (format NIL "~A_~A" MKT N)))))))
```

```
(defmethod preprocess ((a TICKBARGENERATOR) (e MARKETUPDATE))
  (with-slots (COUNTER BUFFER positions) a
              (push 0 positions)
              (setf COUNTER (length BUFFER)))))
```

In this case the agent is not a trading agent and hence the **positions** list only contains zeros. Also as the agent emits the bars to the ***events-queue*** it should not observe any bars by definition.

The FSM representation is very simple and contains only 2 states, **:CALC** that creates the bar from the stream and **:EMIT** when it emits it to the queue:

```
(defmethod setfsm ((a TICKBARGENERATOR))
  (with-slots (MKT N COUNTER BUFFER OP HI LO CL states currentstate
               revalprices transitions positions name) a
    (setf currentstate (first states))
    (setf transitions (list
                       (make-instance
                        'TRANSITION
                        :initialstate :CALC
                        :finalstate :CALC
                        :sensor #'price
                        :predicate #'(lambda (p)
                                       (< COUNTER N))
                        :actuator #'(lambda (p)
                                      (setf CL p)
                                      (setf HI (max HI p))
                                      (setf LO (min LO p))
                                      (push p BUFFER)
                                      (format T
                                              "~S CALC->CALC   ~%"
                                              name)))
                       (make-instance
                        'TRANSITION
                        :initialstate :CALC
                        :finalstate :EMIT
                        :sensor #'price
                        :predicate #'(lambda (p)
                                       (equal COUNTER N))
                        :actuator #'(lambda (p)
                                      (emit a (make-instance
                                               'TICKBAR
                                               :timestamp (first
                                                           (timestamps a))
                                               :security MKT
```

```
                                     :value (list OP HI LO
                                       CL)
                                     :numticks N))
                          (setf BUFFER NIL)
                          (format T
                             "~S CALC->EMIT  ~%"
                             name)))
          (make-instance
           'TRANSITION
            :initialstate :EMIT
            :finalstate :CALC
            :sensor #'price
            :predicate #'(lambda (p)
                             T)
            :actuator #'(lambda (p)
                            (push p BUFFER)
                            (setf OP p)
                            (setf HI p)
                            (setf LO p)
                            (setf CL p)
                            (format T
                                "~S EMIT->CALC   ~%"
                                name)))
          (make-instance
           'TRANSITION
            :initialstate :EMIT
            :finalstate :EMIT
            :sensor #'price
            :predicate #'(lambda (p)
                            NIL)
            :actuator #'(lambda (p)
                            NIL))))))
```

Finally, there is no need for a postprocessor. The other agents in the
agents list would be able to observe the emitted bar as soon as the last
relevant **PRC** event is processed by the bar generator and emitted on the
events queue.

6.4.2 Slicing Price into Boxes

A useful and complementary compression technique focuses solely on the
price dimension. One starts with a price or return scale B and the current
price $P(0)$. The intuitive idea is as follows: Whenever the market is in an
uptrend and does not reverse by more than B from its local high, a series

of ascending boxes of height B are drawn on top of each other. When the market finally reverses by more than B from its top, a new set of descending boxes is drawn one notch to the right. Figure 6.6 gives the FSM representation for the box chart agent and Figure 6.7 the resulting chart example:

Box charts remove the time dimension (be it clock or event time) because each box represents a state of the market where no opposite move occurs relative to the previous trend state (as measured by the box size, i.e., price scale B). The market can stay a long time or a little time in that state. The box charts are useful compression techniques to automate the recognition of chart patterns as we will see in a subsequent chapter.

The size B of the box dictates the price scale of the patterns that appear from such a compression and also, indirectly, their time scale. The relationship between the price and time scales is a function of volatility that varies in time. To produce more consistent price-time scale relationships one can adapt the box size to volatility V. A linear scaling $B_i = \alpha V_{i-1}$ is the simplest example where the next box size is chosen as a function of the average volatility that occured while the market was in the previous box, series of boxes, or a fixed time period.

6.4.3 Market Distributions

Another interesting compression technique is the price distribution over a time period. Namely, one divides the price scale into intervals of length B and fills a horizontal bar between each division as a function of the frequency of occurence of the price in that interval during the time period. Usually the time over which a distribution is accumulated is a trading day.

Figure 6.8 presents the time series of daily price distributions and shows the occurence of unimodal and bimodal daily price distributions. Bimodal distributions occur when news moves the market from one level to another around which the price then oscillates. Using the distributions can be useful for certain intraday mean-reversion models and for some algorithmic execution applications.

6.5 REPRESENTATION

Once data has been sliced and diced by appropriate sampling and compression, different representation techniques can be applied. Representation can be seen as a coding technique and is different for data fed to humans or to machines.

Box Chart Agent

L<H

H-L = S — S is the Size of the Box

Box is either a CROSS (local uptrend) or CIRCLE (local downtrend)

L and H are the Low Level and the High Level of the Current Box

A new CROSS is drawn to the top of current one or to the top right of the current CIRCLE

A new CIRCLE is drawn to the bottom of current one or to the bottom right of the current CROSS

	START	SAME-CROSS	NEW-CROSS-HIGHER	NEW-CROSS-RIGHT	SAME-CIRCLE	NEW-CIRCLE-LOWER	NEW-CIRCLE-RIGHT
START	NIL	NIL	NIL	NIL	NIL	NIL	NIL
SAME-CROSS	T	$L \le p \le H$	T	T	NIL	NIL	NIL
NEW-CROSS-HIGHER	NIL	$p > H$	NIL	NIL	NIL	NIL	NIL
NEW-CROSS-RIGHT	NIL	NIL	NIL	NIL	$p > H$	NIL	NIL
SAME-CIRCLE	NIL	NIL	NIL	NIL	$L \le p \le H$	T	T
NEW-CIRCLE-LOWER	NIL	NIL	NIL	NIL	$p < L$	NIL	NIL
NEW-CIRCLE-RIGHT	NIL	$p < L$	NIL	NIL	NIL	NIL	NIL

FIGURE 6.6 Box Chart Pseudocode

Price	1	2	3	4	5	6	7	8	9	10	11	12	13	14	15	16	17	18	19	20	21
1760																					
1740																					
1720																					
1700												X		X		X					
1680						X						X	O	X	O	X	O				
1660						X	O					X	O	X	O	X	O				
1640						X	O	X				X	O	X	O	X	O				
1620						X	O	X	O	X	O				O	X	O				
1600						X	O	X	O	X					O	X	O				
1580						X	O		O						O	X	O				
1560				X		X									O		O				
1540				X	O	X									O	X					
1520				X	O	X									O	X	O				
1500				X	O	X									O	X	O				
1480				X	O										O	X	O	X			
1460				X											O	X	O	X	O		
1440				X											O	X	O	X	O		
1420				X											O	X	O		O		
1400				X											O	X		O			X
1380				X											O	X		O	X		X
1360				X											O	X		O	X	O	X
1340				X											O			O	X	O	X
1320				X														O		O	
1300				X																	
1280	O			X																	
1260	O			X																	
1240	O			X		X															
1220	O	X		X	O	X															
1200	O	X	O	X	O	X															
1180	O	X	O	X	O	X															
1160	O	X	O	X	O																
1140	O		O	X																	
1120			O	X																	
1100			O	X																	
1080			O	X																	
1060			O																		
1040																					
1020																					

FIGURE 6.7 Box Chart Example

6.5.1 Charts and Technical Analysis

Most commonly, representation is of graphical nature and is designed to help the human trader recognize patterns visually. All the charts shown above are compressed sampled data represented in a particular way as a time series.

The most important feature of a graphically represented time series is the *memory* that is embedded in it. The human eye is very well trained to

740					
735					
730	A				
725	A	B			
720	A	A	B		
715	B				
710	B	C	D		
705	B	B	C	D	D
700	C	C	C	D	
695	D				
690					

FIGURE 6.8 Market Distribution Chart Example

recognize patterns in pictures. Time series are particular pictures that represent an unfolding history. Part of the game is, given such a history sample, to predict the next set of events. This is the central focus of technical analysis.

There is a whole plethora of market patterns that have varying predictive power as to the future evolution of the price action (see Bulkowski, *The Encyclopedia of Chart Patterns*, 2005). The patterns that have proven to have superior predictive power and are amenable to coding efficiently are (1) linear trend channels, (2) breakout from volatility compression (triangles and pennants), (3) breakout or deceleration around support and resistance

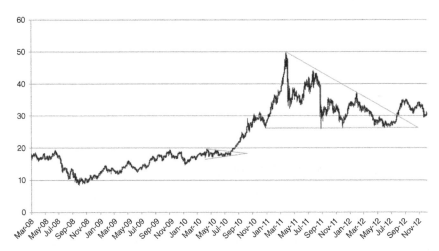

FIGURE 6.9 Examples of Volatility Compression Patterns

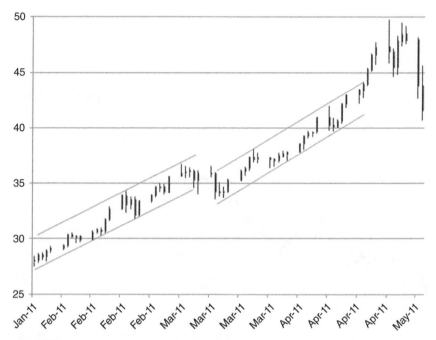

FIGURE 6.10 Examples of Linear Patterns

(including double tops and bottoms, head and shoulders), and (4) trend change via breaking linear trend channels.

The examples given in Figure 6.9 and in Figure 6.10 show several bar and candle charts in time and event sampling that exhibit some common behavioral set up patterns and subsequent market activity. Note that when looking at longer-term charts with large price moves it is more convenient to use a logarithmic scale, as shown in Figure 6.11. The markets tend to move in return space rather than price space at those larger scales and trends that appear nonlinear (exponentially accelerating) on a linear scale become linear on a logarithmic scale.

6.5.2 Translating Patterns into Symbols

Some chart patterns can be recognized algorithmically (examples of code are provided in the next chapter). This opens the door to study whether the occurence of patterns is not random but presents certain statistical rules. One can almost hear the phrase used by some experienced traders: "Hear the market speak." To test such serial correlation one can encode each recognized pattern into a symbol (a letter for example) and study the

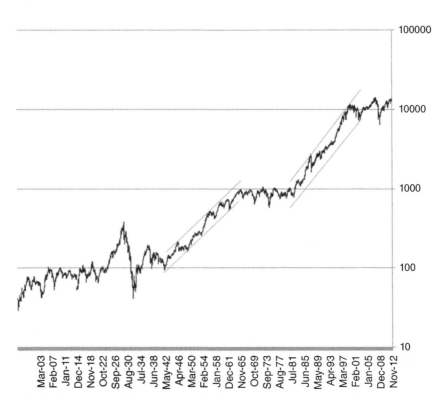

FIGURE 6.11   Example of Trend Channel in Log Scale

statistics of words that are thus generated by the time series of patterns. One can also test for robustness of such analysis by running the test on different markets at different time and event scales.

Figure 6.12 is an example that illustrates the repeated occurence of the following most common pattern:

$$(Volatility\ Contraction) \rightarrow (Trend) \rightarrow (Volatility\ Expansion) \rightarrow \cdots$$

$$\cdots \rightarrow (Range) \rightarrow (Volatility\ Contraction) \rightarrow \cdots$$

6.5.3   Translating News into Numbers

The modern world is awash with news that hits us from all sides: TV, financial news services such as Bloomberg and Reuters, the Internet, and so on. It is impossible to absorb all this data without some filtering. With the

FIGURE 6.12   Contraction-Trend-Expansion-Range Pattern

advent of the streaming news services it has become possible to automatically process that data using language recognition techniques. News pieces are events of a very different nature from prices—they are semantic in nature and communicated to the world in a symbolic language rather than in numeric format.

Language recognition is an active area of research in artificial intelligence. It is a difficult problem because syntax does not imply semantics and phrases usually cannot be taken out of context. The field touches on the most subtle areas of framing and building context (i.e., basic understanding) through learning. Most of computing is performed on numeric problems, and symbolic and semantic problems have always been harder to solve on the prevailing computing architecture. Nontheless languages like LISP (used here) and Prolog have been specifically developed to deal with symbolic problems and the most powerful pattern-matchers and context generators are written in them.

For trading, the most useful understanding of a piece of news is whether the information embedded in it is going to have a positive or negative impact on the price of a security. Some news affects particular securities (like corporate announcements for a stock) and some news affects the market as a whole (like unexpected monetary policy changes). Hence one needs to be able to correlate a semantic datum with a numeric one.

Some reasonably simple techniques have been developed that compute a numerical sentiment index for a given stock. Those techniques process in real time all the news pertaining to that stock and some general news that may affect the whole market. The output of the process for each piece of news is a number that measures the positiveness of the news for that stock. The sentiment index is then computed by adding (integrating) these numbers over time or over a rolling time window.

It is not clear yet how effective such techniques are in systematic trading and research is in progress in this field. There is a prevailing feeling that prices tend to move faster and anticipate news generally. When totally unexpected events occur (shocks to sentiment about a particular stock or to the market as a whole), liquidity dries up very quickly and the reaction to prices can be so violent that one has the impression that the price moves ahead of the news.

6.5.4 Psychology of Data and Alerts

The representation of data has two goals—informative and psychological—and so far I have discussed the informative aspect. The psychological goal is to help traders anticipate better and react to market moves faster. As was pointed out in the Introduction, trading cannot be seen outside of a risk management context. Any representation of data that sharpens the mind with regard to risk management is therefore useful for human traders.

In an open outcry context, the traders could sense the danger and opportunity by the noise level of the pit and the facial expressions of their fellows. In an electronic context that information is not available, but there are ways to substitute it, at least partially.

For example, the increase in market volume and velocity of transactions can be represented graphically. Also, the transactions can be sent to the loudspeaker by a voice synthetizer that can simulate nervousness via the speed of arrival of trades combined with the increase in volume of orders on the book.

Of course, such gadgets may be detrimental to the trader who, instead of keeping a clear head, could be drawn into the market hysteria and overreact. Nevertheless, they can present an advantage by helping a human trader to not be continuously glued to the screen.

One major feature of systematic trading is to remove the psychological element from the trading decision. This does not mean that the psychology of the market should not be an input into the decision making—in fact, it is exactly what makes the various tradable patterns reoccur. Hence measuring such psychological changes is useful.

CHAPTER 7

Basic Trading Strategies

Trading strategies can be classified into two broad categories: directional and contrarian. The category of directional strategies benefits from markets where large moves relative to noise occur regularly. On the other hand, the contrarian strategies benefit from markets where there is a predominance of noise and lack of serial correlation.

The trend-following, acceleration, and breakout strategies can be classified as directional whereas the mean-reversion and market-making strategies are contrarian.

Directional strategies tend to have a low percentage of profitable trades but a high win-to-loss ratio and the distribution of their trade returns has a fat right tail. Contrarian strategies tend to have a high percentage of profitable trades but a low win-to-loss ratio and the distribution of their trade returns has a fat left tail.

7.1 TREND-FOLLOWING

Trend-following strategies are the most popular and widely used by the systematic community. As the old investment adage goes, "The trend is your friend!" Trends have been friends to the CTA community for decades and this is the major reason behind the continous good performance of that investment style.

Ironically, the implicit acceptance by the marginal investor of the teachings of the efficient markets school has been of great help to the trend-followers over the past few decades. Indeed, the less people believe in trends, the easier it is to exploit them, as most people live in denial of their existence. The Introduction touched on why major and minor trends do and should occur in the market when one understands it from the point of view of a complex adaptive system.

How does one capture trends? There are various strategies that are appropriate for the task.

7.1.1 Channel Breakout

Channel breakout strategies are simple and robust. The market is deemed to be in an uptrend if today's price is higher than the highest price over the last N observations, and symmetrically for a downtrend. This indicator is called the Donchian channel after its popularizer, Richard Donchian. A simple strategy would buy on the break of the upper channel and short-sell on the break of the lower channel thus always being in the market.

Variations on the strategy can be numerous. For example, the lookback N can be an increasing function of noise. The logic behind that is that higher nondirectional noise yields higher whipsaw potential and the larger the lookback, the larger the spread between the upper and lower channel become, hence the probability of a whipsaw is reduced.

Another example is a strategy based on two channels, a slow and a fast one. The slow channel is used for entries and the fast one for exits. This strategy allows for neutral states and no positions as long as the market price action is confined within the slow channel. This improvement helps capture a larger proportion of the amplitude of clean trends, that is, trends that have a reasonably stable nondirectional noise level. The combination of those two intuitive ideas is presented here.

Figure 7.1 shows the FSM and the representative statistics of the strategy for an individual market and a portfolio.

7.1.2 Moving Averages

There are various ways to detect trends with moving averages. The moving average is a rolling filter and uptrends are detected when either the price is above the moving average or when the moving average's slope is positive.

There are various definitions of moving averages. The simple moving average is defined by

$$SMA(N, i) = \frac{\sum_{j=0}^{N-1} P(i - j)}{N}$$

An exponential moving average is defined recursively by

$$EMA(\alpha, 0) = P(0) \quad EMA(\alpha, i) = \alpha P(i) + (1 - \alpha)EMA(\alpha, i - 1)$$

CBTR Strategy: Channel Breakout Trend Following							
PFS<S<L<PFL	L is the Slow Highest High and S is the Slow Lowest Low channels						
S<SFS	SFL is the Fast Lowest Low and SFS is the Fast Highest High channels						
SFL<L	PFL, PFS are constants defined at the time of a transition from Init, Stop, Profit to Long or to Short						
	Init	Long	StopFromLong	ProfitFromLong	Short	StopFromShort	ProfitFromShort
Init	]S,L[	NIL	NIL	NIL	NIL	NIL	NIL
Long	[L,PFL[	]SFL,PFL[	[L,PFL[	NIL	[L,PFL[	[L,PFL[	[L,PFL[
StopFromLong	NIL	]S,SFL]	]S,L[	NIL	NIL	NIL	NIL
ProfitFromLong	[PFL,INF[	[PFL,INF[	[PFL,INF[	]S,INF[	[PFL,INF[	[PFL,INF[	[PFL,INF[
Short	]PFS,S]	]PFS,S]	]PFS,S]	]PFS,S]	]PFS,SFS[	]PFS,S]	NIL
StopFromShort	NIL	NIL	NIL	NIL	[SFS,L[	]S,L[	NIL
ProfitFromShort	]-INF,PFS]	]-INF,PFS]	]-INF,PFS]	]-INF,PFS]	]-INF,PFS]	]-INF,PFS]	]-INF,L[

CBTF Representative Statistics		
	PORTF AVG	AUDJPY
TOT_PL	139,991	244,376
PFACT	1.30	1.17
PCT_PROFITABLE	58.30	68.29
AVG_WIN_TO_LOSS	0.89	0.54
TOT_TRD	111	123
AVG_LOGRET	0.13	0.19
WIN_TRD	66	84
LOS_TRD	45	39
POS_PL	1,334,939	1,689,928
NEG_PL	- 1,194,948	-1,445,552
AVG_PL	1,313	1,987
AVG_WIN	20,028	20,118
AVG_LOS	- 26,418	- 37,065
AVG_BAR_IN_TRD	19	15
AVG_BAR_IN_WIN	17	11
AVG_BAR_IN_LOS	22	23
MAX_WIN	34,212	29,158
MAX_LOS	- 77,468	- 103,699
50 Currency Pairs, Daily Sampling, 1997-2008		

FIGURE 7.1 Channel Breakout Trend-Following Strategy

Finally an adaptive moving average $AMA(\alpha(i), i)$ is an EMA with the $\alpha(i)$ a function of time, price, volatility, or other factors, and is the most useful and general concept.

From a filter-theoretic perspective, an SMA has finite memory whereas EMA and AMA have infinite memory (that decays exponentially in time). All moving averages are low pass band filters that attenuate any noise above a certain frequency. For example, for a pure sine wave $P(\omega, t) = A sin(\omega t)$ the N-period $SMA(N, i)$ is identically zero when $\omega = 2\pi/T$, that is, when the sinusoid's period is equal to the lookback of the moving average. In fact, $SMA(N, i)$ significantly attenuates any signal $P(\omega, t)$ with $\omega > \pi/T$. Figure 7.2 shows the attenuation function of a sinusoidal signal of a given frequency by simple and exponential moving averages of $N = 10$ and $\alpha = 2/11$. The attenuation function is shown on a log-scale and represents the resulting relative amplitude of the filtered versus the original signal.

From a practical standpoint, an $SMA(N, i)$ is very similar to an $EMA(2/(N+1), i)$ in the sense that both have approximately a lag of $\lambda = (N-1)/2$. The lag means the following: Let us assume that the price P is constant until time t_{jump} then jumps and stays at Q. Both moving averages will move from value P to value Q and will be close to Q at time $t_{jump} + \lambda$ as Figure 7.3 shows.

Given that an SMA can be well approximated by a constant-α AMA, it makes a lot of sense to adopt the AMA as the principal representative of this family of indicators. Not only it is potentially flexible in the definition of its effective lookback but it is also recursive. The ability to compute indicators recursively is a very big positive in latency-sensitive applications like high-frequency trading and market-making, and this point will be covered in Part Four.

From the definition of the AMA, it is easy to derive that $\Delta AMA > 0$ if $P(i) > AMA(i\text{-}1)$. This means that the position of the price relative to an AMA dictates its slope and provides a way to determine whether the market is in an uptrend or a downtrend.

Moving averages generally provide a more timely measure of a beginning or end of a trend relative to the channels discussed in the previous section.[1] However, the main issue with moving averages is a potential for whipsaw during periods of market congestion, something the channels are less prone to. There are various ways to address it but the principal idea is to perform a calculation of some signal-to-noise ratio (SNR) and only react to trend signals when that ratio is above a certain threshold. There is also room to directly embed that calculation into the AMA so as to vary its sensitivity to price according to the noise level.

As per its name, the two inputs to SNR are calculations of signal and of noise. Signal in the trend-following case will represent the strength of the

---

[1]This observation is purely based on human visual intuition. This book does not define a *trend* other than by a calculation of relevant indicators, so from that perspective a model sees a trend only through the prism of those indicators and not literally, like humans would.

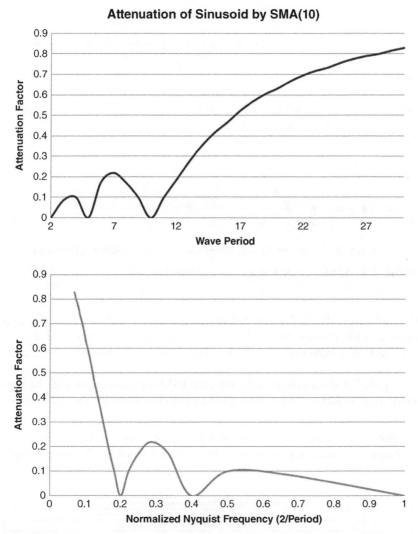

FIGURE 7.2 Frequency Attenuation by SMA(10)

trend as computed by the slope of the *AMA*. Noise can be either a moving average of volatility or of counter-directional volatility as defined below.

AMATR The first model described here uses a symmetric channel around an exponential moving average

$$H(t) = (1 + \beta)EMA(\alpha, t) \quad L(t) = (1 - \beta)EMA(\alpha, t)$$

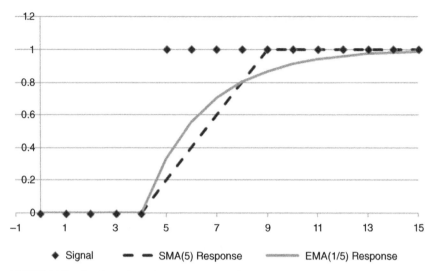

◆ Signal   — — SMA(5) Response   ═══ EMA(1/5) Response

FIGURE 7.3   SMA and EMA Response to a Step Function

This indicator allows for the definition of a trend with sensitivity α and width β. One defines the market to be in an uptrend at time t if $P(t) > H(t)$ and in a downtrend if $P(t) < L(t)$. The model respects the trends so defined.

Figure 7.4 shows the pseudocode, the FSM representation, and the representative statistics of the strategy for an individual market and a portfolio.

AMATR2   The second model uses the power of adaptive moving averages to enhance the accuracy of entries and exits as defined by the above simple

AMATR1 Strategy: Adaptive Moving Average Trend Following							
S<L	L is the H(t) channel and S is the L(t) channel defined in the text						
	Stops and Profits states are never attained						
	Init	Long	StopFromLong	ProfitFromLong	Short	StopFromShort	ProfitFromShort
Init	]S,L[	NIL	NIL	NIL	NIL	NIL	NIL
Long	[L,PFL[	]SFL,PFL[	NIL	NIL	[L,PFL[	NIL	NIL
StopFromLong	NIL	NIL	NIL	NIL	NIL	NIL	NIL
ProfitFromLong	NIL	NIL	NIL	NIL	NIL	NIL	NIL
Short	]PFS,S]	]PFS,S]	NIL	NIL	]PFS,SFS[	NIL	NIL
StopFromShort	NIL	NIL	NIL	NIL	NIL	NIL	NIL
ProfitFromShort	NIL	NIL	NIL	NIL	NIL	NIL	NIL

FIGURE 7.4   Adaptive Moving Average Trend-Following Strategy

model. The intuition about these enhancements comes from the folowing two observations.

Suppose the market is experiencing a directional move that becomes progressively cleaner, meaning that the proportion of counter-directional volatility is decreasing (this is usually the case in short squeezes or asset deleveraging trades). In this case one would benefit from increasing the sensitivity of the *AMA* and decreasing the channel width in order to track the price move more closely for a profit-taking trade. Usually these type of moves end in tears, in the sense that they preclude large counter-moves, hence a higher degree of vigilance and risk management is warranted.

Suppose, on the contrary, that the market is experiencing a directional move that is becoming progressively messier, meaning that the proportion of counter-directional volatility is increasing (this is usually the case in trend continuations or potential trend reversals that are not associated with blowout tops or bottoms). In this case, one would benefit from decreasing the sensitivity of the *AMA* while increasing the channel width in order to reduce the probability of a whipsaw once the trade is exited.

To formalize, define the upside and downside deviations as the same sensitivity moving averages of relative price appreciations and depreciations from one observation to another

$$D^+(0) = 0 \quad D^+(t) = \alpha(t-1)max\left(\frac{P(t)-P(t-1)}{P(t-1)}, 0\right)$$
$$+ (1-\alpha(t-1))D^+(t-1)$$

$$D^-(0) = 0 \quad D^-(t) = -\alpha(t-1)min\left(\frac{P(t)-P(t-1)}{P(t-1)}, 0\right)$$
$$+ (1-\alpha(t-1))D^-(t-1)$$

These deviations represent the noise element in the *SNR*, but conditional on the trend state. The signal is represented by the strength of the trend as computed by the absolute value of the *AMA* slope.

The *AMA* is computed by

$$AMA(0) = P(0) \quad AMA(t) = \alpha(t-1)P(t) + (1-\alpha(t-1))AMA(t-1)$$

and the channels

$$H(t) = (1+\beta_H(t-1))AMA(t) \quad L(t) = (1-\beta_L(t-1))AMA(t)$$

with now variable functions for sensitivity $\alpha(t)$. For a scale constant β, the upper and lower channels are defined to be

$$\beta_H(t) = \beta D^- \quad \beta_L(t) = \beta D^+$$

The upper channel's width to the *AMA* is proportional to the downside deviation because the higher the deviation the higher probability that an upmove will abort. Vice versa for the lower channel. The signal-to-noise ratio calculations are state dependent:

$$SNR(t) = \frac{(P(t) - AMA(t-1))/AMA(t-1)}{\beta D^-(t)} \quad If\, P(t) > H(t)$$

$$SNR(t) = \frac{-(P(t) - AMA(t-1))/AMA(t-1)}{\beta D^-(t)} \quad If\, P(t) < L(t)$$

$$SNR(t) = 0 \quad otherwise.$$

Finally the overall sensitivity $\alpha(t)$ is determined via the following function of $SNR(t)$:

$$\alpha(t) = \alpha_{min} + (\alpha_{max} - \alpha_{min}) * Arctan(\gamma SNR(t))$$

The trick is not only for the moving average and the channel to be adaptive to the change of the signal-to-noise ratio but to make the *SNR* dependent on the state of the model. This means that once the strategy exits after a protracted up-move (and a buy signal), the channel parameters for the potential subsequent short entry will be wider, thus lowering the probability of whipsaw if the uptrend were to continue. When a down-move starts, the lower channel will adapt closer to the price action, thus increasing the probability of a short entry proportional to the cleanliness of the down-move. The FSM and representative statistics for the AMATR2 strategy is shown in Figure 7.5.

7.1.3 Swing Breakout

This strategy is based on the observation that markets have trends, trends have certain widths around them, and when the market breaks such a trend channel, the trend usually changes in the direction of the break.

The difficulty is that the volatility tends to persist, so the scale of those trend channels tends to change. Take α and β, two scale parameters. They represent, respectively, the expected width and price extension of a move, in rolling volatility terms and as percentage of price levels.

AMATR2 Strategy: Adaptive Moving Average Trend Following						
PFS<S<L<PFL	L is the H(t) channel and S is the L(t) channel defined in the text					
S<SFS	SFS, SFL can be introduced as volatility spreads to the AMA					
SFL < L	PFL, PFS can be constants defined at the time of a transition from Init, Stop, Profit to Long or to Short					
	Init	Long	StopFromLong	ProfitFromLong	Short	StopFromShort	ProfitFromShort
Init	]S,L[	NIL	NIL	NIL	NIL	NIL	NIL
Long	[L,PFL[	]SFL,PFL[	[L,PFL[	NIL	[L,PFL[	[L,PFL[	[L,PFL[
StopFromLong	NIL	]S,SFL[	]S,L[	NIL	NIL	NIL	NIL
ProfitFromLong	[PFL,INF[	[PFL,INF[	[PFL,INF[	]S,INF[	[PFL,INF[	[PFL,INF[	[PFL,INF[
Short	]PFS,S]	]PFS,S]	]PFS,S]	]PFS,S]	]PFS,SFS[	]PFS,S]	NIL
StopFromShort	NIL	NIL	NIL	NIL	[SFS,L[	]S,L[	NIL
ProfitFromShort	]-INF,PFS]	]-INF,PFS]	]-INF,PFS]	]-INF,PFS]	]-INF,PFS]	]-INF,PFS]	]-INF,L[

AMATR2 Representative Statistics		
	PORTF_AVG	AUDUSD
TOT_PL	369,960	331,350
PFACT	1.59	1.56
PCT_PROFITABLE	42.60	41.18
AVG_WIN_TO_LOSS	1.67	2.23
TOT_TRD	38	51
AVG_LOGRET	0.39	0.58
WIN_TRD	16	21
LOS_TRD	22	30
POS_PL	1,057,500	922,500
NEG_PL	- 687,540	- 591,150
AVG_PL	8,607	6,497
AVG_WIN	51,107	43,929
AVG_LOS	- 29,663	- 19,705
AVG_BAR_IN_TRD	15	19
AVG_BAR_IN_WIN	23	30
AVG_BAR_IN_LOS	10	11
MAX_WIN	270,313	363,450
MAX_LOS	- 118,907	- 53,250
50 Currency Pairs, Daily Sampling, 1997-2008		

FIGURE 7.5 Adaptive Moving Average Trend-Following Strategy 2

At time 0, the strategy starts in the *INITVOL* state and first collects data for an interval of time T to determine the rolling volatility parameter $V_T(T)$. Once done, it moves to the *INIT* state and sets up a symmetric channel

$$S = P(T)/(1 + V(T)\alpha/2) \quad L = P(T) * (1 + V(T)\alpha/2).$$

Let us assume that at some point $t_0 > T$, the symmetric channel is breached on the upside, that is, $P(t_0) > L$. Then, the state of the model changes to $LONG$. The model will be now seeking to either take profit at

$$PFL = P(t_0) * (1 + V_T(t_0)\beta)$$

or to reverse position to a short at S.

As the price $P(t)$ rises, $S(t)$ ratchets up accordingly:

$$S(t) = max(P(\tau)|\tau \in [t_0, t])/(1 + V_T(t_0)\alpha)$$

If the model does not take profit and at some point t_1, $P(t_1) < S(t_1)$ then the model reverses its position and goes into the $SHORT$ state.

Then it will seek either to take profits on the shorts or go long. The long entry level becomes

$$L(t) = min(P(\tau)|\tau \in [t_1, t]) * (1 + V_T(t_1)\alpha)$$

and the profit from short

$$PFS = P(t_1)/(1 + V_T(t_1)\beta)$$

Suppose, instead, that the model does take profits when it is in the $LONG$ state, that is, the price $P(t_1) > PFL$. The model goes flat and moves back to the $INIT$ state, by resetting a symmetric L, S channel around $P(t_1)$.

It is important to note two elements here. First, any allusion to time should be interpreted as either clock or event time. The strategy can be set up for both. Second, this strategy is actually independent of any measure of time, as long as the scaling $V_T(t)$ can be computed. In a sense, the strategy is akin to trading up and down moves in a box chart, where the size of the box resets at each swing according to V_T.

Figure 7.6 shows the FSM representation and the representative statistics of the strategy for an individual market and a portfolio.

7.2 ACCELERATION

Acceleration patterns are relatively rare and can be violent. They are usually driven by forced stop-outs and feed on themselves. They were explained in the first chapter as a sudden switch from a cooperative accumulation to a noncooperative divestment game.

PFS<S<L<PFL	SWBR Strategy: Swing Breakout						
	L and S are defined in the text						
	Stop states are never attained						
	PFL, PFS are constants defined at the time of a transition from Init, Stop, Profit to Long or to Short						
	Init	Long	StopFromLong	ProfitFromLong	Short	StopFromShort	ProfitFromShort
Init	]S,L[	NIL	NIL	NIL	NIL	NIL	NIL
Long	[L,PFL[	]SFL,PFL[	NIL	NIL	[L,PFL[	NIL	[L,PFL[
StopFromLong	NIL	NIL	NIL	NIL	NIL	NIL	NIL
ProfitFromLong	[PFL,INF[	[PFL,INF[	NIL	]S,INF[	[PFL,INF[	NIL	[PFL,INF[
Short	]PFS,S]	]PFS,S]	NIL	]PFS,S]	]PFS,SFS[	NIL	NIL
StopFromShort	NIL	NIL	NIL	NIL	NIL	NIL	NIL
ProfitFromShort	]-INF,PFS]	]-INF,PFS]	NIL	]-INF,PFS]	]-INF,PFS]	NIL	]-INF,L[

SWBR Breakout Strategy		
	PORTF_AVG	EUR_USD
TOT_PL	678,372	507,968
PFACT	1.13	1.17
PCT_PROFITABLE	39.84	39.91
AVG_WIN_TO_LOSS	1.71	1.76
TOT_TRD	7,963	8,283
AVG_LOGRET	0.01	0.01
WIN_TRD	3,171	3,306
LOS_TRD	4,792	4,977
POS_PL	5,559,410	3,529,965
NEG_PL	- 4,881,037	- 3,021,997
AVG_PL	87	61
AVG_WIN	1,761	1,068
AVG_LOS	- 1,040	- 607
AVG_BAR_IN_TRD	2	2
AVG_BAR_IN_WIN	3	3
AVG_BAR_IN_LOS	2	2
MAX_WIN	11,169	5,966
MAX_LOS	- 12,012	- 5,447
5 Currencies, 1 minute data, Mar-2009 - Mar-2010		

FIGURE 7.6 Swing Breakout Strategy

7.2.1 Trend Asymmetry

This game-changing dynamic explains trend asymmetry in asset markets. Equities, high yield bonds and currencies, and other risky assets tend to fall much faster than they rise. Investment grade bonds tend to do the reverse, and so do commodities that are prone to shortages.

Hence those asymmetries in behavior ought to be taken into account during strategy building. One should not, in general, expect that parameters should be the same for, say, a long-only and a short-only trend-following strategy, when estimated in clock time.

However, the acceleration events are less pronounced when seen in event time, unless they contain gaps due to liquidity shortages in the market. Hence there is an avenue of trading the acceleration patterns thanks to this asymmetry of time versus event representation.

7.2.2 The Shadow Index

For nonlinear trends in time and areas of high probability, how are reversals detected? To gain intuition, first consider the difference, when looking at a bar chart, of a linear trend versus a congestion: One observes that, on the same time interval, there is a divergence between the degree of overlap of bars, as seen projected onto the price axis (as if a light was shining on them from the right). For a trending market, that overlap, or shadow, is lighter than for a congested market. This gives rise to the shadow index

$$SI(1, N) = \frac{2 \sum_{i<j} Overlap(Bar_i, Bar_j)}{N(N-1)(HH - LL)}$$

Here if a bar is represented by the [L,H] interval, $Overlap(Bar_i, Bar_j) = \max(\min(H_i, H_j) - \max(L_i, L_j), 0)$ is the length of the intersection of the two intervals, HH is the highest high, and LL is the lowest low. Figure 7.7 shows a representative graph of the Shadow Index under the price bar chart.

When the market is in a strong gappy uptrend, the shadow index is zero. When the market is in a complete stall, the shadow index is 1. Otherwise it mean-reverts between those two extremes as trends come and go.

However, to study accelerations in clock time, one needs to filter out linear trends. For this one can take a moving average $S_i = SMA(Pivot, N)(i)$ of the bar pivot prices and look at the de-trended shadow index:

$$DSI(1, N) = \frac{2 \sum_{i<j} Overlap(Bar'_i, Bar'_j)}{N(N-1)(HH' - LL')}$$

where

$$Bar'_i = (O', H', L', C') = (O_i - S_i, H_i - S_i, L_i - S_i, C_i - S_i)$$

and $HH' = max(H')$ and $LL' = min(L')$.

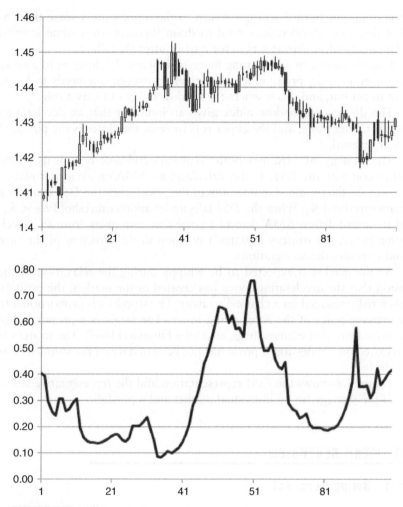

FIGURE 7.7 Shadow Index

Now, when the market is in a linear trend or a congestion, the *DSI* will be high. On the other hand, it will be low when the market accelerates away from a linear trend. So a pattern of mean-reversion exists for the *DSI* but the times when it is low are rare, because so are accelerations.

7.2.3 Trading Acceleration

Accelerating moves usually end in tears. Someone gets stopped out at the worst possible price, and then the market mean-reverts. Regret sets in, and players that got burned will not return to the market for a some time, in either direction. Accelerations tend to drain liquidity for a some interval and a directionless market sets in for a while after the fallout.

Latching on to an accelerating move is similar to latching on to a trend (and in event time, pretty much the same). However, one needs to know when to get out, and this is where the shadow index can play a role.

The de-trended shadow index gives an indicator that an accelerating move is taking place, and the closer it is to zero, the closer is the potential violent reversal.

The strategy $ACMR$, uses both event bars and time bars. It uses time bars to compute the DSI. It also calculates an AMA on event bar pivots, to gauge the finer-grained momentum of the price, when the DSI is under a certain threshold K_1. When the DSI falls under another threshold $K_2 < K_I$, and the event-driven AMA detects a persistent turn away from the accelerating move, the strategy initiates a position in the direction of the turn (counter-trades the acceleration).

As the market is expected to be whippy during the relaxation of the tension that the accelerating move has created in the market, the position is then risk-managed on a channel strategy. The stop-loss is proportional to the extreme point of the accelerating move. The target is a proportion of the move from that extreme (e.g., around a Fibonacci level). The strategy is also exited on a time-stop if profit has not been taken and the stop-loss was not elected.

Figure 7.8 shows the FSM representation and the representative statistics of the strategy for an individual market and a portfolio.

7.3 MEAN-REVERSION

7.3.1 Swing Reversal

This strategy is the mean-reversion counterpart to the $SWBR$ encountered above. The idea is that even though trends occur at certain time and price scales, mean-reversion patterns occur at lower time and price scales. Taking the analogy with box charts when discussing $SWBR$, this strategy aims at trading in the box rather than trading breakouts from a box.

The α and β scale parameters now represent, respectively, the expected width of the mean-reversion box and maximal allowed breakout from the box (stop-loss level). They are again scaling the rolling volatility and the percentage of prices.

At time 0, the strategy starts in the $INITVOL$ state and first collects data for an interval of time T to determine the rolling volatility parameter

Basic Trading Strategies **119**

ACMR Strategy: Acceleration Relaxation Mean Reversion (Long-only version)						
SFL<L<PFL	DSI, AMA, SLF and PFL are defined in the text					
P>AMA	TD is Time in Trade and TMAX is the time stop					
K1>K2	Short-only version is defined in a similar way					
	Init	SetupLong	Long	StopFromLong	ProfitFromLong	TimeStop
Init	DSI>K2	DSI<=K2	NIL	NIL	NIL	NIL
SetUpLong	DSI>K1	DSI<=K1 P< AMA	DSI<=K1 P>= AMA	NIL	NIL	NIL
Long	NIL	NIL	TD<TMAX SFL<P<PFL	TD<TMAX P<SFL	TD<TMAX P<PFL	TD>=TMAX
StopFromLong	T	NIL	NIL	NIL	NIL	NIL
ProfitFromLong	T	NIL	NIL	NIL	NIL	NIL
TimeStop	T	NIL	NIL	NIL	NIL	NIL

ACMR Representative Statistics		
	PORTF AVG	AUDJPY
TOT_PL	17,252	33,741
PFACT	4.49	1.70
PCT_PROFITABLE	53.38	57.14
AVG_WIN_TO_LOSS	1.47	1.27
TOT_TRD	16	7
AVG_LOGRET	0.21	0.46
WIN_TRD	8	4
LOS_TRD	8	3
POS_PL	104,883	82,196
NEG_PL	- 87,631	- 48,455
AVG_PL	2,076	4,820
AVG_WIN	11,970	20,549
AVG_LOS	- 10,439	- 16,152
AVG_BAR_IN_TRD	3	3
AVG_BAR_IN_WIN	3	3
AVG_BAR_IN_LOS	3	3
MAX_WIN	34,164	45,897
MAX_LOS	- 29,982	- 35,925
50 Currency Pairs, Daily Sampling, 1997-2008		

FIGURE 7.8 Acceleration Relaxation Strategy

$V_T(T)$, Once done, it moves to the $INIT$ state and sets up a symmetric channel

$$L = P(T)/(1 + V(T)\alpha/2) \quad S = P(T) * (1 + V(T)\alpha/2)$$

Let us assume that at some point $t_0 > T$, the symmetric channel is breached on the downside, that is, $P(t_0) < L$. Then, the state of the model changes to $LONG$. The model will be now seeking to either stop-loss at

$$SFL = P(t_0)/(1 + V_T(t_0)\beta)$$

or to reverse position to a short at S.

As the price $P(t)$ falls, $S(t)$ ratchets down accordingly:

$$S(t) = min(P(\tau)|\tau \in [t_0, t]) * (1 + V_T(t_0)\alpha)$$

If the model does not stop out and at some point t_1, $P(t_1) > S(t_1)$ then the model reverses its position and goes into the $SHORT$ state.

Then it will seek either to stop-loss from the shorts or go long. The long entry level becomes

$$L(t) = max(P(\tau)|\tau \in [t_1, t])/(1 + V_T(t_1)\alpha)$$

and the stop from short

$$SFS = P(t_1) * (1 + V_T(t_1)\beta)$$

Suppose, instead, that the model does stop out when it is in the $LONG$ state, that is, the price $P(t_1) < SFL$. The model goes flat and moves back to the $INIT$ state, by resetting a symmetric S, L channel around $P(t_1)$.

Figure 7.9 shows the FSM representation, and the representative statistics of the strategy for an individual market and a portfolio.

7.3.2 Range Projection

The range projection model $RPMR$ projects both the average price and the daily range forward, so as to build a channel that is expected to intersect tomorrow's range. The idea is then to always buy the low channel and sell the high channel. If the market has a steady momentum in its average price, then the ratchet-up of the projected ranges will compensate for this momentum.

SWMR Strategy: Swing Mean Reversion							
SFL<L<S<SFS	L and S are defined in the text						
	Profit states are never attained						
	SFL, SFS are constants defined at the time of a transition from Init, Stop, Profit to Long or to Short						
	Init	Long	StopFromLong	ProfitFromLong	Short	StopFromShort	ProfitFromShort
Init	]L,S[	NIL	NIL	NIL	NIL	NIL	NIL
Long	]SFL,L]	]SFL,PFL[	NIL	NIL	]SFL,L]	]SFL,L]	NIL
StopFromLong	]-INF,SFL]	]-INF,SFL]	]-INF,S[	NIL	]-INF,SFL]	]-INF,SFL]	NIL
ProfitFromLong	NIL	NIL	NIL	NIL	NIL	NIL	NIL
Short	[S,SFS[	[S,SFS[	[S,SFS[	NIL	]PFS,SFS[	NIL	NIL
StopFromShort	[SFS,INF[	[SFS,INF[	[SFS,INF[	NIL	[SFS,INF[	]L,INF[	NIL
ProfitFromShort	NIL	NIL	NIL	NIL	NIL	NIL	NIL

SWMR Representative Statistics		
	PORTF AVG	AUDJPY
TOT_PL	196,227	976,505
PFACT	1.24	1.77
PCT_PROFITABLE	63.89	66.35
AVG_WIN_TO_LOSS	0.68	0.90
TOT_TRD	99	104
AVG_LOGRET	0.18	0.97
WIN_TRD	63	69
LOS_TRD	36	35
POS_PL	1,269,446	2,242,839
NEG_PL	- 1,073,219	-1,266,334
AVG_PL	1,700	9,389
AVG_WIN	20,050	32,505
AVG_LOS	- 30,485	- 36,181
AVG_BAR_IN_TRD	24	23
AVG_BAR_IN_WIN	16	15
AVG_BAR_IN_LOS	38	39
MAX_WIN	89,668	182,845
MAX_LOS	- 134,788	- 160,386
50 Currency Pairs, Daily Sampling, 1997-2008		

FIGURE 7.9 Swing Reversal Strategy

Suppose that one observes bars Bar_i in clock or event time. Then one can calculate $S_i = SMA(Pivot, N)(i)$ the moving average of bar pivots, and $R_i = SMA(TR, N)(i)$ the moving average of percent ranges

$$TR = 2\frac{H - L}{H + L}$$

One then defines the channel center, high, and low for the next day as

$$CC_{i+1} = Open_{i+1} + (S_i - S_{i-N+1})/N$$

$$CH_{i+1} = CC_{i+1}(1 + TR_i/2) \quad CL_{i+1} = CC_{i+1}/(1 + TR_i/2)$$

$$SFS_{i+1} = CC_{i+1}\left(1 + \frac{2}{3}TR_i\right) \quad SFL_{i+1} = CC_{i+1}\Big/\left(1 + \frac{2}{3}TR_i\right)$$

At the open of each day, limit orders are put in the market to sell at the CH_{i+1} and buy at CL_{i+1}. Stop-losses are then set up by an additional 1/6 of the expected range away, at the *SFS* and *SFL* levels. If the model is not stopped out and has not taken profit on the opposite side of the range, it is exited at the close of the day.

Figure 7.10 shows the FSM representation, and the representative statistics of the strategy for an individual market and a portfolio.

7.4 INTRADAY PATTERNS

7.4.1 Openings

One of the historically popular strategies traded by locals is the opening range breakout (ORB). The idea is to monitor closely the first few minutes of an open outcry trading session and go in the direction of the breakout for a while. The intuition comes from the fact that overnight, when the market was closed, the information that could not be expressed or risk-managed would be done so around the open of the new session.

In modern times however, with the 24 hour trading session in almost all major futures there is less pent-up information for the day session. So in those markets, it is less obvious as to what the opening means. Individual equities and several non-U.S. futures still do not trade overnight, so in those markets the ORB strategy may still make sense.

7.4.2 Seasonality of Volatility

Throughout the 24-hour trading session, the volatility of intraday prices has some recurring patterns. This is seen quite clearly in different FX rates where ranges for each consecutive 5-minute interval in the trading day were sampled and averaged. Figure 7.11 shows the average intraday volatility of a few different FX rates. One notices that Asian currencies tend to be more active during the Asian daytime, whereas the Canadian dollar is asleep then, and wakes up in the North American morning. Some currencies, like the Euro or the Yen, are active throughout the day but with troughs of activity, just before Europe starts its day, then just before the United States comes in, then finally between the U.S. close and the Asian open.

			RPMR Strategy: Range Projection Mean Reversion				
SFL<L<S<SFS			L is CL(t) and S is CH(T) defined in the text				
			Profit states are never attained				
			SFL(t), SFS(t) are defined in the text				
	Init	Long	StopFromLong	ProfitFromLong	Short	StopFromShort	ProfitFromShort
Init	]L,S[	NIL	NIL	NIL	NIL	NIL	NIL
Long	]SFL,L]	]SFL,PFL[	NIL	NIL	]SFL,L]	]SFL,L]	NIL
StopFromLong	]-INF,SFL]	]-INF,SFL]	]-INF,S[	NIL	]-INF,SFL]	]-INF,SFL]	NIL
ProfitFromLong	NIL	NIL	NIL	NIL	NIL	NIL	NIL
Short	[S,SFS[	[S,SFS[	[S,SFS[	NIL	]PFS,SFS[	NIL	NIL
StopFromShort	[SFS,INF[	[SFS,INF[	[SFS,INF[	NIL	[SFS,INF[	]L,INF[	NIL
ProfitFromShort	NIL	NIL	NIL	NIL	NIL	NIL	NIL

RPMR Representative Statistics		
	PORTF AVG	AUDJPY
TOT_PL	183,618	634,814
PFACT	1.14	1.25
PCT_PROFITABLE	54.10	55.58
AVG_WIN_TO_LOSS	0.96	1.00
TOT_TRD	402	421
AVG_LOGRET	0.05	0.14
WIN_TRD	217	234
LOS_TRD	185	187
POS_PL	2,013,322	3,167,236
NEG_PL	- 1,829,704	-2,532,422
AVG_PL	484	1,508
AVG_WIN	9,224	13,535
AVG_LOS	- 9,804	- 13,542
AVG_BAR_IN_TRD	4	4
AVG_BAR_IN_WIN	3	3
AVG_BAR_IN_LOS	4	4
MAX_WIN	59,626	110,935
MAX_LOS	- 82,435	- 118,812
50 Currency Pairs, Daily Sampling, 1997-2008		

FIGURE 7.10   Range Projection Reversal Strategy

Hence a variation on the ORB strategy in a 24-hour market is a volatility breakout strategy that re-sets the opening range around the times when volatility is low (if, at that day and time, the volatility is indeed low). It then keeps positions at most until the new time zone starts, and re-sets the ranges again.

Figure 7.12 shows the FSM representation, and the representative performance of the strategy for a portfolio.

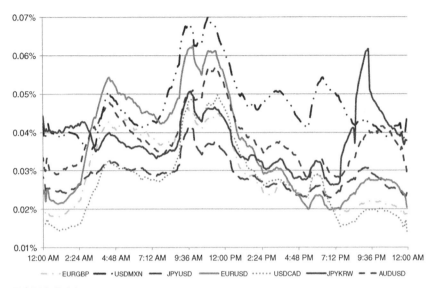

FIGURE 7.11 Examples of Intraday Seasonality of Volatility

7.5 NEWS-DRIVEN STRATEGIES

7.5.1 Expectations vs. Reality

When an event is expected, the market tries to anticipate it and positions the risk bearing in a way that is compatible with the expectation being realized (central scenario). However, when reality ends up different from expectations, the markets react to adapt to the new information. This is similar to the well-known Bayesian approach of changing probability assessments dynamically when observing new events.

Earnings reports, non-farm payrolls, monetary policy changes, elections, distillate inventories, to name a few, all have market impact if they come at a significant spread from expectations.

I and Veredas [See "Macro Surprises and Short-Term Behavior in Bond Futures" CORE 2002-37] have performed a study on the impact of various economic number releases on the U.S. bond market. The study showed that there is some significant impact in the first hour from certain data releases, and that impact is proportional to the gap between the previously expected number and the release (after adjusting for revisions).

However, it is important to point out that the severity of the impact for the same expectational gap is a function of the current macroeconomic context and the focus of the market on this or that particular number. The non-farm payrolls and the CPI tend to be the most robust as far as the effect

ORB: Opening Range Breakout Strategy					
Rule1: Buy above R1, Take Profits at R2>R1					
Rule2: Sell Below S1, Take Profits at S2>S1					
	Init	**Long**	**Short**	**FlatFromLong**	**FlatFromShort**
Init	S1<P<R1	MOC	MOC	S1<P<R1	S1<P<R1
Long	R1<P<R2	S1<P<R2	R1<P<R2	NIL	R1<P<R2
Short	S2<P<S1	S2<P<S1	S2<P<R1	S2<P<S1	NIL
FlatFromLong	P>R2	P>R2	P>R2	P>R1	P>R2
FlatFromShort	P>S2	P>S2	P>S2	P<S2	P<S1

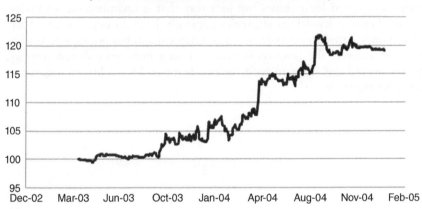

NAV of ORB model traded on 15 Futures
(Realized Statistics: Return=6%,Vol=8%)

FIGURE 7.12 Opening Range Breakout Strategy

of surprises on the short-term reaction of the bond market. But there are times when no one cares about numbers, and the market is just powering ahead in one direction or another.

7.5.2 Ontology-Driven Strategies

It was alluded to in the Introduction that an increasing amount of symbolic data coming from news agencies is being processed in real time, and is being used for generating trading signals.

Real-time algorithms for written and spoken language recognition have been in existence for some time, spurred by the necessity of intelligence agencies to automatically deal with the explosion of information flowing from the Internet.

Language semantic analysis is a very tricky business because of so much aliasing (using the same words for different meanings and different phrases for the same meanings). So the context of a discourse is very important to grasp before attempting to do any mechanical analysis.

Some language-processing algorithms do not pretend to understand the full semantics of a piece of news, but compute a sentiment index by basically counting positive and negative news. The interpretation is based on pre-classifying some patterns of speech and usage of some words into categories that are robust to context (i.e., they would be considered as positive or negative independently of the context).

These sentiment indices (and most important, the changes thereof) are being used for individual equity trading. However, there have not been any conclusive results one way or the other. Usually prices change before news comes out (or at least comes out in a way that is unambiguous to understand), hence price-driven strategies generally have an edge on ontology-driven ones. In whatever context, once a news signal has been given and the position entered, the position is managed on a pure price-driven strategy, as one would not want to wait for our favorite TV anchor to suggest us covering the trade.

CHAPTER 8

Architecture for Market-Making

T he transformation of the marketplace spurred by technological progress has dramatically changed the operation of liquidity-providing activities. Open outcry has mostly been replaced by silent matching engines at the exchanges and the function of a specialist or local has been diluted. In some markets, hedge funds now provide more liquidity than other market participants. Electronic market-making has become a very profitable game but only for businesses that have superior access to transactions or to flow.

8.1 TRADITIONAL MARKET-MAKING: THE SPECIALISTS

Traditionally, the market-maker's hypothesis is that its client flow is on average two-way and balanced. The market-maker maintains the order book by aggregating client requests. One client wants to buy at 50 while the other wants to sell at 52. As far as the market-maker is concerned, it sees 51 as mid-price. A third client comes and needs to sell. He asks, "Where is the market?" without showing his hand, and the market-maker replies 50.5–51.5, ensuring he's quoting a fair bid-ask around the mid. The sale is done at 50.5 and the market-maker now carries the stock, while posting the trade on the tape. Next, the first client gets itchy and sees that the market had moved his way. He asks, "Where is your best offer?" and the market-maker replies 50.75. Seeing that the price is still close enough, the client says, "Mine!" and the market-maker sells him the stock for a 25 cent profit.

In the illustration above, the market-maker took the risk of carrying the inventory, and got paid for it, because the clients had immediacy of execution needs. It is a real risk, because the following situation could have happened. After the first sale, suppose that the second client panics and sees 50.5 printed. He calls and asks, "Where is your best bid?!" The market-maker replies 50.25 to which the client shouts, "Yours and cancel my 52 offer!" Now the market-maker is stitched with double inventory at an average price of 50.375. If a selling panic ensues, he is traditionally obligated to provide an orderly market no matter what, at his own expense.

The idea is that, over time, those drawdowns are averaged out, and the market-maker makes an average of a fraction of the bid-offer on each trade. Hence market-makers are incentivized to trade as much as possible but need capital behind them to survive drawdowns.

The traditional market-making model is to continuously provide liquidity around a fair mid-price that the market-maker calculates as being the weighted average of its order book entries or expected client flow. This is a model that works for specialists, that is, businesses that have the monopoly on dealing in one security, but may not work for other liquidity-providing activities.

8.2 CONDITIONAL MARKET-MAKING: OPEN OUTCRY

The open outcry model is different from the specialist model. An open outcry pit is a collection of locals competing for the flow that is generated outside the pit by the clients of the exchange and internally by the locals themselves. The order book is not explicitly seen by anyone and specific orders get communicated by brokers into the pit as they come from the particular clients of that broker.

Each local behaves like a conditional specialist. Not a single local possesses the full information as to the aggregate client order book so everyone needs to observe what other locals are doing and react accordingly. The liquidity provision becomes more dis-intermediated and the provision of orderly market by one individual is replaced by a self-organizing crowd.

It is useful to learn the pit trading styles from the locals themselves, to get some further ideas on designing market-making strategies [see Hoffman and Baccetti, 1999]. Those styles constitute a broader set of strategies than the specialists'. Indeed, locals used to characterized themselves by several trading styles, namely edge scalper, transition scalper, momentum scalper, contrarian scalper, position trader, and spreader.

Edge scalpers use strategies that are the closest to the traditional specialist model, where the local tries to extract a fraction of the bid-ask from a high volume of frequent trades, by joining as many bids and offers as possible.

Transition scalpers do cross the bid-offer and go to market from time to time, either to exit their inventory or to take a very short term view on the direction.

Momentum and contrarian scalpers exploit a larger scale of moves but go home flat, whereas position traders take longer-term views and may carry positions overnight or for several days.

Spreaders take relative view positions on pairs of contracts, either between different future delivery dates or between different assets, and effectively market-make the spread.

The open outcry markets in futures used to have only the pit session before electronic trading started dominating the marketplace. At that time, the pit session was it, and a lot of price dynamics was a function of the time of day, and accordingly, of the number of locals present in the pit. The opening was a very important time when all the locals would be in the pit, and many short-term strategies were developed by the locals, based on the opening range and the behavior of the price breaking that range.

So one sees, by this account, that the pit is actually an amalgam of traders that provides liquidity to the marketplace in various degrees (or commitments) and sometimes takes liquidity away. Liquidity becomes partially conditional because not a single individual is obligated to provide orderly markets, although the exchange has put in place particular incentives. With the coming of electronic exchanges those incentives have been quantified more concretely than in an open outcry environment.

8.3 ELECTRONIC MARKET-MAKING

The introduction of computers into the marketplace has changed the liquidity provision mechanisms and the incentive model of the market-making community. It has improved some aspects of it but in some other ways it has not, and this has to do with a relative lack of evolutionary time since the transformation of exchanges into electronic commerce networks.

The main change is that everyone can see the aggregate order book but the marketplace has become completely anonymous. So everyone gets access to specialist type of information but no one knows who's trading.

What is seen in the order book does not represent the true size and liquidity out there. This is because participants can hide their orders via iceberg and other algorithms. This is not dissimilar from before, where brokers would not necessarily disclose all at once the extent of their customers' interests to the specialist or the pit.

Electronic markets give the possibility to anyone and their broker to post limit orders, which is the main tool for market-making. However, in order to be able to participate in the flow, the bids and offers need to be very competitive and be top of the market[1] for a good proportion of the time. Hence one has to be fast enough to route orders (new orders and cancel-replaces) in order not to be out-competed. The technological edge in processing and connectivity speed has replaced the edge that local traders had by positioning themselves in advantageous positions in the pit, close to floor brokers.

But it is not just speed that counts in the competitive landscape. Speed is a factor because of the first in-first out (FIFO) principle that ECN matching engines are based on. However, despite the FIFO, on some exchanges order priority is given to a group of leading market-makers (LMMs). This means that if an LMM joins your top-of-the-market bid or offer, it will be apportioned a certain size ahead of you, even if you've placed your order before.

If $X\%$ is the proportion of order priority aggregately given to LMMs in a market then, on average, their executed volume will be a comparable percentage. The incentives of LMMs are in the form of reduced or waived exchange fees (but not clearing fees). The LMM's level of commitment to the exchange is calculated as a combination of its participation in terms of frequency of quoting, volume, and tightness of spreads posted.

In certain markets LMMs enjoy not only the reduced fees and allocation prioritization, but also the ability to handle (place, cancel, or replace) mass orders in one message. This is particularly handy in options market-making where bids and offers for a whole grid of expirations and strikes need to be re-computed at almost every change of the price of the underlying.

LMMs are usually very well capitalized and technologically savvy, and hence have come to dominate many trading venues. This means that unless one is an LMM on an exchange, one's edge may be greatly reduced as far as profitable pure market-making is concerned, and that edge is inversely proportional to the share of LMMs' and one's speed to market.

In FX and OTC markets (mainly fixed income) the picture is altogether different. That arena is not centralized, and several ECNs compete for global transaction volume. Many of these ECNs are either bank market-making engines or amalgamations thereof, and do not provide much leeway for people to route resting limit orders. This is because there is no incentive for banks to open up that market, and they continue to take advantage of the edge provided to them by a whole range of their clients who need immediacy of execution. Banks have natural FX and fixed income customer flow that helps them to market-make just on that flow.

---

[1]Tightest bid or offer.

Some trading venues like HotSpotFX and FXAll have created aggregators that allow banks and other participants to compete for transaction volume, at the same time providing a decent liquidity stream to the end-user. However, it is still nontrivial to compete for liquidity in such venues because there are no superior access or lower fee incentives for people who would be committed to providing continuous two-way markets. Banks do it because they do it in any case for their customers and their own FX platforms, so their marginal cost of piping streams to such an ECN is mimimal. For a non-bank customer the fee structure may be prohibitive because give-up, clearing, and custody fees are charged as a percentage of the trade value. The value extracted per trade from a customer's trading activity should be more than the sum of these frictional fees, and quite often that sum is larger than the bid-offer spread. When banks self-clear and self-custody their own trades, their frictional marginal fee is almost nil.

Hence, to be profitable in the modern market-making arena, one needs an increasingly subtler approach that takes into account larger-scale factors in the millisecond-driven pure edge scalping activities. This means that the market-making model should be overlayed by a longer-term strategy that would help to tilt the inventory in the direction of the longer-term move as defined by that strategy.

8.4 MIXED MARKET-MAKING MODEL

Figure 8.1 shows the finite state machine transition matrix (predicates and actuators) of a stylized market-making agent with 7 states. In plain words, the agent is continuously quoting a two-way market $O = ((b, s_b), (a, s_a))$ of bid and ask orders (price and size). The sizes and prices depend on its state, the last quote (trade), and the apparent imbalance in the order book (difference between either top bid and ask sizes or aggregate bid and ask sizes

SMM Strategy: Simple Market-Making						
S<K	I is the Inventory					
	S and K are explained in the text					
	The resulting bid-ask quoting strategy in each state is explained in the text					
	Init	AccumulateLong	ReduceLong	StopFromLong	AccumulateShort	ReduceShort	StopFromShort
Init	I = 0	I > 0	NIL	NIL	I < 0	NIL	NIL
AccumulateLong	I = 0	0 < I < S	S <= I <K	I >= K	NIL	NIL	NIL
ReduceLong	I = 0	0 < I < S	S <= I <K	I >= K	NIL	NIL	NIL
StopFromLong	T	NIL	NIL	NIL	NIL	NIL	NIL
AccumulateShort	I = 0	NIL	NIL	NIL	-S < I < 0	-K <= I < -S	I < -K
ReduceShort	I = 0	NIL	NIL	NIL	-S < I < 0	-K <= I < -S	I < -K
StopFromShort	T	NIL	NIL	NIL	NIL	NIL	NIL

FIGURE 8.1 Basic Market-Making Strategy

or size-weighted aggregate bid and ask quotes—the reader can experiment with a number of indicators).

The goal of the agent is to make money by buying at its bid and selling at its offer as often as possible, while keeping the inventory under control. For simplicity, assume that the market's order book is balanced (similar size on bid and ask). Our agent starts with zero inventory $I = 0$ in the $Init$ state by joining the top of the market's best bid and ask in size S.

Assume the agent has executed part of his bid, and now carries positive inventory $I > 0$. It transitions to the $Accumulate Long$ state where $0 < I < S < K$, which opens the agent to potentially increase its long inventory. The agent would join the market bid for the size $S - I$ and join the market offer with size S. At that point the agent may stay in that state, or if it's lucky, flip its inventory and end up in the $-S < I < 0$ and $Accumulate Short$ state.

When the agent does not manage to sell out, and its inventory becomes $I > S$, then it transitions to the $Reduce Long$ state, where it would quote a bid below the top bid, and offer I at least at the market offer or more aggressively (if possible). It becomes a more aggressive seller, and if it suddenly detects that more trades are happening at the previous bid, then it would attempt to altogether scratch the trade and hit the bid with size I.

Finally, if the above had not worked, and the agent accumulated inventory to its risk-bearing limit of $I >= K$, it will pull the bid altogether, and will proceed to hit the market with size K, by crossing the spread. This is the $StopFrom Long$ state that lasts till $I = 0$ and the agent comes back to the $Init$ state. The agent had to lose the edge to survive the unfortunate situation of being long in a fast falling market and preserve its capital.

The agent then returns into the $Init$ state. At that point the optimal and maximal exposures S and K may be adjusted in function of the PL of the agent. These numbers may also be adjusted each time the inventory flips sign.

This basic FSM skeleton of a market-making model with stop-loss has been the starting point for several of my investigations. It provides a framework to implement the conditional market-making idea alluded to at the end of the last section that is dubbed the mixed market-making model or simply the $M4$.

Namely, the agent's actuator $O(t) = ((b, s_b), (a, s_a))$ becomes not just a function of the immediate local information coming from the order book, but also takes into account the location of the price path from a larger-scale perspective. Intuitively, if one thinks that the market is at a support level, which, if broken, may lead to a large sell-off, then the agent should endeavor to position itself as a much better seller, and pull all its bids, when it detects the break starting to happen.

That information is not a priori contained in the order book, simply because the order book does not show the market participants' stop-loss orders. When the market breaks support, the hidden stops get triggered but at that point, even if the order book shows a flurry of at-market sells, it may be way too late for the agent to pull or reduce its bid. Hence longer-term models and chart patterns can help in the discovery of stops, or, at least, point out zones of high probability for market turns or breaks.

Some of the strategies discussed in the previous chapter are good candidates as overlay or signalling tools for designing the $M4$ model. Here an example is presented demonstrating how a longer-term model interacts with a market-making model by sending its state and level information.

A market-making strategy is by nature a mean-reversion strategy. This means that, on average, it will lose money in situations where the market experiances a breakout or an accelerating trend. Mean-reversion strategies work best when the market is in a congestion and where the momentum relative to the noise is small. Hence embedding trend or impulse information into a market-making model helps to mitigate those situations.

The $AMATR$ adaptive moving average trend-following strategy is a candidate for such an addition. This strategy will compute its indicators on the top of the book mid-price updates **mid** for every tick. It could also use the size-weighted mid price (**bidavgprc+askavgprc**)/2.

The change of state of $AMATR$ is communicated via a **COMM** event to the $M4$ strategy via the procedure described in the Chapter 5 ("Inter-Agent Communications"). The goal of this signalling is for the $M4$ strategy be aligned with the positive or negative momentum detected by $AMATR$.

If the state of the $AMATR$ is **LONG** then $M4$ will be incentivized to be, on average, in a positive inventory situation $I > 0$. This means that if it happens to be in the *AccumulateShort* or *ReduceShort* states, it will bid more aggressively and offer less aggressively than if $AMATR$ was in the **FLAT** state. If the $M4$ strategy happens to be in the *AccumulateLong* or *ReduceLong* state, then the procedure by which it posts the two-way orders is unaffected (neutral). The decision matrix of the bidding and offering behavior of $M4$ is a function of its state and the state of $AMATR$ is shown in Figure 8.2.

Signaling Matrix from the AMATR Agent to the M4 Agent							
B<A	BM and OM are prevailing market best bid and ask						
BM<AM	B and A are the quoted bid and ask by the M4 strategy						
	Init	AccumulateLong	ReduceLong	StopFromLong	AccumulateShort	ReduceShort	StopFromShort
AMATR_SHORT	Neutral	B > BM	A > AM	Neutral	A < AM	B < AM	Neutral
AMATR_LONG	Neutral	B > BM	A > AM	Neutral	A > AM	B > AM	Neutral

FIGURE 8.2 Conditional Market-Making Example

One sees here the power and flexibility of the agent-based approach to model design and building. What is important here is that the combination of the event-driven FSM representation of decision making with the inter-agent communication paradigm creates a very modular and scalable approach. The full power of this approach is further clarified in Part Two, where adaptation within swarm systems of agents is discussed.

8.5   AN ARCHITECTURE FOR A MARKET-MAKING DESK

This section presents a high-level view of the architecture for conditional market-making in the context of a large institution that processes customer flow and has the ability to carry inventory on its books (banks and large hedge funds).

A flow chart of information, control, and data repositories is given in Figure 8.3 and the points of application of various quantitative methods are annotated. All real-time control arrows are shown in bold. The numbers correspond to the specific quantitative methodologies in the boxes and are explained as follows:

- The current street-quoted and futures market prices, as well as their histories, determine, along with some external variables, a market state. This market state can be quantified as a set of numbers attached to every traded or quoted asset. Those numbers for example can indicate conditional probabilities of continuation of current trends in price level and volatility for the next period. For simplicity, one can think of the market state as over-bought, over-sold, or neutral, both in the price and volatility spaces. The quantitative models used here include purely price-based systematic (e.g., momentum, mean-reversion, pattern) methodologies. It is important that the models help to quantify expected amplitudes and frequencies of market moves and are used in the calculation of optimal risk-bearing in the next step. The $AMATR$ model discussed above is an example. The addition of external variables, for example time of important data releases, can subsume certain purely price-based models and force the optimal risk-bearing to be more or less conservative.
- The market state then allows the determination of a theoretically optimal portfolio for the back-book (inventory). It is performed through a constrained optimization and is essentially a dimensionality reduction. The objective function is to maximize the overall market-making

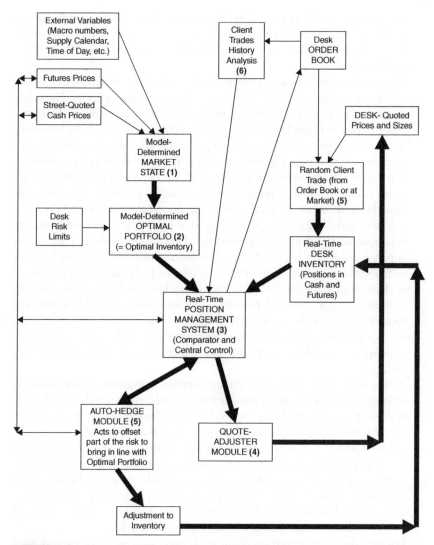

FIGURE 8.3 Flow Chart for a Market-Making Business

desk return-to-risk ratio. The return is given by both the expected degree of market re-pricing (determined by the market state and the implied mean-reversion time) and the expected transaction volume for the desk. The constraints are the overall desk risk limits, sector risk limits, and sector minimal holdings (long or short) that ensure that expected client demand or supply in that sector can be satisfied over the next time period. For simplicity, if one is in an over-bought state in one of the sectors, then optimal holdings in that sector should be short, as the desk positions itself to bid on excess supply as and when the market turns.

- Once a client performs a trade against the desk, the inventory changes, in absolute terms and relative terms to the optimal portfolio. The trade can be either expected, that is, coming from a prior resting order in the order book, or it can be unexpected and transacted directly by the client against desk-quoted prices. At this point the information is aggregated into the position management system, which is essentially a conditional comparator. Its main function is to decide the degree to which the change in inventory is wanted relative to the optimal portfolio. It is possible that the desk wants to accumulate risk in certain sectors and decrease risk in others. The information about that particular client trade history may also tilt the degree of optimal risk-bearing of the desk, if the client is perceived to trade on information successfully and may trade again in the same direction. The unwanted part of the desk excess inventory is then dealt with by the auto-hedge module, both in futures and in cash against the street, if possible. The auto-hedge module would try to scratch out of the unwanted inventory. The wanted part is kept on the books, and the models that determine the market state determine appropriate stop-loss and profit-taking levels that are added to the desk order book.

- At the same time, and while the auto-hedge is performed, the position management system alters the state of the desk-quoted prices and sizes. It does it so as to position itself relative to the street as a better buyer, better seller, aggressive, neutral, or passive in the particular security, sector, or spread. The inputs to that quote-adjuster module are real-time street and future prices, inventory, and market state. The module monitors real-time street bid-offers and sizes in order to gauge liquidity and flow away from the desk. The example of such a change in quoting was given in the last section, which discussed the decision matrix of the $M4$ model in function of the state of the $AMATR$ model.

- Both the auto-hedge and the client trade execution modules are endowed with classical execution algorithms that enable constraints to be set on price, volume, and speed of execution. The difference being that the algorithms within the auto-hedge module are controlled directly by the position management system, whereas the client sets his algorithms independently.

- Finally every client trade is added to the trade database, then analyzed via classical data-mining techniques against price history to determine which clients are better market-predictors or have predictable behavioral patterns. This analysis is distilled into a set of risk flags that is input into the position management system, and indirectly influences the auto-hedge module and the quote-adjuster module.

Although the architecture presented here is an abstract skeleton, the main important drivers of success of a professional market-making operation are clearly itemized. The agent-based paradigm along with the implementation design patterns should give the reader a solid base for building or bettering such a market-making business.

CHAPTER 9

Combining Strategies into Portfolios

There are two main types of portfolio aggregation methods, namely combining strategies that are operating on one security and combining agents that are operating on different securities.

9.1 AGGREGATE AGENTS

A portfolio of agents a_i operating on the same security can be represented by another trading agent, called the aggregate agent. In real trading, the aggregate agent is the one that usually emits the trading instructions that are the result of the aggregation of trading instructions coming from individual agents. It is defined as a subclass of **AGENT** by:

```
(defclass AGGREGATEAGENT (AGENT)
  ((members
    :accessor members
    :initarg :members
    :initform NIL)))
```

The **members** field is just a time series of the list of agents that are aggregated. The reason **members** is a reverse-chronological list of members is because the aggregation process may not be static in time. This gives the flexibility to deal with swarm systems in Part Two.

In order to instantiate a class, assume that a_i's are collected into the ***agents*** list. Then one would invoke a command similar to:

```
(defparameter *agag*
  (make-instance 'AGGREGATEAGENT
```

```
                :name "MyAggregateAgent"
                :members (list *agents*))))
(push *agag* *aggregateagents*)
```

The aggregate agent has no logic by itself, outside of aggregating all the individual desired market positions and orders. Hence its **update** method is:

```
(defmethod update ((a AGGREGATEAGENT) (e MARKETUPDATE))
  (push (reduce #'+
                (mapcar #'(lambda (m) (car (positions m)))
                        (car (members a))))
        (positions a))
  (setf (orders a) (reduce #'append
                           (mapcar #'orders
                                   (car (members a)))))
  (format T "MAIN complete for agent~S and event~S~%" a e))
```

In the above, `(car (members a))` represents the list of latest members of the aggregate agent. The resulting desired market position is the sum of its members' positions. The outstanding orders is the union of outstanding orders of the members.

From a computational perspective, the aggregate agent needs to be calculated right after the individual members have been updated. Hence if one were to parallelize the computation of the **consume** methods across ***agents***, the aggregate agents need to wait for the individiual threads to finish before proceeding to their own **consume** calculation. This is the reason why it is better to keep them in two separate lists, ***agents*** and ***aggregateagents***.

If one desires to trade a portfolio of agents, the logic of aggregating them into one single aggregate agent is to:

- Reduce transaction costs
- Be able to automatically generate all relevant trade statistics without any extra machinery
- Risk manage the portfolio of agents as one

Indeed it could well happen that upon receiving a market update event, one agent needs to buy and another needs to sell. The net position is unchanged, so the aggregate agent does not emit any market orders. However, if there were no aggregation then a buy and a sell order would be generated by the individual agents, which would result in the trading system giving away at least one bid-offer spread to the market.

In Part Four, this aggregation is discussed in the context of the aggregation/disaggregation layer, which comes with its own subtleties. Once an execution for the aggregate agent had been received by the OMS, every single member agent needs to be communicated its respective fill in order to continue operating and making decisions.

9.2 OPTIMAL PORTFOLIOS

There are various classical and less classical approaches to combine strategies into portfolios. The most classical comes from modern portfolio theory (MPT) that was originally designed for optimizing long-only static asset allocation decisions.

The MPT's idea is, in a nutshell, as follows. Take a set of assets A_i. Assume that for the next foreseeable future, their expected total returns vector $E = E(R_i)$, is constant. The covariance matrix of their returns, K, where $K_{ij} = Cov(R_i, R_j)$, is assumed to be constant as well.

The central question is how to choose the allocation vector $w = \{w_i\}$ so that the portfolio $A(w) = \sum w_i A_i$ has the best expected reward-to-risk characteristics. This optimality is defined by finding the highest reward for a given risk, or the lowest risk for the given reward. The MPT defines reward as total return $R(A)$ and risk as the volatility $V(R)$ of the return. The optimality criterion is equivalent to maximizing the mean-variance functional

$$F(w) = R(A(w)) - \lambda V(R(w))$$

where $\lambda > 0$ is a risk-aversion parameter. Then the optimal portfolio $A^* = \sum w_i^* A_i$ is found to be such that w is proportional to $K^{-1} E(R)$.

As much as assets themselves do not exhibit stable statistics, the trading strategies have a much better track record than long-only holdings. Hence there is scope for an application of MPT ideas to portfolios of strategies, be they operating on one security or across a variety.

I, however, prefer to assemble portfolios of strategies on one security via nonparametric techniques that take into account particular trade statistics. As will be seen in the next chapter, the trading agents calculate automatically the statistics on average win (W), average loss (L), average time in winning trade (T_W), average time in no trade (T_0), average loss in losing trade (T_L), probability of win (P_W), and probability of loss (P_L).

Those statistics can be assembled into the stylized equity curves that consist of repeating the pattern of fall by $-L * P_L$ on an interval of length

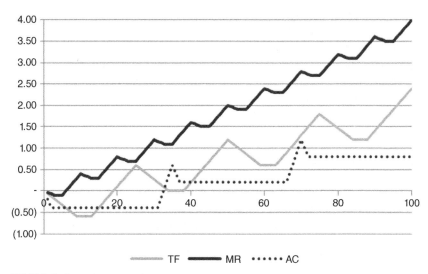

FIGURE 9.1   Stylized Equity Curves

T_L, followed by a flat line on the interval of length T_0, followed by a rise by $W * P_W$ on an interval of length T_W.

As seen in Figure 9.1, the trend-following, mean-reverting, and acceleration strategies are all seen to have different patterns of growth of their stylized equity curves. For example, the time T_0 for acceleration models is usually much larger than for trend-following models, which is itself larger than for mean-reversion models (which are almost always in a trade).

Combining those stylized equity curves gives a different angle on how to analyze the expected statistics of a portfolio of models.

9.3   RISK-MANAGEMENT OF A PORTFOLIO OF MODELS

The MPT has many variations on the theme, but all basically come down to multiplying the inverse of the covariance matrix by the vector of expected returns. The main risk in using MPT is getting the expectations vector wrong. The second risk is getting the covariances wrong.

As mentioned previously, the markets do not exhibit many static statistics to the world, and are continuously changing and evolving. Hence MPT is only useful for designing portfolios on periods of time when one is certain that those statistics will not vary.

The 60-40 Rule for running balanced portfolios has wrecked havoc in the defined benefit pension fund system in many municipalities and states in the United States. It came from using MPT on an extrapolation of the rally in equities since the 1950s, with expectations that equities will go on returning 10 percent to 12 percent forever. Equities have been in a bear market in Japan since 1990 and in the United States and Euroland since 2001, and registered drawdowns ranging from 40 percent to 90 percent from their peaks. As a result, some pension funds are now only 60 percent funded, and this is not even including a correct marking-to-market of their liabilities (discounting by the much lower interest rates the world is experiencing currently).

Hence risk management of portfolios is of the utmost importance, be it static mutual fund–like asset holdings or a dynamic portfolio of trading strategies in leveraged markets.

Part Two will focus on adaptive methods I have developed to mitigate the downside risk of either individual strategies or portfolios, and that discussion is deferred to then.

CHAPTER 10

Simulating Agent-Based Strategies

T he agent-based representation of trading strategies introduced in this book naturally yields a distributed event-driven approach to simulation. Each agent consumes events that are relevant to it and potentially emits messages to other agents. At a cost of added complexity in writing the disciplined FSMs and inter-agent communication protocols that don't fall through the cracks, one can gain a lot of flexibility and freedom. The same code can be used for backward-testing, forward-testing, and real-world trading. In the real-trading implementation, the agents also communicate with the outside world to perform trading and middle-office tasks. An event-driven approach to simulation is the closest thing to the real world because the real world works in an event-driven fashion. Most of the code written for the simulator can be re-used in the real-time implementation so that when models go live there is no risk of mistakes introduced by rewriting code.

Before delving into the details of the process, I will first enumerate the four major types of simulations that can be considered while researching the suitability of trading strategies. The goal is to find a subset of strategies that are expected to provide robust profitable results. Hence backward and forward tests can be run to:

1. Simulate different instances of the same class of agent on one market. The goal is to find optimal parameters for such a class for that market.
2. Simulate different instances of the same class of agent on different markets. The goal is to find optimal parameters on average for the collection of markets.

3. Simulate instances of different sets of inter-communicating agents for one market. The goal is to find optimal communication parameters for such a collection of agents on that market.
4. Simulate instances of different sets of inter-communicating agents for different combinations of markets. The goal is to find optimal communication parameters on average for those agents on that selection of markets.

10.1 THE SIMULATION PROBLEM

It is important to realize that trading agents, be they human or machines, cannot be seen in isolation from the market, because once they start trading, they become an integral part of the market and directly influence its future. The market *is* the collection of agents.

Hence, if an agent cannot be seen outside of the market, then it cannot ultimately be simulated without taking into account how the market would react to that agent. The situation is similar to physics where it is hard to design experiments on isolated systems. Not many things are actually isolated in our interconnected universe. Hence physicists create idealized thought experiments to work out certain concepts but it is very difficult to perform idealized observational experiments. At quantum mechanical scales, the observer disturbs the object of its observation by the mere fact of observing it.

Of course, there are simplifying assumptions allowing one to get away from simulating the whole world in one go. In physics, if an object is large enough, then shedding light on it will not perceptibly change its momentum, and one can assume that quantum phenomena could be ignored. In trading, if an agent is small enough, then one can assume that the impact of its trading size on the market would be negligible.

Hence the complete simulation framework in the context of automated trading should strive to model:

- The agent's reaction to the ECN's price updates and to agent-to-agent communications, inclusive of slippage and missed trades.
- The agent's reaction to a range of technical glitches related to communications with the ECN, inclusive of order acknowledgment delays and order rejects.
- The ECN's reaction to the agent's trading inclusive of delayed market impact and other agents' learning and adaptation behavior.

This chapter focuses on the first aspect of simulation, namely the analysis of the performance of agents when one assumes that the ECN is perfect in the sense that:

- No Impact: The agents' action in placing orders and performing trades does not impact the ECN's behavior.
- No Delay: The ECN acknowledges immediately any order placement by the agents.
- No Rejects: The ECN does not reject any of the agents' orders

The framework presented here is applicable to a wide range of strategies and data sets. Most price-taking strategies can be simulated to a reasonable degree of accuracy by modeling partial fills, slippage, and some execution algorithms (discussed mostly in Part Three).

Limit-order–driven strategies are inherently more difficult to simulate because of the uncertainty of the time and size of the execution associated with such orders.

A lot of the real-world complexity can be rendered by connecting to the test environments provided by the ECNs. These test environments attempt to create realistic situations related to glitches and latency in the communications infrastructure. However, prior to connectiong to such an environment, an order management system needs to be developed to keep track of all the resting orders and state of the execution. That in itself is a nontrivial task as shown in Part Four. The complete simulation process that is based on an FSM representation of the coupled (OMS – Strategy) system is deferred to there.

10.2 MODELING THE ORDER MANAGEMENT SYSTEM

The simulation environment used here, on the other hand, assumes perfect ECN behavior. It is handy for back- and forward-testing a whole range of strategies of which the performance is not severely impacted by the subtle imperfections in communicating with ECNs.

This chapter presents a simplified version of the OMS that is sufficient for this context. Here the OMS is endowed with minimal functionality to handle aggressive orders, algorithms based on aggressive orders, and some passive orders.

It is assumed here that orders placed by the OMS into the ECN are acknowledged instantaneously and that no orders are ever rejected. The complexity associated with receiving delayed acknowledgments, rejections, and delayed rejections is discussed in Part Four.

10.2.1 Orders and Algorithms

When making decisions after consuming events, the trading agent emits orders to the ECN. Those orders fall into two major categories:

1. Aggressive Orders. These are used to change the agent's position at a point in time by taking some of the available liquidity in a security while paying at least the bid-ask spread. The aggressive orders are executed via stop, at market, stop-limit, immediate-or-cancel, market-on-open, and market-on-close orders.
2. Passive Orders. Those are placed by the agent into the security's order book at the ECN and are expressed via limit orders.

There are several ways by which an agent may place the order into the ECN and those ways depend on the ECN's functionality. Some ECNs are pure matching engines that mostly accept limit orders from the participants (this is the case with most exchanges). Some ECNs only accept price-taking orders because the ECN's operator is the market-maker (as is the case with several FX trading venues that originate from banks).

Hence not all types of orders can be placed with just any ECN and the simulation environment should take this into account. For example, there is no obvious way, as a client, of placing a limit order into a bank's FX market-making stream. The bank makes money from market-making and so all the agents connecting to that stream are de facto price takers.

The execution algorithms ("algos") is a layer of functionality that allows a wide variety of orders to be placed into exchanges.

A simple example of an execution algorithm is the stop order. It does not naturally exist in a matching engine of an exchange—it is not a resting order. Stops do not appear in the order book before they are actually executed. They are in fact limit orders that are placed into the matching engine the moment a price trigger happens. The limit price is such that the order can sweep the necessary liquidity in the order book to fill the size. If there is not enough size or if one wants to limit the price impact, the order is broken into various tranches until it is filled.

Another example of an algo is a synthetic limit order in an ECN that does not support passive orders. If one wanted to place a sell limit at a price P, one could keep placing aggressive sells as long as the ECN is quoting the bid side at P or better, until all the desired order size is filled.

More sophisticated algos are discussed in Part Three. For example, large institutional equity and ETF orders are usually placed using volume-weighted average price (VWAP) or time-weighted average price (TWAP) algos. The agent can decide on what algo to use in placing an order, hence an algo should be reflected in the information set that constitutes the order.

The **ORDER** class is a subclass of **MARKETUPDATE** and inherits the **timestamp**, **value**, and **security** fields:

```
(defclass ORDER (MARKETUPDATE)
  ((ordertype
    :accessor ordertype
    :initarg :ordertype)
   (orderquantity
    :accessor orderquantity
    :initarg :orderquantity)
   (orderprice
    :accessor orderprice
    :initarg :orderprice)
   (algoinstance
    :accessor algoinstance
    :initarg :algoinstance)))
```

The **algoinstance** field points to the particular instance of the **ALGO** class that the agent wants to use:

```
(defclass ALGO ()
  ((algotype
    :accessor algotype
    :initarg :algotype)))
```

The **algotype** field identifies the nature of the algo and is useful for the simulation of slippage. In this particular context, algos can fall into the **:AGGRESSIVE** or **:PASSIVE** categories.

10.2.2 Simulating Slippage

The matter of slippage is covered in detail in Part Three where the goal is to design algos that minimize market impact. Slippage can come from various sources but it mostly stems from either lack of liquidity or lack of access to liquidity. Slippage can come from aggressive orders that are not executed at the expected price or from passive orders that are not executed at the expected size.

In the current simulation environment, slippage models some likely effects that the agent's trading implies on the execution price. The **SIMUL** algo contains a slippage response function and is defined as the subclass:

```
(defclass SIMUL (ALGO)
  ((slippage
    :accessor slippage
    :initarg :slippage
    :initform #'slippagefunction)))
```

The **slippagefunction**, in turn, needs to be set up for potentially every security in the simulation. It could be a function of time of day or other factors known to affect liquidity. By default it takes the event, the size of the order, and the order type as arguments. Time information and security name can be extracted directly from the event. A simple example is:

```
(defun slippagefunction (e size ordertype)
  (* (signum size) 0.01))
```

This slippage function would bump every price by one percent in the direction of the trade, independent of the security and order type. The following function, for example, bumps AAPL 0.2 basis points for limit orders and 2 basis points for all others (stops) in the direction of the trade. It accounts for twice the above slippage for MSFT:

```
(defun slippagefunction (e size ordertype)
  (let ((s (+ 1 (abs (/ size 100000)))))
    (* (signum size)
       (case-equal (security e)
                   ("AAPL" (case ordertype
                             ((:LMT :LMT_ON_OPEN :LMT_ON_CLOSE)
                              (* 0.00002 s))
                             (otherwise
                              (* 0.0002 s))))
                   ("MSFT" (case ordertype
                             ((:LMT :LMT_ON_OPEN :LMT_ON_CLOSE)
                              (* 0.00004 s))
                             (otherwise
                              (* 0.0004 s))))
                   (t 0)))))
```

This function is applied to adjust the resulting price of the transaction via the generic function **price** that takes the optional arguments of the slippage function, the size, and the order type. The price adjustment is made via the function

```
(defun adjustprice (p slippagefunc e size ordertype)
  (* p (+ 1 (if slippagefunc
                (funcall slippagefunc
                         e
                         size
                         ordertype)
           0)))))
```

and the **price** methods are as follows:

```
(defmethod price ((e PRC) &key (slippagefunc NIL) (size 0)
(ordertype NIL))
  (let ((p (car (value e))))
    (adjustprice p slippagefunc e size ordertype)))

(defmethod price ((e BAR) &key (slippagefunc NIL) (size 0)
(ordertype NIL))
  (let ((p (case ordertype
             ((:STP_ON_OPEN :LMT_ON_OPEN) (o e))
             ((:STP_ON_CLOSE :LMT_ON_CLOSE) (c e))
             (otherwise (pivot e)))))
    (adjustprice p slippagefunc (security e) size ordertype)))

(defmethod price ((e BOOK) &key (slippagefunc NIL) (size 0)
(ordertype NIL))
  (let ((p (if (zerop size)
               (mid e)
             (if (> size 0)
                 (askbest e)
               (bidbest e)))))
    (adjustprice p slippagefunc (security e) size ordertype)))
```

The method **BAR** allows for execution either on the close or the open of a bar.

10.2.3   Simulating Order Placement

In the simulation environment the agent keeps track of its active orders in the **orders** list. When it decides on an order to place, it simply pushes an instance of the **ORDER** object onto its **orders** list via the generic function **sendorder**:

```
(defmethod sendorder ((a AGENT) (e MARKETUPDATE) &key opc oqt otp oid)
  (push (make-instance
           'ORDER
         :timestamp (timestamp e)
         :value oid
         :security (security e)
         :ordertype otp
         :orderquantity oqt
         :orderprice opc
         :algoinstance (make-instance
                         'SIMUL
                       :algotype (case otp
                                   ((:STP :IOC :MOC :MOO) :AGGRESSIVE)
                                   ((:LMT) :PASSIVE)))))
    (orders a)))
```

Here it emits either a passive or aggressive **SIMUL** algo. That algo type is then used by the slippage function to adjust the trade price accordingly.

There are three places in the event consumption cycle by the agent where orders can be emitted:

1. In the FSM Transitions **actuator** functions. Passive orders should be emitted when transitions happen.
2. In the **update :after** method. The immediate change in the agent's desired market position is being generated at the level of the FSM transition, and the resulting agressive order can be dealt with after the FSM is processed and before postprocessing.
3. In the aggregator. When several agents are trading in the same security it is also possible to route all the agents' positions into an aggregator so that the slippage is minimized. Such aggregators are discussed in Part Two.

The following methods are used to change and cancel existing orders and are most useful for handling passive orders that have not been executed yet:

```
(defmethod changeorder ((a AGENT) (e MARKETUPDATE) &key new-opc new-oqt
new-otp old-oid)
  (let ((o (car (remove-if-not #'(lambda (x) (equal (value x) old-oid))
                       (orders a))))
        (restorders (remove-if #'(lambda (x) (equal (value x) old-oid))
                       (orders a))))
```

```
(when new-opc (setf (orderprice o) new-opc))
(when new-oqt (setf (orderquantity o) new-oqt))
(when new-otp (setf (ordertype o) new-otp))
(setf (timestamp o) (timestamp e))
(setf (orders a) (append (list o) restorders)))))

(defmethod cancelorder ((a AGENT) old-oid)
  (setf (orders a)  (remove-if #'(lambda (x) (equal (value x) old-oid))
                               (orders a))))
```

Once the agent generates the orders, they are passed to the order management system simulator for execution.

10.2.4 Simulating Order Execution

In the real world, an order placed with the ECN generates (generally) a partial fill and a remaining working order that stays at the ECN. The simulation environment presented here models such effects by introducing the **execute** generic function that returns two values, namely the executed trade and the remaining order.

For the slippage-endowed **SIMUL** algo there is no remaining working order but on the other hand the price of the execution is being adjusted by the slippage function in the direction of the trade:

```
(defmethod execute ((o ORDER) (l SIMUL) (e MARKETUPDATE))
  (values
   (list (make-TRADE :timestamp (timestamp e)
                     :price (price e
                                   :slippagefunc (slippage l)
                                   :size (orderquantity o)
                                   :ordertype (ordertype o))
                     :quantity (orderquantity o)))
   NIL))
```

If, for example, one has access to order book update events, one can model an aggressive algo that sweeps the book up to a certain depth (if needed) until it has finished filling the order. The algo class **AGRESSOR** contains a field for maximum depth of book sweep:

```
(defclass AGRESSOR (ALGO)
  ((maxdepth
    :accessor maxdepth
    :initarg :maxdepth)))
```

The **execute** method can be defined as follows for this class:

```
(defun lift-quotes (quoteslist quantity max-depth)
  (let* ((f (first quoteslist))
         (q (second f))
         (result (list f))
         excess)
    (for (i 1 (- max-depth 1))
         (when (<= q  quantity)
           (incf q (second (nth i quoteslist)))
           (push (nth i quoteslist) result)))
    (setf excess (- (sum-list result #'second) quantity))
    (when (> excess 0)
      (decf (second (first result)) excess))
    result))


(defmethod execute ((o ORDER) (l AGRESSOR) (e BOOK))
  (let* ((q (orderquantity o))
         (bookside (if (> q 0) (second (value e)) (first (value e))))
         (sweep (lift-quotes bookside q (maxdepth l)))
         (trds (mapcar #'(lambda (x) (make-trade
                                      :timestamp (timestamp e)
                                      :price (first x)
                                      :quantity (* (signum q)
                                                   (second x))))
                       sweep))
         (sweepsize (sum-list sweep #'second))
         (shortfall (- q sweepsize)))
    (values
      trds
      (if (zerop shortfall)
          NIL
        (make-instance
          'ORDER
          :timestamp (timestamp e)
          :value (value o)
          :security (security e)
          :orderprice (orderprice o)
          :orderquantity shortfall
          :ordertype (ordertype o)
          :algoinstance l)))))
```

The **AGGRESSOR** algo does not need any explicit slippage functions because, via its recursive operation, it generates slippage by going beyond the best bid-offers (according to its order size relative to the order book liquidity).

10.2.5 A Model for the OMS

The order management system handles the execution logic of the current orders of the agent. In the real world the OMS serves two major purposes:

1. It communicates orders from the agent to the ECN.
2. It communicates fills from the ECN back to the agent.

Because of this dual functionality, in the simulation environment the OMS is called at different points in the event consumption cycle. It takes an optional argument **algocategory** that enables it to process only a subset of the active orders at a point in time. That subset can be all passive or all agressive orders, for example.

```
(defmethod oms ((a AGENT) (e MARKETUPDATE) &key (algocategory :ALL))
   (let* ((categoryp #'(lambda (x) (if (equal algocategory :ALL)
                                        T
                                (equal (algotype (algoinstance x))
                                       algocategory)))))
            (notcategoryp #'(lambda (x) (not (funcall categoryp x))))
            (bins (classify (orders a) (list categoryp notcategoryp)))
            (categoryorders (first bins))
            (noncategoryorders (second bins))
            (newcategoryorders NIL))
     (dolist (o categoryorders)
       (when (equal (security o)
                    (security e))
         (multiple-value-bind
             (executions remainingorder)
             (execute o (algoinstance o) e)
           (when executions
             (push-list executions (trades a))
             (push (compute-tradestats (trades a)) (tradestats a)))
           (when remainingorder
             (push remainingorder newcategoryorders)))))
     (setf (orders a)
       (append newcategoryorders
               noncategoryorders))))
```

The OMS method first classifies all the agent's active orders into orders corresponding to the chosen category and the remainder. For every order in the category of interest the **execute** method is called when the market update event is for the same security as the order was given for. This method returns the list of partial fills that is appended to the agent's **trades** list, and the remaining unfilled order, if any. If there are any new fills, then the **compute-tradestats** function adds the trade statistics to the agent's **tradestats** list.

The resulting active orders for the agent become the set of unfilled orders in the category and the set of orders that were not in the category of interest. The OMS then passes control back to the agent's **update** method.

10.2.6 Operating the OMS

When the agent starts a new market update event consumption cycle, the method **update :before** is invoked first. At that point the OMS is called, before any preprocessing begins, to check whether any active orders can be executed on the new event. Those orders come from the previous cycle and are the set of unfilled passive and aggressive orders. Hence the **oms** method is invoked with **algocategory** equal to **:ALL**:

```
(defmethod update :before ((a AGENT) (e MARKETUPDATE))
  (when (null (timestamps a))
    (push 0 (pls a))
    (push 0 (fitnesses a)))
  (push (timestamp e) (timestamps a))
  (push (price e) (revalprices a))
  (oms a e :algocategory :ALL)
  (preprocess a e)
  (format T "BEFORE method completed for agent  A and event
  A %" a e))
```

During the agent's decision-making stage of the event consumption cycle, a new set of orders may be added to the active orders list. This could be directly at the level of the **actuator** stage of the FSM transitions or it could be after the FSM had been processed and the desired market position of the agent changed via the **positions** list. The **update :after** method, by default, generates an aggressive order if the agent has changed its desired position:

```
(defmethod update :after ((a AGENT) (e MARKETUPDATE))
  (let* ((L (length (timestamps a)))
         (lastposition (first (positions a)))
         (prevposition (if (< L 2)
                           0
                           (second (positions a))))
         (tradequantity (- lastposition prevposition))
```

```
          (lastprice (first (revalprices a)))
          (prevprice (if (< L 2)
                         0
                         (second (revalprices a))))
          (pl (if (< L 2)
                  0
                  (* prevposition (- lastprice prevprice)))))))
    (push pl (pls a))
      (unless (zerop tradequantity)
        (sendorder a e
                   :opc (price e)
                   :oqt tradequantity
                   :otp :STP
                   :oid :POSCHG)
        (format T "generated aggressive order for  S for
          quantity  S %" a tradequantity))
      (postprocess a e)
      (format T "AFTER method completed for agent  A and
        event  A %" a e)))
```

When the agent consumes an event and decides to change its market position, it places the new aggressive order in its **orders** list. The OMS will attempt to execute that order when the agent observes the next market update event.

This is a pessimistic execution model because the agent does not execute the change in position on the same event that prompted that change, but has to wait until the next one. One could think that this is overly restrictive; however, it provides a more realistic framework.

For example, if one wants to model a strategy that trades at the close of a trading day, then rather than sampling the closing price, one should sample an interval of prices just before the close. In reality it is difficult to always trade at the close and not necessarily advisable.

As a second example, if one uses **BARs** then one could model execution at the open of the next bar given a change of position computed at the close of the previous bar. Putting the OMS at the head of the event consumption cycle is compatible with such realistic execution logic rather than the less realistic hope to be executing at the close.

It is also important to point out that the modeled OMS is supposed to operate on a timescale that is an order of magnitude smaller than that of the potential state changes of the agent. Situations where the OMS cannot be de-coupled from the FSM of the agent are discussed in Part Four.

10.3 RUNNING SIMULATIONS

To set up a simulation environment, assume that a set of strategies have been coded into trading agents and tested. For example, the strategies discussed in Chapter 7 are good candidates that can be tested on various parameter sets, markets, and timescales. The complete simulation process is:

- Instantiate each agent class with the relevant parameters and group them into the ***agents*** list.
- Collect a timestamp-ordered list into the ***events*** list of market update events to be supplied to the simulator. For simplicity, all the events should be instances of the same subclass of **MARKETUPDATE** but can carry information on different securities. In this book at least three basic subclasses can be handled by the trading agents (**PRC, BOOK,** and **BAR**) but the framework given here gives readers the stepping stone to extend it at their will.
- Run the **run-simulation** function on the ***events*** argument. At the end of the simulation, all PL and trade statistics time series remain stored in each agent's relevant fields (**pls, trades, tradestats**).
- Run an analysis function **analyze** that will output relevant statistics and show optimal parameter combinations.

The **run-simulation** routine introduced in Chapter 5 is the core general process that performs the simulation task:

```
(defun run-simulation (events)
  (dolist (a *agents*)
    (initialize a))
  (setf *events-queue* events)
  (while *events-queue*
    (let ((e (pop *events-queue*)))
      (dolist (a *agents*)
        (consume a e)))))
```

Given that the central simulation routine is already written, the focus now is on setting up all the data relevant to the simulation and on the analysis of simulation results.

10.3.1 Setting Up a Back-Test

Assume, for simplicity, that one has collected a time series of prices for a certain security (here we take AAPL and MSFT for example). Those time series, for simplicity, are stored in flat files **AAPL.txt** and **MSFT.txt** that reside

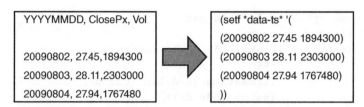

FIGURE 10.1 LISP Quote Recap Data Representation

in the directory represented by the string ***data-dir-string***. Each line is composed of a timestamp, a price, and a transaction volume. These time series are exactly like quote recap tables that all the major data providers publish (e.g., Bloomberg, Reuters, or the exchanges themselves). An excerpt from such a quote recap is given in Figure 10.1.

The goal is to produce from that data a combined time-ordered list of **PRC** events for AAPL and MSFT in order to initialize the ***events*** list.

An efficient way of doing it in LISP is to initially transform the flat data files into LISP programs in order to use the powerful **load** function. The reader is reminded that one of the cardinal strengths of LISP, and a feature that distinguishes it from all other computer languages written to date, is the fact that data and programs in LISP have the same structure, namely they are lists.[1]

Hence via a scripting language like either PERL or AWK one creates two new files **AAPL.lisp** and **MSFT.lisp** that look like Figure 10.1.

This way an amorphous flat file is transformed into a LISP program that sets a variable called ***data-ts*** to a list of lists, each one representing a timestamp, price, and volume update. All one needs now is to execute that program by simply loading it:

```
(defparameter *data-ts* NIL)
(defparameter *data-dir-string* " /datafiles")

(defun create-events-list (data-name &key (data-dir
                                            *data-dir-string*)
                                           (start-D NIL)
                                           (end-D NIL))
  (let ((data-path (make-pathname
                    :directory data-dir
                    :name data-name
                    :type "lisp")))
```

---

[1] This is also true for Scheme, a language based on LISP.

```
(when (probe-file data-path)
  (load data-path)
  (mapcar #'(lambda (d) (make-instance
              'PRC
              :timestamp (u-d-h-m (car d))
              :value (cdr d)))
          (remove-if #'(lambda (x) (or (if start-D
                                           (< (first x) start-D))
                                       (if end-D (>
                                         (first x) end-D))))
                     *data-ts*)))))
```

In order to operate the file loader to create the ***events*** list one evaluates
the following forms:

```
(defparameter *MSFT-events* (create-events-list "MSFT"))

(defparameter *AAPL-events* (create-events-list "AAPL"))

(setf *events* (sort (union *MSFT-events* *AAPL-events*)
                     #'(lambda (x y)
                         (< (timestamp x) (timestamp y)))))
```

The last action takes the set union and sorts it chronologically according to
timestamp. The ***events*** list is now ready to be passed as argument to the
run-simulation routine simply by evaluating the form

```
(run-simulation *events*)
```

10.3.2 Setting Up a Forward Test

Running simulations forward in time is mechanically the same process as
running back tests. Instead of populating the ***events*** list by a past history
of events, one needs to produce a possible future path of such events.

    In order to generate such possible future paths, one needs to think care-
fully about which elements of the dynamics of the markets one wants to realistically reproduce. A lot of financial theory has been based on overly simplifying assumptions of normality on the distributional side and of Markov
property on the time-interdependence side. Although, by the central limit
theorem, these properties may hold at long timescales, these scales may not
be relevant to any trader's lifetime. As pointed out several times before, the
market presents features of a complex system that is far from equilibrium.

In such a system, features tend to occur according to a power law, and innovations are far from being normally distributed and time-independent.

If markets were normally distributed and Markovian, then one could easily generate paths by a straightforward Monte Carlo method, modeling a stochastic process

$$dP(t) = \alpha(P, t) + \sigma(P, t)dX(t)$$

where $dX \in N(0, 1)$ is a normally distributed innovation. In order to use such a representation, besides assuming normality, one has to further assume a *model* of the market dynamics by having a prior idea of the class of functions that the drift α and the volatility σ belong to. In other words, one needs to have an a priori idea of the functional and parametric form of those functions. Then one can proceed to estimate these parameters (up to a certain accuracy) by standard statistical methods (e.g., maximum likelihood).

In absence of such a priori insight, one can adopt a purely phenomenological stance and derive a set of paths that have very similar features to the ones coming from an observed path. This is achieved by reshuffling observed data in a certain way and these types of methods are sometimes referred to as *bootstrapping*. The question is, what may be those features of interest? They could be:

- Distribution of innovations. As there is no model of the market, there is no a priori vision as to what the distribution of price innovations should be, hence one may as well take an observed distribution as starting point, and assume that this feature remains the same for a possible future path.
- Directional clustering. The market has experienced a certain behavior in time. Namely, a certain concentration of positive innovations may have reflected certain uptrends. This serial correlation may be a feature of interest for modeling possible paths.
- Amplitude clustering. The market may have experienced periods of high and low volatility. This may be reflected by a feature that the innovations tend to cluster in time, either on the distribution's tail or on the distribution's body, with transitions between body and tail being of lower probability.

Hence the following phenomenological reshuffling algorithm is introduced, with aim to generating possible future paths that preserve the above features relative to a historically observed path.

To set up the reshuffling algorithm, suppose a history of prices P_i where $i = 0..N$ had been observed. This history yields data that can be used to reproduce the features just enumerated. First one derives the distribution of percentage innovations:

$$D = \{R_i\} \quad R_{i+1} = \frac{P_{i+1} - P_i}{P_i} \quad i = 0..N-1$$

This distribution can be classified, for example, into 4 subsets

$$D = T^- \cup B^- \cup B^+ \cup T^+$$

where Ts are the tails and Bs are the bodies of the distribution. The criterion could be quartiles of the negative and positive subsets of innovations, for example. Having partitioned the distribution in such a way, one can deal with directional and amplitude clustering in the following manner. Given the observed path P_i, one derives the symbolic time series that corresponds to the location of the innovation relative to the above classification:

$$\{L_i\} \quad R_i \in L_i \quad L_i \in \{T^-, B^-, B^+, T^+\}$$

This symbolic series shows the path of the history through the distribution but not the size of the innovation. One can now produce a new time series Q by randomly drawing from the distribution's subsets:

$$Q_0 = RND \quad Q_{i+1} = Q_i * S_{i+1} \quad S_{i+1} \in L_{i+1}$$

Each path starts at a random point $RND > 0$. By construction, the time series Q has the same three features as the original series P, namely the same distribution and directional and amplitude clustering of returns.

The above algorithm gives a basis to built simulated future paths of price events (without volume information). Studying the joint distribution of quotes and volumes one can, in a similar way, forward-simulate full price and volume quotes **PRC**. Finally, studying the distribution of mid-prices, ranges, and locations of open and close relative to the range in percentage terms, one can forward-simulate a stream of **BAR**s.

10.4 ANALYSIS OF RESULTS

Once the simulation finishes, all the trade statistics and PL data pertaining to each agent remains saved in the agent's **pls** and **tradestats** fields. Hence an analyzer needs to be provided that extracts that data and repackages it into a useable format at the end of the simulation run.

The basic statistics that an agent is judged on fall into the continuous and the per-trade categories. Here the very basic functions are presented, mainly to show how to extract data from the agents. The reader, no doubt, would be able, on this basis, to build an analysis package or use other third-party tools like Matlab.

10.4.1 Continuous Statistics

The **pls** list contains the agent's history of PL increments that is calculated for each relevant market update event, in the **update :after** method.

Metrics like the maximal drawdown, information ratio, and return-to-drawdown ratio can be easily derived from the **pls** list. If the agent is compared to a benchmark, then the relative upside and downside capture statistics can also be computed, taking into account the return stream from the benchmark on the same simulation period.

A joint concurrent simulation of a portfolio of agents opens the door to the correlation and cointegration analysis of PLs as discussed in the last chapter, as well as to the overall PL analysis stemming from the aggregation of the individual information into an instance of the **AGGREGATEAGENT** class.

To plot the time series of the statistics, one can use the following method that calls on the **ts-plot** function that plots a time series on the users GUI. This function is implementation dependent and is left to the reader's design. Here the **what** keyword determines the trade statistic to run:

```
(defmethod graph-stats ((a AGENT) what)
  (ts-plot (timestamps a)
           (case what
             (:cpl (rc-integrate (trunc (pls a))))
             (:fit (trunc (fitnesses a)))
             (:prc (revalprices a))
             (:pls (trunc (pls a)))
             (:pos (positions a)))))
```

The function **rc-integrate** creates the time-series of a consecutively integrated reverse-chronological vector of real values (see Appendix), and **:cpl** stands for plotting cumulative PL since inception. Here the time series are plot against the same timescale as provided by the ***events*** stream.

10.4.2 Per-Trade Statistics

The **tradestats** field contains the most important per-trade statistics on each agent. It is a reverse-chronological timeseries of **TRADESTAT** structures containing the statistics at each recalculation of the agent:

```
(defstruct TRADESTAT
  percent-profitable
  win-to-loss
  average-logret
  tot-pl
  average-duration
  pos-pl
  neg-pl
  profit-factor)
```

The function **compute-tradestats** is responsible for this calculation at each new trade, and is called in the **oms** method, as soon as order executions are received by it.

Of course, for most purposes of analysis, the first data point (last in time!) of **tradestats** is relevant, as it contains the accumulated statistics on the full simulation run. However, in Part Two, the rolling statistics are relevant for the agent's **fitness** calculation, and that is an integral part of an adaptive swarm system. Hence the agents have been designed ab initio for storing the time series of structures representing their trade statistics.

Those statistics ignore the continuous repricing information of the position between position changes and focus only on extracting the information from trade events and prices associated with those events.

The statistics are the percent profitable, the win/loss ratio, the average logarithmic return per trade, the total, positive, and negative PLs, the profit factor, and the average trade duration (in clock time or event count time, depending on the nature of the timestamps associated with the market update events).

To plot the time series of trade statistics against the timescale provided by the times of the trades one can use the following method.

```
(defmethod graph-tradestats ((a AGENT) what)
  (with-slots (trades tradestats) a
    (ts-plot (mapcar #'trade-timestamp trades)
             (case what
               (:tpl (mapcar #'tradestat-tot-pl tradestats))
               (:lrt (mapcar #'tradestat-average-logret tradestats))
               (:prc (mapcar #'trade-price trades))
               (:qnt (mapcar #'trade-quantity trades))))))
```

10.4.3 Parameter Search and Optimization

The traditional methods of model discovery entail a search in the parameter space of the model, once the inuition about the dynamic properties of the model have been implemented in code. All the models considered in the Chapter 7 are parametric. For example, the lookback periods of the fast and slow channels in the channel breakout system are the model's parameters.

Chapter 3 gave an example on how to define parametric families of agents stemming from the same class. For example, a one-dimensional family was defined for the **SIMPLEMODEL** agent class:

```
(for (i 10 110)
     (push (make-instance
            'SIMPLEMODEL
            :L i)
           *agents*))
```

Once the simulation has been run, the statistics can be retrieved into a list by a series of simple functions for further analysis. For the above example, to get the list of parameter and final trade PL pairs, one can invoke the following form:

```
(let ((results NIL))
  (dolist (a *agents*)
    (push (list (L a)
                (tradestats-tot-pl (first (tradestats a))))
          results))
  results)
```

It was noted above that the first element in the reverse-chronological **tradestats** list is the **TRADESTAT** structure that corresponds to the last computation of the trades statistics.

This list can be graphed as a function of the parameter *L*. For models that have two relevant parameters, a heat map can be displayed and analyzed for the desired statistics. Of course, visualizing data for three parameters or more becomes a challenge, but various solutions such as Matlab provide a reasonably easy-to-use functionality to represent graphically three-dimensional slices (heat map) through multidimensional data.

Programatically, to find a subset of top-performing agents is relatively straightforward. The function **cluster-agents** returns a clustering of any trade statistic according to bins defined by splitting the range of observed values equally in **num-bins** intervals.

```
(defun cluster-agents (agents what num-bins)
  (labels ((getstat (a)
                (let ((ts (first (tradestats a))))
                  (case what
                      (:tpl (tradestat-tot-pl ts))
                      (:lrt (tradestat-average-logret ts))
                      (:wtl (tradestat-win-to-loss ts))
                      (:pcp (tradestat-percent-profitable ts))
                      (:pff (tradestat-profit-factor ts)))))))
          (let* ((stats (mapcar #'getstat agents))
                 (minstats (min-list stats))
                 (maxstats (max-list stats)))
            (multiple-value-bind
              (numeric-predicates bins)
              (interval-division-predicates-bins
               minstats maxstats num-bins)
              (let* ((agent-predicates
                       (mapcar #'(lambda (p)
                                    #'(lambda (a)
                                        (funcall p (getstat a))))
                               numeric-predicates))
                     (agent-clusters
                       (classify agents agent-predicates)))
                (values bins agent-clusters))))))
```

This function would be invoked by evaluating, for example:

```
(cluster-agents *agents* :tpl 10)
```

It calculates the minimal and maximal values for the given statistic across agents and proceeds by splitting that interval in **num-bins** equal length bins and computes the associate predicates **numeric-predictates** to determine whether a number is in a given bin. The function **interval-division-predicates-bins** returns the predictates and the bins (intervals):

```
(defun interval-division-predicates-bins (min-lvl max-lvl num-bins)
  (let ((predicates-list NIL)
        (bins-list NIL)
        (subdivision (/ (- max-lvl min-lvl) num-bins))
        (first-pred #'(lambda (x) (< x min-lvl)))
        (first-bin (list :MIN_INF min-lvl))
        (last-pred #'(lambda (x) (>= x max-lvl)))
        (last-bin (list max-lvl :PLUS_INF)))
```

```
(list-append predicates-list first-pred)
(list-append bins-list first-bin)
(dotimes (i num-bins)
  (let* ((bin-left (+ min-lvl (* i subdivision)))
         (bin-right (+ bin-left subdivision)))
    (list-append predicates-list #'(lambda (x)
                                     (and (>= x bin-left)
                                          (< x bin-right))))
    (list-append bins-list (list bin-left bin-right))))
(list-append predicates-list last-pred)
(list-append bins-list last-bin)
(values predicates-list bins-list)))
```

Those predicates are then transformed to **agent-predicates** that calculate whether the agent's statistic of interest is in a given interval (bin). This is done by composing the standard numeric predicates by the **getstat** local function. Finally the agents cluster list is computed via the very general **classify** function. This function takes a list of things and predicates on those things, then returns the list of bins that correspond to things to which a consecutive predicate applies:

```
(defun classify (objects-list predicates-list)
  (let ((bins-list NIL))
    (dolist (pred predicates-list)
      (let ((p-bin NIL))
        (dolist (obj objects-list)
          (when (funcall pred obj)
        (list-append p-bin obj)))
    (list-append bins-list p-bin)))
  (values bins-list)))
```

Because the numeric predicates were defined on nonoverlapping bins that cover the real line, the resulting bins are nonoverlapping, hence the classification is exhaustive and without intersections.

The automation of such classification is an important tool for high frequency trading, as will be seen in Part Two.

10.5   DEGREES OF OVER-FITTING

However realistic the simulation process adopted, one can never escape a certain degree of data mining and over-fitting. Over-fitting appears in at least three ways, two of which can be addressed but the third one less likely:

1. However much data one processes, the choices of optimal parameters and portfolio combinations are not necessarily stable in time. Market regimes change sometimes to something that has never been seen before. To address some of this concern, Part Two develops an adaptive agent framework that helps mitigate such regime changes and ensure at least a graceful decay of strategies (rather than blow-ups).
2. Even if the above concern is addressed and confidence in the robustness of the model is gained, there is no guarantee that the trader (be it automatic or human) would necessarily perform with the same discipline in the future. For humans, the learning process comes with time, but no one is infallible and awake and ready to trade 24 hours a day. Electronic automated trading environments also experience power downs and disconnects. Part Four develops a framework for minimizing such operational problems.
3. Assume now that items 1 and 2 have been addressed and that one has built a robust adaptive automated trading framework tested on an ECN's simulated environment. At that point one is a long way ahead (and I of course hope that this book contributed to the success!). But one is not fully there yet because of the fact that the market, as discussed in the Introduction, is a complex adaptive system. The fact that the trading system is now a member of the market means that the market has changed, and will have to adapt to it, in its own unpredictable way. Of course, such nonlinear feedback is small when the system's trade size is small relative to the whole volume turned around by the other participants. Part Three presents some trading execution algorithms that are designed to minimize the market impact. However, the limitation is inherent in the nature of the market itself, and no one can do anything about it. One has to accept a certain degree of market uncertainty, however well-researched and designed is the framework. At the end of the day, no pain, no gain and no pay, no play!

With this healthy balance of enthusiasm and fatalism it is now time to attack the topic of adaptation.

Evolving Strategies

With the agent-based framework introduced in Part One for the basic estimation techniques, indicators, and models, we are ready to move on to the next level of sophistication. Part Two introduces a series of concepts that help tackle the higher complexity of the markets at lower timescales. Those timescales have become increasingly dominated by electronic trading and reflect the growing competition for liquidity and speed of execution.

The arms race unfolding in this area is creating an environment where patterns are more transient and behavior less stable and participants learn from each other faster. More efficient computing and execution technologies are fighting to match the increasing flow of information and orders.

Thus the high frequency world presents novel opportunities and poses at the same time new challenges. To navigate successfully the ever-evolving markets, I further draw on concepts that come from evolutionary theory and learning in order to endow strategies with the characteristics of flexibility and adaptability.

The crux of the matter lies in designing trading systems that exhibit at the same time opportunism, robustness, and flexibility. Opportunism means the ability to continually find new money-making opportunities. Robustness means to efficiently latch on to those opportunities while they last, and flexibility means to gracefully survive regime changes when these opportunities go away. The confluence of these three attributes is a difficult task to achieve in one single design and this part focuses on some of the progress I have made in this direction.

In reality, the distinctions between the three goals are more blurred than at first sight. Humans and animals combine them unconsiously. The phrase that comes to mind when one thinks about this goal is for the trading system to have characteristics of an autonomous adaptive agent (an AAA). The ideal result is, of course, to have an AAA that generates stable positive performance over time. The framework for autonomous agents has been introduced in Part One and here it is expanded to contain elements of adaptation.

The modern paradigm that I feel is ultimately appropriate to tackle the problem is artificial life. AL itself is very much a work in progress and a hot topic of current research. It blends ideas from biology, theory of complex systems, control theory, and robotics. It allows us to disentangle adaptation and learning and recombine them at will into evolutionary models that include shares of Darwinian and Lamarkian ideas. Most and foremost it is the science of artificial autonomous agents. It does not claim to be solving or even addressing the hard semantic problems that artificial intelligence is attempting to tackle. Yet it sheds a lot of light on the emergence of self-organization and behavioral complexity in animal-like digital creatures and provides very efficient ways of constructing such creatures.

Coming back to the three fundamental goals of the AAA, opportunism is the difficult part as it is the most human and nonobjective of the three. It entails more than a random or blind search for strategies and is based partly on intuition of what should work and partly on prior knowledge of what has worked. Some of this prior knowledge is taken in the form of pre-existing possible strategies from Part One.

Assuming that the set of opportunities is finite and known (and thus does not need to be continuously discovered), the main challenge then becomes to design a strategy that will optimally exploit the current best opportunity or pattern and gracefully transition to the next behavior when needed. The focus here is to discuss several possible avenues to achieve such control.

This set of opportunities is represented by a set of strategies that are compatible with certain repeated market regimes. It is argued that the concept of regime (and changes of regime) can be seen through the prism of a strategy compatible with it. Different classes of trading models can in general provide robust indicators of such different types of regimes. To figure out what regime is most likely to be in force, scale-invariant fitness measures for strategies are introduced. The concept of fitness feedback control is the first step toward ensuring graceful degradation of performance of a single strategy that finds itself negatively affected by a market regime it is not adapted to.

Building up from the study of regime persistence viewed through those scale-invariant fitnesses, automated model-switching algorithms are implemented. Those aggregate agents are called swarm systems and provide an adaptation method that is based on switching decisions within a parametrized population based on simple individual models. This meta-process is simple from a control-theoretic perspective but provides already nontrivial gains in performance relative to static choices we explored in Part One.

The next step comes from embedding more complexity into the switching strategy itself by explicitly introducing reinforcement learning techniques into the swarm decision making. We discuss here the main concepts of supervised and reinforcement learning and comment on the subtle interplay between adaptation and learning in an evolutionary context. The idea behind the concept of the learning swarm is to introduce a continuous exploration versus exploitation activity that searches for the best control parameters while the market is cycling through different regimes.

Hence, in a nutshell, instead of embedding complexity into one agent, one uses a whole swarm of agents to create a set of potential behaviors. The agent swarm then chooses a subset of the fittest that is then implemented in real trading.

The strength of this methodology lies in its openness to innovation. Humans can continuously contribute new ideas to the swarm that it will or will not decide to allocate some risk to, depending on performance. I am currently exploring ideas from certain AL techniques to automatically search for new potential behaviors to add to the swarm.

I hope that this part endows the reader with a solid start for the further exploration and design of profitable and robust adaptative trading agents.

CHAPTER 11

Strategies for Adaptation

P art One introduced the agent-based representation of a trading strategy and an architrecture for running concurrently a set of trading agents. In this framework, the agents are operating autonomously and may communicate with each other. Part Two builds on that design to endow the trading agents with adaptive features, either as a group or as individuals.

First of all, the problem needs to be framed correctly in order to have a clear picture of the goals and benefits of an adaptive behavior. Then one needs to formulate the external constraints or features that the strategies should be adapting to.

11.1 AVENUES FOR ADAPTATIONS

What, first of all, is *adaptation*, and to what?

There are three main universal aspects of systems that exhibit adaptive behavior:

1. The system is endowed with a reserve of potential strategies or tactics.
2. The system is endowed with a set of criteria, driven by internal or external factors, for making choices between these strategies at any point in time.
3. The system makes those choices in order to achieve a certain goal under a certain set of constraints.

For a trading agent, be it human or robot, to exhibit adaptive behavior is to be able to change its trading strategy or tactics when certain market or PL factors warrant it, while maintaining the goal of profitability under constraint of maximal allowed drawdown. This reserve of strategies can be, for example, a parametric family of strategies of the same kind, or a discrete set of semantically different strategies.

Given the preceding, there are three principal ways to set up an adaptive trading system:

1. *Swarm:* Here the different potential strategies are represented by a set of nonadaptive (constant parameters) agents running in parallel in paper trading mode. Every agent's performance is assessed in real time according to a certain criterion, and a subset of well-performing agents is allowed to trade.
2. *Smart:* Here the single agent learns to change its internal strategy via a reinforcement mechanism that rewards it for good behavior and takes points away for bad behavior.
3. *Scary:* This is the swarm of smart agents!

An analogy can be drawn with ways that people manage trading businesses. The swarm model is similar to a large trading operation with lots of traders with diverse styles. They are all good at certain things, but not at others. One trader is good at capturing trends in commodities, another is great at exploiting discrepancies between swaptions and caps, yet another refuses point blank to take a view on the direction of the stock market and is only interested in trading the spread between companies in the beverage sector. But the beer trader cannot tell a cap from a sock, the vol trader thinks people get life for selling crack spreads, and the sugar trader can't figure out why Chablis should cost more than Ribena. So each trader sticks to its own style.

As it happens, for each style and asset class, there are periods when that style is profitable and periods when it is not. Commodities do not trend all the time, correlation is not mispriced that often, and no, unfortunately, juice is usually not pricier than wine. So the CIO comes in, takes a look at the relative merits of this or that style, and allocates risk between the traders. The CIO does not fire traders if they don't perform all the time, but just reduces their risk until they become profitable again.

Compare this to a super-smart hedge fund manager. He does not need anyone around him, just a bunch of screens and donuts. He's traded lots of different markets, survived a couple of crashes and his own blow-ups, and learned when to call and when to fold. Like Mr. Keynes, he'll change when the facts change.

Then imagine putting a group of super-smart managers together. They need to be reined in, from time to time, by an even smarter CIO, who channels their hyperinflated egos into a cooperative world domination process by steering them away from stealing each other's donuts and risk allocation. This swarm of masters of the universe can quickly become scary, but at this point it is just, thankfully, science fiction!

Part Two discusses both the swarm and the smart systems while I continue my work on the scary ones.

Given the conceptual understanding of these possible approaches to adaptation, one still needs to formulate the goals and the constraints of an adaptive trading strategy to be able to implement those ideas.

11.2 THE CYBERNETICS OF TRADING

One of the aims of this book is to demonstrate to the reader that designing trading strategies based on the autonomous adaptive agent paradigm provides a basis on which a robust trading business can be constructed. Built-in robustness should be a key feature of any serious automated trading business and an important factor of its long-term survivability.

Part One addressed the question of completeness by introducing the FSM representation of the control system of an agent. Completeness is a first step toward robustness, as it ensures operational continuity in whatever state of the world the agent finds itself in.

The robustness discussed here pertains to the strategy's performance, that is, its money-making capability across different market regimes. The goal is to come up with an architecture that ensures the strategy's adaptation or, at worst, graceful decay when the market regime changes.

The AAA approach brings forth concepts of adaptation for the design of self-correcting strategies that are more robust than the traditional constant parameter strategies discussed in Part One.

Adaptive and self-correcting systems are characterized by control mechanisms that have a series of feedbacks. These feedbacks dynamically change the parameters of the system in order to achieve certain implicit or explicit goals. The feedbacks usually compare a current observed external state of the system with a desired state, and change the internal control parameters so as to reduce the distance between those states. This concept is at the essence of cybernetics, and is epitomized by Figure 11.1.

For example, the **AGRESSOR** algo encountered in Chapter 10 was built exactly on the above principle of feedback. The desired state is a certain market position, the current state is the actual position, and the control mechanism is to issue an order quantity for the difference between the two. When executions come, either the desire is fulfilled, or there is a shortfall and another order is emitted recursively to cover the shortfall.

In a device, like a thermostat, the goal is very clear and so is the mechanism. Even filling a sink involves feedback: There is a source with a tap, a sink with a plug, and someone tells us the amount of water needed. Easy.

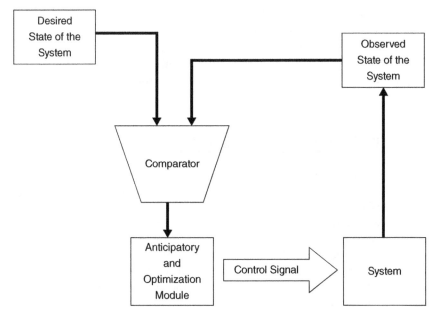

FIGURE 11.1   General Cybernetic Feedback

But now take a trading strategy. What is its goal? It is to make money. There is a sink where it can lose money, so it needs to implement a plug. Its decision-making mechanism may be a source, but it is an uncertain, leaky tap that can sometimes pour money straight down the sink hole. Although the principle of feedback is very intuitive, it is not always obvious how to pose the problem correctly in order to implement it efficiently.

My stance is that capital preservation is a primary goal in trading, and capital growth is second in line. Of course, there is no free lunch, and there is no growth without risk. One has to pay to play, but one also needs to be able to stay in the game long enough in order to have a chance to win. Managing downside risks relative to potential gains should be the *guiding principle* for a successful and robust trading business.

Given that the ultimate goal of the strategy is to make money, and that the strategy needs some breathing space to take risks, how then one is to measure the distance between the actual and the desired state? Is the strategy achieving its goal?

Herein lies part of the problem, but also part of the solution. It is the vagueness in the definition of external state that lies at the root of the difficulty in designing the control loop.

In the discussion regarding the swarm paradigm of adaptation, on what basis would the CIO decide to reallocate risk from a trader who underperforms to a trader who performs better? Is it with a concrete performance goal in mind or a certain benchmark?

From the questions above, the intuition arises that the concept of the external state of a strategy is related to some criterion that measures its behavior. To implement the adaptation feedback loop one then would need to understand how far the current behavior deviates from the desired behavior. A numeric criterion that measures the behavior of a decision-making strategy is called a fitness measure.

The concept of fitness comes from the evolutionary ideas of Darwin and Lamark, and was formalized when genetic algorithms were introduced into computer science in the 1960s. Ranking simulated organsims by fitness provides a numeric selection criterion that helps retain the best subset of the population at each genetic algorithm iteration.

In absence of a guaranteed source of profit, the principles that apply for designing an adaptive control system for a trading agent are not based on the concept of optimal goal. One cannot demand from a trader to make a guaranteed million, unlike a thermostat that will, under most circumstances, achieve the temperature in the room to be 20°C. Instead, similar to the evolutionary theory, the design for adaptation is based on a criterion that compares relative behaviors, and dynamically chooses the best.

In the next chapter, various possible fitness measures are discussed for the purpose of evaluating and comparing trading strategies. A basic adaptation mechanism, the fitness feedback control (FFC), is introduced.

The fitness feedback control mechanism allows the market risk exposure of a trading agent to be adapted to its own theoretical performance that comes from paper trading. It creates a simple adaptation of the agent to the current market state. It is basically a switch that turns the agent's risk-taking off when it stops performing, and turns it back on when it starts performing again.

The idea behind the FFC, although simple, is the first step toward ensuring robustness, because it reduces drawdowns of any trading strategy that has persistent up-run and drawdown behavior.

The behavior of nonadaptive strategies is closely related to the behavior of the markets and the implicit market states. Markets often go through regime changes, and a particular strategy goes in and out of favor, reflecting subtle changes in a particular market feature that it tries to exploit. Hence it is argued that the most efficient way of looking at market regimes is through the prism of a diversified set of nonadaptive models.

Putting the above intuitions together, a swarm trading methodology is formalized. It works by dynamically supplying risk capital to a subset of strategies out of a pool of potentials, based on the feedback provided by the individual fitnesses. The swarm decision-making process itself can be evaluated by computing a measure of its efficiency over a wide variety of model sets and market regime switches.

Further on, concepts are discussed pertaining to the design of a trading agent using the smart paradigm of adaptation, where a reinforcement learning mechanism is directly embodied into an agent's control system.

CHAPTER 12

Feedback and Control

T his chapter introduces the concept of fitness feedback control. It is the basic adaptation mechanism of a trading agent to its own performance and forms the basis on which robust trading strategies are built.

12.1 LOOKING AT MARKETS THROUGH MODELS

At any point in time, the central question for a robot is how to optimally use its actuators in response to a stimulus from a sensor, in order to maximize the probability of achieving a certain pre-stated goal.

Similarly, for a trading agent, the central question is what position to have in the market in response to new information arriving, in order to maximize the probability of return under a risk constraint.

12.1.1 Internal World

The important point to notice is that the internal world of any AAA can be quite different from the real world in its fullness. Let us start with humans who only can sense a small part of the electromagnetic spectrum. Insects perceive hardly any colors. Plants do not have any eyes so they sense the light in a very different way than we do, yet many flowers tend to follow the sun and close themselves at night. Bacteria have chemical sensors that help them to move in the direction of nutrients. Similarly, robots sense their position and obstacles from a variety of sonars and cameras. Although the perceptions and internal represenations of real-world facts are very different in different species, they are nevertheless sufficient to achieve each organism's goal.

Trading strategies use a variety of filters, measures, and indicators to decide on their market positioning. Their internal world representation consists of detecting the current state of the market, according to their vision. That state is different in nature from what humans would perceive. To give a concrete example, take the simplest trend-following system based on a single moving-average. By merely glancing at the price charts, humans can see trends very clearly and in their fullness. The trading strategy, on the other hand, sees only a binary set of states $\{Downtrend : (P <= MA), Uptrend : (P > MA)\}$. There is a definite loss of fidelity from the human visual perception of the full picture of the trend to the binary decision set the model sees.

In robotics, the description of the world based on the human perception is called distal, and the one based on the robot's representation is called proximal. The aim is, of course, to build sensors for the AAAs that closely reflect the human vision of the world, achieved via our brains' full information-processing capabilities. This is the same goal in any advanced technology that is designed to assist and supersede humans in daily tasks.

In the systematic trading endeavor, several avenues that bring one closer to that goal are discussed below. Namely, in this and next chapter an implicit approach is built on a feedback between strategy performance and strategy behavior. Then later on, an explicit approach based on pattern recognition and learning algorithms is explored.

12.1.2 Strategies as Generalized Filters

As pointed out previously, the dynamics of markets exhibit a fair share of instability and complexity. The purely statistical analysis of price dynamics certainly helps in understanding some of that complexity, but gives little clue as to how to exploit it efficiently. At the end of the day, statistics are statistics and do not fully answer the immediate fundamental question of control in trading: "What should my position be right now?"

In order to elucidate the solution to this problem one should first ask, "What should the strategy observe and adapt to?" Intuitively, one thinks of observing a market regime and adapting to a regime change, for example choosing a trend-following approach in a trending market and switching to a mean-reversion strategy in a sideways market. Hence part of the task is to elucidate a workable concept of market regime.

Part One explored various types of simple nonadaptive strategies that are particularly suited to certain market environments. If that environment changes, the strategies tend to perform poorly and go into drawdown. Instead of saying, "The market is in a trending regime because I see a trend," one could also say, "My trend-following strategy is performing well *hence* the market is in a trending regime." Thus one could replace a subjective concept of a market regime by a concrete observable performance measure stemming from a strategy that is tuned to perform well in such regimes.

Why was the human observation of a trend qualified as being subjective? Simply because, despite the fact that most people see trends (including the efficient market theorists even though they won't admit it), they do not see them exactly the same, that is, not everyone would agree where exactly a trend starts or finishes. As alluded to previously, our internal world comes from observing with our eyes and interpreting, or modeling, the external world with our minds. Despite the fairly high degree of coherence of perceptions of the external world by our society, it is still the case that internal representations vary from one individual to another. This is why visual pattern recognition is difficult to formalize as was discussed in an earlier chapter.

12.1.3 Implicit Market Regimes

The basic thesis of this section is that a workable concept of market regime is already embedded in the performance of a simple nonadaptive strategy, and that regime changes can be inferred from the change in performance of such a strategy. This implicit approach is efficient in three major ways:

1. It reduces the complexity of the sensing problem by internalizing the concept of market regime into a suitable numeric fitness measure.
2. It tackles regime changes via the observation of suitable changes in that fitness measure.
3. It allows implementation of the fitness feedback control on the strategy, which enhances its reward-to-risk ratio by reducing drawdowns.

Figure 12.1 illustrates the first point, where the fitness measure is simply the performance equity curve. One observes that the performance over time of the above strategy exhibits noisy trends. Those trends are reflecting the fact that the market regime changes, and the strategy goes periodically in and out of favor. Here it can be clearly seen why that is the case: The market goes visually from trending to consolidations, and the strategy either latches on to the trend or gets whipsawed.

On the other hand, analyze Figure 12.2, showing a different strategy. Here time is event time, that is, new trade. It is much less obvious as to why the strategy has such swings in performance. It is visually very difficult to

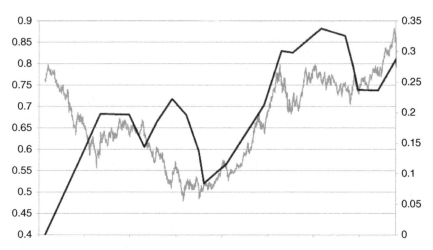

FIGURE 12.1   Trend-Following Strategy and Price Action

say that the market behaves differently in periods of up-run and drawdown of the strategy, yet something subtle is happening. This is a mean-reversion strategy that is tuned to a certain interval of frequencies, and it happens that the market has been changing the oscillation frequency in a way barely perceptible to the human observer.

The second example illustrates well a situation happening in high-frequency systematic trading. The intraday price action has periodic bursts

FIGURE 12.2   Mean-Reversion Strategy and Price Action

of volatility and regimes change quickly. It is very difficult to produce a responsive and timely statistical technique that would efficiently indicate that a change in regime is happening. On the other hand, a trading strategy gives one a very clear numeric answer as to whether the market is in a state that corresponds to the range of regimes compatible with the strategy.

12.1.4 Persistence of Regimes

Let us come back, in the graphs preceding, to the extended up-runs and drawdowns of the equity curve. This is happening because the losing and winning trades of the strategies tend to be clustered in time. Each performance cluster corresponds to a particular implicit regime of the market, and the persistence of such a regime is categorized by the size of the respective cluster (i.e., the cluster's extent in clock or event time). Figure 12.3 makes this concept more visual by showing explicitly the clusterings of winning and losing trades (boxed).

This persistence of regimes implicit in the clustering of winners and losers is observed across a variety of strategies. In Figure 12.4 the performance graphs of various strategies from Part One are shown.

A natural question then arises: If there is a persistence of market regime that is reflected in the persistence of up-runs and drawdowns of the equity

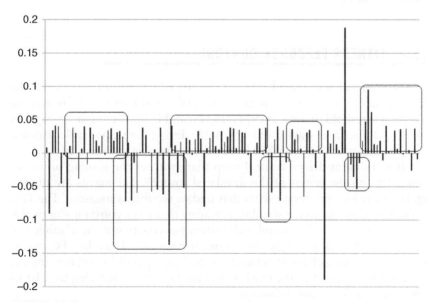

FIGURE 12.3   Clustering of Winning and Losing Trades

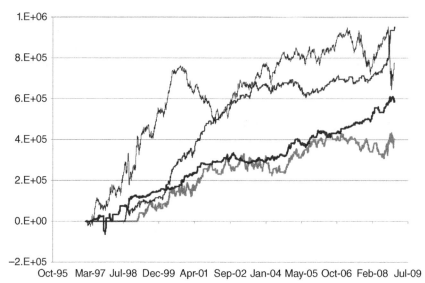

FIGURE 12.4 Strategies Up-Runs and Drawdowns

curve, how can such persistence be exploited for achieving enhanced performance of such a strategy?

12.2 FITNESS FEEDBACK CONTROL

The fitness feedback control (FFC) is the procedure that turns on or off the risk-taking of a strategy when its measure of fitness rises or falls relative to a certain threshold. It aims at exploiting favorable (implicit) market regimes for the strategy and staying out of trouble during the unfavorable regimes. The FFC algorithm is described by the block diagram in Figure 12.5.

It is an event-driven control loop that switches the trading on or off depending on the fitness of the simulated strategy. The events are market update or trade execution events that update the fitness measure. The FFC collects statistics from the simulated strategy that has a constant size or risk allocation per trade. The simulated strategy runs continuously, whether real trades are allowed or not by the control mechanism. Thus the FFC can be seen as a switch mechanism between the real-time parallel simulator and the same strategy traded in the market. For the benefit of later chapters, let us introduce the following definitions.

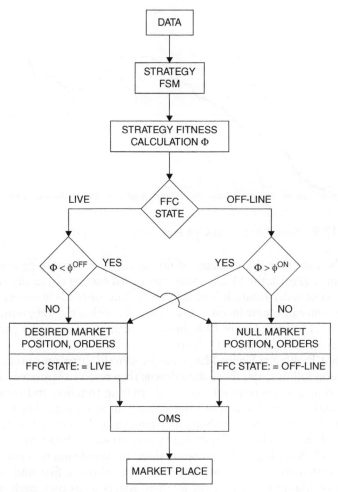

FIGURE 12.5 Block Diagram of Trading Strategy as an AAA

Definition 2. Take a strategy S and an FFC based on the fitness function Φ resulting in the FFC-controlled strategy $FFC(S)$. A recalculation event ρ is any event that updates the S's state and/or the fitness Φ. A paper trading event π is a recalculation event that induces a change in the theoretical position of S. A trading event τ is a recalculation event that induces a change in the market position in $FFC(S)$.

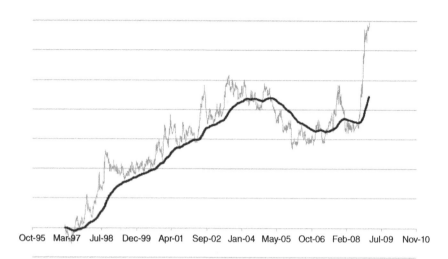

Oct-95   Mar-97   Jul-98   Dec-99   Apr-01   Sep-02   Jan-04   May-05   Oct-06   Feb-08   Jul-09   Nov-10

FIGURE 12.6   Some Long-Term CTA Performance

In the case that the measure of fitness is either the raw or smoothed performance (P&L), the FFC is sometimes called *trading the equity curve* in the context of hedge funds. It is used by some fund-of-funds investors to take profits or enter into new investments, especially within the long-term trend-following CTA space. Figure 12.6 shows an example of an equity curve of a long-term trend-following CTA fund.

Indeed, looking at Figure 12.6, it can be seen that after up-runs in equity, a correction follows, and those drawdowns then resolve themselves into the next up-run. This corresponds to the alternating trending and congestion regimes that are correlated across the majority of assets traded by CTAs. As CTAs can be equally long or short, they tend to latch to both uptrends and downtrends while getting whipsawed by congestions in between.

The FFC is an important stepping stone for the design of a robust and efficient systematic trading infrastructure. It is also the first and simplest example of adaptation, where the strategy adapts to its own performance. The concrete implementation of it in the context of high-frequency trading is discussed in Part Four. The next subsection makes explicit the appropriate fitness measures to use in an FFC.

12.2.1   Measures of Fitness

Coming back to the AAA paradigm, the concept of fitness is any measure that numerically evaluates the quality of the behavior of an agent. It is used to rank agents by the quality of their behavior. In a very general sense, a fitness should measure a behavioral signal-to-noise ratio, and should aim to quantify how well the agent performs in an uncertain environment, in relation to its goal.

In the context of trading strategies, the fitness should provide a reward-to-risk measure that allows judgement of the current quality of the strategy, and allows comparison across agents that operate on different time and price scales. Hence there is a requirement for the fitness measure to be as scale-independent as possible. This will appear clear in the next chapter, where an adaptive trading system is designed with, at its core, an FFC implementation of the switch between individual nonadaptive agents.

Part One discussed various measures of strategy risk, performance, and reward-to-risk ratio. These statistics broadly fall into two categories:

1. Continuous Statistics: These measures compute statistics by taking a time interval (e.g., a week) and sampling mark-to-market P&L at regular subintervals (e.g., minutes or ticks). Examples are continuous NAV, Sharpe, omega, Sortino, return-to-drawdown, and so on.
2. Per-Trade Statistics: These measures compute statistics by taking a series of trades (strategy events). Examples are trade NAV, percent profitable, profit factor, average logarithmic return, and so on.

To gain intuition regarding the choice of the above statistics for candidate fitness measures, it makes sense to compare the simplest measure of fitness, the equity curve (NAV or cumulative P&L), in clock time and strategy event time for a low-frequency and a high-frequency strategy. Such comparison is shown in Figures 12.7 and 12.8.

For the long-term trend-following strategy, the equity curve seems by and large smoother in event time but the jury is out. The large step up in the equity curve due to catching the outsize trend in the middle of the graph is magnified in event time.

For the high-frequency strategy, the equity curve seems much smoother in event time than in clock time. The main reason is that at those price scales, the markets experience periodic pockets of activity and increased volatility, and the amount of events (trades) per unit of clock time varies. This is especially true for strategies that aim at exploiting such volatility, like this example of high-frequency mean-reverting strategy. As seen in Part One, when one looks at tick charts in tick time versus intraday charts based on a regular time division, one observes a much greater smoothness in price action.

Thus the appropriate time representation of the performance of the strategy is a function of its nature. Here are some stylized facts about what one should expect the equity curves to be for the broad class of trend-following and mean-reverting strategies. These two are characterized by

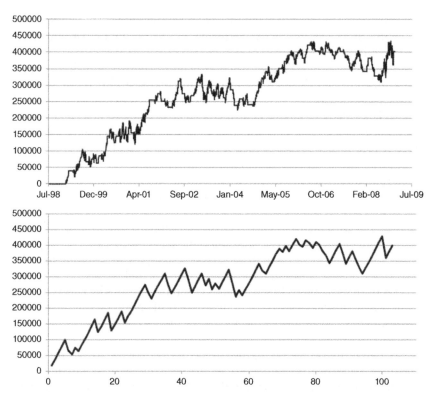

FIGURE 12.7   NAV in Clock and Strategy Event Time for TF Strategy

the difference in the win/loss ratios and percentage of profitable trades. TF strategies tend to have a high win/loss of 2 to 3 and a low percent profitable of 35 to 45 percent. MR strategies tend to have a low win/loss of 0.8 to 1.2 and a high percent profitable of 55 to 65 percent. Their stylized equity curves have been discussed in Chapter 9 and are shown in Figure 9.1.

From stochastic control theory it is known that the smoother the process, the more effective it is to potentially control [see Astrom, 1996]. The reason for this is that a higher signal-to-noise ratio gives higher predictability of the future path of the process. Hence the smoother the fitness measure, the more effective the fitness feedback control should be based on that fitness. In my own experience, the appropriate fitness measure to implement the control is a function of the frequency and nature of the strategy. For mean-reversion trading, event-driven fitness measures are the most appropriate, whereas for momentum trading, clock-time periodically resampled measures are the smoothest.

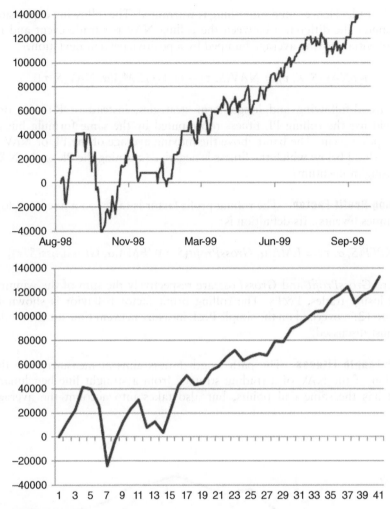

FIGURE 12.8　NAV in Clock and Strategy Event Time for MR Strategy

Some appropriate scale-invariant measures of fitness are given below. To be clear, call S a trading strategy (agent), e a market update event, τ a trading event, $NAV(S, \tau)$ is the rebased cumulative total return since inception, and $EMA(\alpha, x)$ is an exponential moving average of a variable x.

Rolling Trade NAV　One of the first signs of trouble occurs when the NAV starts to inch down. NAV by itself is a noisy indicator of persistence of performance, because not a single strategy is expected to make money on every single trade. Hence some smoothing is warranted. The following expression computes the difference between the rolling NAV per trade event and its exponential moving average bumped by a positive percent deviation.

$$RTNAV(S, \lambda, \tau) = NAV(S, \tau) - (1 + \lambda)EMA(\alpha, NAV(S, \tau))$$

For trend-following and longer-term strategies, instead of RTNAV one should use the rolling PL fitness recomputed by the same formula but at each price event. The band above the moving average of the PL or NAV is a threshold below which the fitness is negative (meaning the PL or the NAV is losing momentum).

Rolling Profit Factor   The rolling profit factor is taken on a fixed window of trades (events). Its definition is

$$RPFF(S, \alpha, \tau) = EMA(\alpha, GrossProfit(S, \tau))/EMA(\alpha, GrossLoss(S, \tau))$$

where *GrossProfit* and *GrossLoss* are respectively the sum of the winning and losing trades, P&Ls. The rolling profit factor behavior is shown in Figure 12.9, overlaid on the simple P&L measure in event time for the model we just discussed.

Path-Length Fitness   The path length fitness aims at measuring the deviation of the NAV of a trading strategy from a straight line benchmark that has the same end points, but also takes into account the average

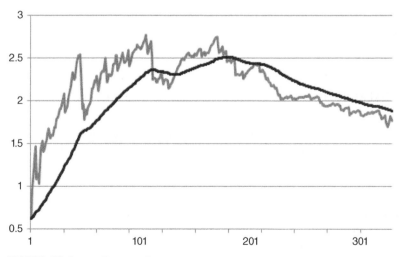

FIGURE 12.9   Rolling Profit Factor in Strategy Event Time

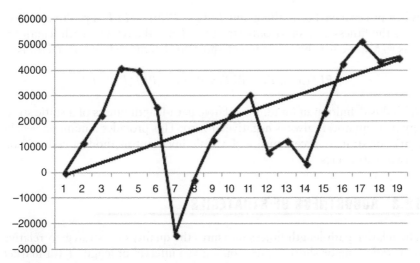

FIGURE 12.10 Path Length Fitness Measure

return over that period, so that low or negative return is penalized. It can be computed either at every trade or at every market update event. The definition is as follows: take the last T event observations (either market updates or trades), then

$$PLF(S, 0, T) = (\frac{NAV(S, T)}{NAV(S, 0)} - 1)^{\frac{1}{T}} \frac{\sqrt{T^2 + (NAV(S, T) - NAV(S, 0))^2}}{L[NAV(S), 0, T]}$$

The first term is the period average return, or the slope of the straight line between the beginning and end points of the *NAV* path. The second term is the ratio of lengths between the straight line path and the realized path, as shown in Figure 12.10.

The shortest path between two points is a straight line. This is the benchmark for an ideal strategy that has the same average period return as the given strategy. Intuitively, the longer it takes for the strategy to go from one point to the other, the less in tune it is with the market.

This fitness measure is scale-invariant and allows comparison of strategies operating on different frequencies.

Relative Path-Length Fitness Actively traded strategies are usually compared with a static long-only or short-only benchmark (index). The path-length fitness of such a strategy can be computed by exactly the same formula as above using the price process $P(t)$ itself instead of the *NAV*. That fitness of the price path itself will be denoted by $PLF(P, 0, T)$. When $P(T) > P(0)$, *SPLF* is positive and reflects the path-length fitness of a long-only strategy.

When prices have been falling and $P(T) < P(0)$, $-SPLF$ is positive and reflects the fitness of a short-only strategy. Hence the relative path-length fitness to a static benchmark (long or short, as determined ex post facto) is:

$$RPLF(S, 0, T) = PLF(S, 0, T) - |PLF(P, 0, T)|$$

With this definition in mind, the relative path-length fitness of a static strategy (benchmark) is always negative or zero. This provides a numeric benchmark for strategy acceptance and a scale-invariant method of comparison between strategies.

12.3 ROBUSTNESS OF STRATEGIES

The relative path-length fitness measures the quality of a strategy S relative to a static long or short strategy on a given interval of length T (of market update events).

As markets change, a strategy may go in and out of favor, and this is reflected by the fact that its fitness, taken on a rolling interval $[t, t + T]$, will fluctuate.

A measure of robustness of the strategy can be obtained by gathering the statistics of the fitness measure on a large amount of past or forward-simulated intervals. Namely, take the set of market update paths on an interval of length T:

$$\Pi = \{P_i(t)|t \in [0, T]\}$$

Assume that the set of paths is chosen such that the distribution of $P(T) - P(0)$ is symmetric around zero (there is the same amount of upward-sloping as there is downward-sloping paths and the slopes are distributed symmetrically). Compute $D(S)$ the distribution of fitnesses $RPLF(S, 0, T)$ on those paths. Robustness is defined as the difference between the positive and negative masses of the distribution:

$$R(S) = D^+(S) - D^-(S)$$

By definition, the robustness of a static long-only or short-only strategy is zero. This implicitly says that static strategies are brittle and this fact has been tested time and time again in the real world.[1]

---

[1] As mentioned before, pension funds have been the major victims of the fallacy of the efficient market hypothesis that prophesizes static asset allocations.

To say that $R(S) = 0.5$ is equivalent to saying that S outperforms any static strategy 50 percent of the time.

This measure of robustness is a good starting point for studying adaptation of strategies to market conditions.

12.4 EFFICIENCY OF CONTROL

Given a fitness measure Φ, the FFC mechanism transforms a strategy S, that runs continuously in paper trading mode, into a strategy $FFC(S, \Phi)$ that is executed in the market. The fitness measure triggers the control of the position size of the traded strategy.

12.4.1 Triggering Control

As seen in Figure 12.5 that shows the FFC decision process, the control is triggered, and the model $FFC(S, \Phi)$ is stopped from real trading, when the measure of fitness of S falls under a certain threshold:

$$FFC^{OFF} = \{\Phi(S) < \phi^{OFF}\}$$

At that point the $FFC(S, \Phi)$ strategy is flattened and no residual orders remain in the market. The $FFC(S, \Phi)$ is re-launched on the event when the fitness of S passes above a threshold:

$$FFC^{ON} = \{\Phi(S) > \phi^{ON}\}.$$

Intuitively $\phi^{ON} - \phi^{OFF}$ corresponds to the volatility of the rolling fitness measure $\Phi(S)(t)$. Spacing the triggers apart by that measure helps avoid control whipsaws. The difference $\phi^{ON} - \phi^{OFF} > 0$ between the two triggers should be bigger than the absolute value of the marginal fitness that an average winning or losing trade would generate.

Otherwise, one could be constantly going in and out of the strategy in situations where the winning and losing trades are of the same magnitude and follow each other (are intermeshed). This type of situation occurs at the borders of the clusters of winning and losing trades, that is, at the transition areas between regimes.

So the FFC control mechanism is not just based on the choice of Φ but on the choice of the full control triple $\Psi = (\Phi, \phi^{ON}, \phi^{OFF})$.

12.4.2 Measuring Efficiency of Control

The question naturally arises as to how efficient the FFC control mechanism itself is given the control triple Ψ.

Intuitively, for a particular strategy S, one could use the robustness measure R above to compare the distribution of fitnesses of S and of $FFC(S, \Psi)$, on the same set of price paths Π, namely

$$Eff(FFC(S, \Psi)) = R(FFC(S, \Psi)) - R(S)$$

As discussed, the measure of robustness R is based on the particular $RPLF$ fitness that compares the path of the NAV of a strategy to the path of prices P on which the strategy operates.

As an example, take S to be a static long-only strategy. It has, by construction, $R(S) = 0$. Take

$$\Psi = (RTNAVF(S, 0, \alpha), 0, 0)$$

Here the control fitness is chosen as the rolling PL fitness with $\lambda = 0$. The thresholding parameters ϕ^{ON} and ϕ^{OFF} are both zero. Also choose α and T in such a way that the effective lookback period $N = 2/\alpha - 1$ is of an order of magnitude smaller than T. The $FFC(S, \Psi)$ is basically a long-only trend-following system that is long when $P(t) > EMA(\alpha, P(t))$ and flat otherwise.

The following Figure 12.11 shows the distribution $D(FFC(S, \Psi))$ of the relative path-length fitness. This compares with $D(S) = \delta(0)$ which is the

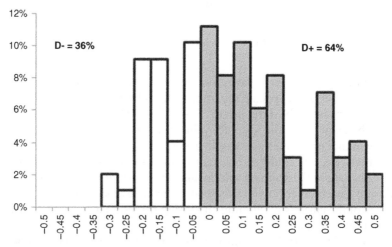

FIGURE 12.11 Fitness Distribution for FFC Applied to Static Strategy

Dirac mass at 0 by construction. One sees that $R(FFC(S, \Psi)) > 0$, hence $Eff(FFC(S, \Psi)) > 0$.

So a brittle, static, long-only strategy was transformed, via a very simple FFC process, into something more robust, namely a long-only trend-following strategy based on an exponential moving average of prices.

Of course, judging the efficiency of a control process on only one behavior is not enough. The point about control is that all kinds of behaviors should be rectifiable, at least to an extent.

Hence, to really judge efficiency of control, one should compute

$$Eff(FFC(\Psi)) = Average\{Eff(FFC(S, \Psi))|S \in Strat\}$$

where *Strat* is a large set of different strategies.

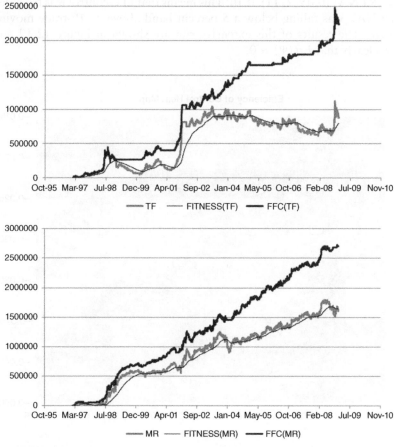

FIGURE 12.12 FFC Test Results for a Particular Control Triple

12.4.3 Test Results

This is of course a daunting task, but it is an important step that I have performed for studying adaptation. The interesting and encouraging result is that the FFC is indeed efficient, when Φ is the $RTNAV$ or the $RPFF$ computed on a reasonable lookback period (10–20 trade events).

To set up the extensive test, I took five parametric families of strategies, $CBTR(f, s)$, $AMATR(\alpha, \beta)$, $SWTR(\alpha, \beta)$, $SWMR(\alpha, \beta)$, and $PCMR(\alpha, \beta)$. This constituted 100 strategies per parametric family, hence 500 strategies in total. 200 paths were chosen of such a length that each strategy had no less than 100 trades per path. Hence the sample consisted of 200,000 individual strategy runs (S and $FFC(S, \Psi)$) and corresponding efficiency of control measures per strategy, $Eff(S, \Psi)$. The fitness triple $\Psi = (RTNAV(0.05, 2/11), 0, 0)$. This means that FFC control was triggered when NAV was falling below a 5 percent band above its 10-trade moving average. The results of this extensive run are shown in Figure 12.12 and show clearly that $Eff(\Psi) > 0$.

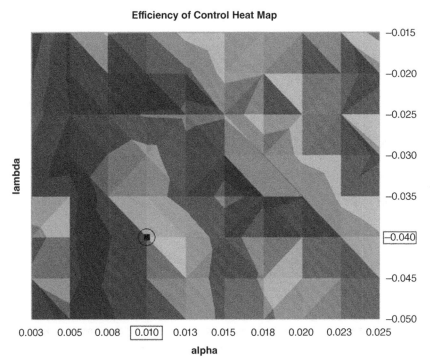

Efficiency of Control Heat Map

FIGURE 12.13 Heat Map of Control Efficiency

12.4.4 Optimizing Control Parameters

The extensive run above was performed for a particular triple Ψ. The *RTNAV* fitness function had fixed lookback period $\alpha = 2/11$ corresponding to averaging 10 trade events, and the $\lambda = 5$ percent. Also the trigger to start and stop FFC were respectively $RTNAV < 0$ and $RTNAV > 0$, that is, $\phi^{ON} = \phi^{OFF} = 0$.

The goal is to find the optimal triple Ψ^* for which the $Eff(\Psi^*)$ is maximal. This is of course a very computationally heavy problem because it involves running the above extensive simulation on a whole multidimensional grid of parameters. Simplifying the problem and keeping the fitness trigger levels at zero, $(\phi^{ON} = \phi^{OFF} = 0)$, one is left with a two-dimensional family of control triples $\Psi(\alpha, \lambda)$.

A heat map of $Eff(\Psi(\alpha, \beta))$ is given in Figure 12.13. It shows that the area of the peak of control efficiency is reasonably spread out around the optimal pair (α^*, λ^*).

CHAPTER 13

Simple Swarm Systems

This chapter presents two versions of automated trading systems that are direct applications of the research performed on the fitness feedback control and strategy switching. I nicknamed an original implementation of this system "The Swarm," and the name stuck. These systems are the precursors of more complex methodologies discussed in the next chapters that contain learning feedbacks at the agent and meta levels. Thus this chapter is just the starting point, the skeleton upon which a full fledged swarm of scary trade-bots can be built.

All the architectural subtleties of such systems are discussed in Part Four and many concepts introduced here are important components for efficient and robust implementation.

13.1   SWITCHING STRATEGIES

This section introduces the usage of the FFC for managing transitions between market regimes. The market regime was defined indirectly by putting the emphasis on the performance of a certain strategy that is supposed to perform in that regime. If that strategy performs well, then the market is in the sought-after regime. Thus the strategy acts as a filter to discover what regime the market happens to be in. More generally, a strategy can be seen as a filter with the pass-band corresponding to the range of market regimes where it performs.

If one can identify a diverse enough family of strategies that cover most of the market regimes, then an automatic switching mechanism between these strategies can be created, in order to achieve a robust continuous performance during the transitions from one market regime to another. This concept lies at the heart of the swarm systems discussed in this chapter. Here the ground work is laid by discussing the mechanism of switching between two strategies.

13.1.1   Switching between Regimes

Consider the price chart in Figure 13.1, where one can visually see trends and congestion phases. Choose a mean-reverting strategy SWMR and one trend-following strategy AMATR that were introduced in Part One. One can study the difference in their performances over time, with particular focus on periods when their $RTNAV$ fitness measures are turning, as seen in Figure 13.1.

The two strategies have mostly nonintersecting zones of their positive and negative performance—this exactly fits the intuition that the two strategies are supposed to perform in complementary market regimes.

As seen in the last chapter, the $RTNAV$ can provide an efficient fitness criterion for the FFC mechanism. This measure can also be used to rank the strategies, in order to decide which to trade at a given point in time. This intuition gives rise to the strategy switch algorithm (SSA) described in Figure 13.2.

Figure 13.3 presents a comparison of the risk-reward statistics of:

- The sum of the original uncontrolled strategies (this is the classic approach in systematic trading to find a set of negatively correlated strategies and combine them in an independent linear sum)
- The sum of the strategies where FFC is applied individually and independently
- The SSA

It can be seen that the result of the FFC provides an improvement over the linear sum and the switch methodology provides a further improvement.

13.1.2   Switching within the Same Regime

Consider again the price chart in Figure 13.1 where one can clearly see trends and congestion phases. If one now takes two mean-reverting strategies of the same parametric family SWMR discussed in Part One, one can also study the difference in their performances and the particular times when their $RTNAV$s are turning. Figure 13.4 illustrates this.

It can be seen that the two strategies have a large intersection of their positive and negative performance zones in clock time as measured by the

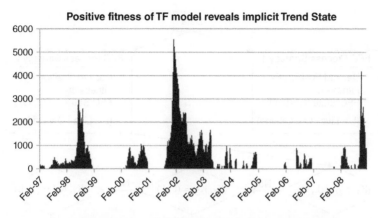

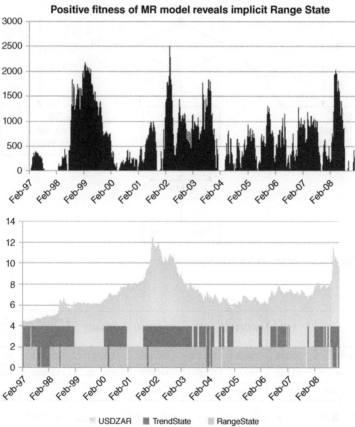

FIGURE 13.1 Fitnesses of MR and TF Strategies and Implicit Market Regimes

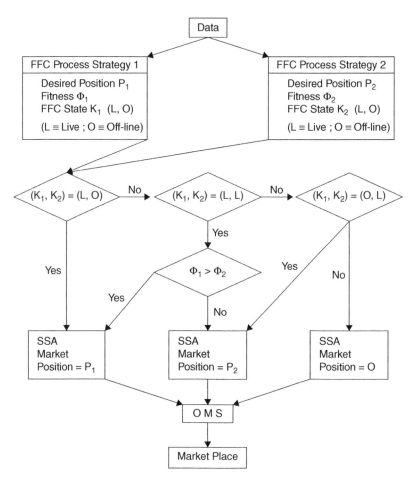

FIGURE 13.2   Strategy Switch Algorithm

	TF	FFC(TF)	MR	FFC(MR)	TF+MR	FFC(TF)+ FFC(MR)	SSA (TF,MR)
Avg PL	76,393	186,359	135,315	219,464	211,708	405,823	354,360
Avg Vol	183,885	160,175	175,954	140,627	236,423	207,605	186,363
Information Ratio	0.42	1.16	0.77	1.56	0.90	1.95	1.90

FIGURE 13.3   Comparative Statistics of MR and TF Strategies and SSA

RTNAV, indicating that they see broadly the same market regime and transitions. Nevertheless, they differ in the timing of their performance turning points, the absolute value of their equity curves, and in the amount of events per unit of clock time (which reflects their different mean-reversion speeds). The statistics of the three combinations are compared in Figure 13.5.

The switch provides an improvment over the individual FFC-filtered trading strategies. It better exploits the same class of market regimes, namely the mean-reverting states.

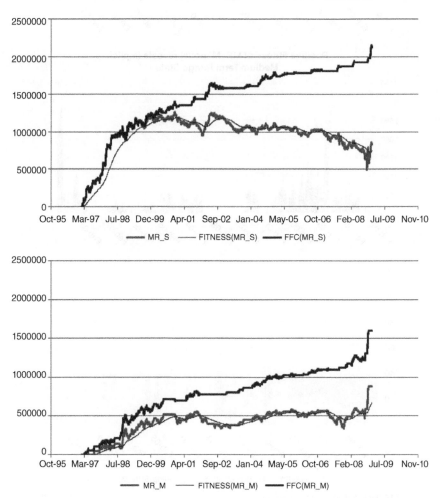

FIGURE 13.4 Fitnesses of MR Strategies from Same Family

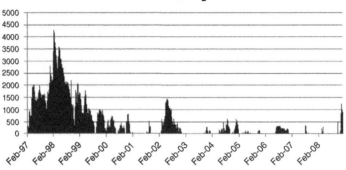

Positive fitness of MR_S model reveals implicit
Short Term Range State

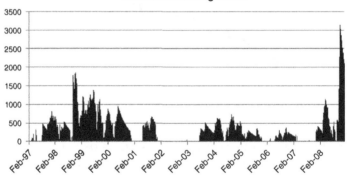

Positive fitness of MR_M model reveals implicit
Medium Term Range State

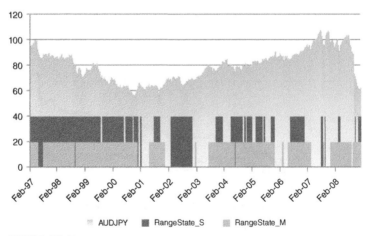

FIGURE 13.4 *(Continued)*

	MR_S	FFC(MR_S)	MR_M	FFC(MR_M)	MR_S+MR_M	FFC(MR_S) + FFC(MR_M)	SSA(MR_S, MR_M)
Avg PL	64,452	169,368	71,198	129,303	135,650	298,672	249,602
Avg Vol	176,394	127,458	134,108	116,531	229,261	170,208	143,950
Information Ratio	0.37	1.33	0.53	1.11	0.59	1.75	1.73

FIGURE 13.5 Comparative Statistics of Different MR Strategies and SSA

This idea is generalized below and gives rise to the maximizing swarm process. It results in switching to the best performer within a parametric family of strategies in order to increase the performance further.

13.1.3 Mechanics of Switching and Transaction Costs

Continuously switching (trading in and out) between strategies can be a costly exercise if not performed properly and can erase any gains from the improved methodology. Hence one needs to understand carefully how is it to be implemented to reduce those costs to a minimum.

The first point to notice is that the methodology always operates in trade event time and not clock time. The fitness measure, namely the $RTNAV$, is only changing when the new realized or simulated trade information comes in.

The block diagram in Figure 13.6 illustrates the high-level architecture of the event-driven choice process. The important architectural feature is that the switch resides between the price feed and the order management system and gives the net total desired market position. The OMS is a comparator that brings in line the existing and desired model positions.

The above feature is particularly important in mean-reversion strategies, which tend to reverse the whole position in one trade (as opposed to say trade out of a long then take the short position). Sometimes either the FFC alone or the switch warrants an exit from the strategy, when a reversal trade needs to occur. As the FFC and switch operate as a concurrent simulator, they would give this information on the same price tick as would a stand-alone strategy trigger a reversal.

In many situations the effect of the switch on the market is nil. In particular, in the case of switching within the same parametric mean-reverting set of strategies, one is tuning to subtle changes in mean-reversion frequencies of the market. Very often the new optimal model has the same desired position as the previously traded (optimal) one.

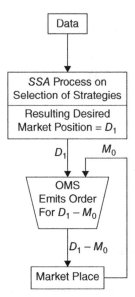

FIGURE 13.6 Diagram of the Switch Process

13.2 STRATEGY NEIGHBORHOODS

Via the computation of their fitness, individual strategies provide a mechanism to decide on the prevailing implicit market regime. The FFC allows limiting the drawdowns of the strategy when that regime changes, but also turning the strategy on when the regime comes back.

If one has at one's disposal enough varied strategies to cover most known market regimes, one could, theoretically, transition from a strategy to another via the FFC-based switch introduced in the last section. This would be possible if the time (or number of events) it takes to transition is much smaller than the extent in time (or events) of the individual regimes, that is, if the FFC provides efficient enough control for the switch.

There is however a certain amount fuzziness in the behavior of the strategies, as well as in the human perception of regimes. From the human perception perspective, this was seen when studying the mean-reversion strategy in the previous section. It was noticed how it went in and out of favor, despite the fact that changes in the market's oscillation frequency were not perceptible to the eye. A strategy tuned to a slightly different frequency would have performed in a similar way, but gone in and out of favor at different times. On the other hand, the trend-following strategy was shown to perform well

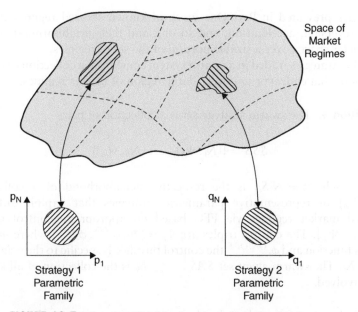

Space of
Market
Regimes

p_N

p_1

Strategy 1
Parametric
Family

q_N

q_1

Strategy 2
Parametric
Family

FIGURE 13.7 Strategy Neighborhoods and Market Regimes

across a series of trending regimes that were perceived differently by the eye and had different measures of signal-to-noise ratio.

From this one can deduce that the neighborhood of a strategy in the space of its parameters covers a neighborhood of similar market regimes as shown in Figure 13.7. Each strategy is a filter with a pass-band corresponding to the set of market regimes where it performs. Intuitively, the mapping between strategies and regimes that favor those strategies is continuous (in the topological sense of the word).

Definition 3. Take a parametrically defined strategy $S(p_1, \ldots, p_n)$ and intervals $I_i = [p_i - a_i, p_1 + a_i]$ around each parameter value. The neighborhood of S is the set

$$N[S] = \{S(q_1, \ldots, q_n) | q_i \in I_i\}$$

For practical computational purposes, a large discrete subset of the hypercube $N[S]$ is chosen, instead of the whole continuous set.

This continuity can be exploited by covering large areas of known market regimes by a series of strategy neighborhoods. The different types of strategies presented in Part One work in known stylized regimes (trend, mean-reversion, acceleration, and so on), and their neighborhoods in the parameter space cover a sizable portion of the set of regimes.

The strategies traded in a swarm system come from a collection of neighborhoods that endeavor to cover a large region of market regimes.

Definition 4. The swarm strategy set is a collection of pairs

$$SSS = \{(N_1, \Psi_1), \ldots, (N_m, \Psi_m)\}$$

where each $N_i = N[S_i]$ is the respective neighborhood of a collection $\{S_1, ...S_m\}$ of representative parametric strategies that exploit different stylized market regimes via FFC based on appropriate control triples $\{\Psi_1, \ldots, \Psi_m\}$. The control triples are $\Psi_i = (\Phi_i, \phi_i^{ON}, \phi_i^{OFF})$ where Φ_i is a fitness function and $\phi_i^{ON, OFF}$ the control thresholds specific to the neighborhood N_i. The swarm agent set $SAS = \cup_{i=1}^{m} N_i$ is the collection of all strategies involved.

Notice that for each stylized regime, one can choose the most appropriate fitness function. The appropriatness is based on the efficiency of the control mechanism discussed previously. For example, for mean-reversion regimes, fitness functions based on trading events appear to be efficient, whereas for momentum strategies, fitness functions based on time are efficient.

13.3 CHOICE OF A SIMPLE INDIVIDUAL FROM A POPULATION

In Figure 13.8, a hypothetical path in time of the unfolding market regime is indicated. The switching mechanism introduced in the last chapter allows lifting that path back to the space of strategies. This is the essence of the swarm systems. They exploit this continuity and covering property, and allow for automatically tuning into the prevailing market regime by either trading all the fit strategies, or continuously switching to the fittest strategy in each relevant neighborhood.

Of course, as the market is a complex adaptive system, the set of all possible regimes is not known. This does not mean that the exercise is futile. It allows performance of real-time risk management that adapts to the new and unfolding circumstances. If the market regime is not covered by the set of the swarm's strategy neighborhoods, then the swarm would stay out of

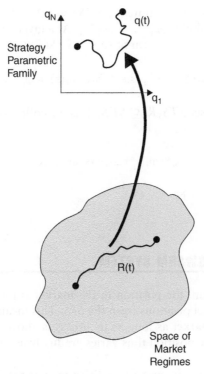

FIGURE 13.8 Path of Market
Regimes Lifted into the Space of
Strategies

trouble by turning all the strategies off until the regime changes back to one
of the covered ones.

Before moving on, it is useful to define the concurrent versions of the
events defined for a single FFC in the last chapter. Namely, for a single strategy S, the recalculation, paper trading, and trading events were defined.

Definition 5. Take a swarm strategy set SSS. At each market data update
event e the concurrent recalculation event $R(e)$ is the union of concurrent
individual recalculation events $\rho(s, e)$ for each strategy $s \in SAS$. The concurrent paper trading event $\Pi(e)$ is the union of concurrent individual paper
trading events $\pi(s, e)$.

The following definitions formalize the two sets that define the choice
of strategies used in the two swarm systems presented here.

Definition 6. Take a swarm strategy set $SSS = \{(N_1, \Psi_1), \dots, (N_m, \Psi_m)\}$ and respective FFC thresholds $\{\phi_1^{ON}, \dots, \phi_m^{ON}\}$. At a given concurrent recalculation event event $R(e)$, the swarm fit subset $SFS(R) \subseteq SAS$ is defined as

$$SFS = \cup_{i=1}^m \left\{ s | s \in N_i \& \Phi_i(s) > \phi_i^{ON} \right\}$$

The swarm top subset $STS(R) \subseteq SFS(R)$ is the collection of strategies with maximal fitness

$$STS = \cup_{i=1}^m \left\{ s_i^* | s_i^* \in N_i \& \Phi_i(s_i^*) = max(\Phi_i(s_i) | s_i \in N_i) \& \Phi_i(s_i^*) > \phi_i^{ON} \right\}$$

in each neighborhood $N_i \subset SAS$.

13.4 ADDITIVE SWARM SYSTEM

In an additive swarm, the position in the market is the arithmetic sum of the individiual model positions from the *SFS*. This means that a model will participate in the market as long as its fitness is above its threshold of acceptability ϕ^{ON}. The position thus varies gradually as the *SFS* changes.

Definition 7. *Additive Swarm System.* Every member of the *SFS* is participating in the trading process. This is just a linear combination of FFC-filtered strategies independent of which strategy subset they belong to. The sizing of each strategy is comparatively small (because many would be traded at the same time) and the overall sizing of the portfolio changes almost continuously.

Figure 13.9 shows the event-driven diagram of the linear swarm, which is the simplest of the two systems discussed here.

The four main steps of the algorithm are explained as follows:

1. Each market data update e yields a concurrent recalculation event $R(e)$ on the set of participating strategies SAS.
2. Each strategy S is an agent that listens to the data update and recalculates its state and desired position via its FSM. It also updates its fitness function Φ. Those two steps constitute an individual recalculation event $\rho(e)$. This recalculation event is done in parallel, but synchronized so that all the FSMs and fitnesses of the strategies are updated by the end of this step.

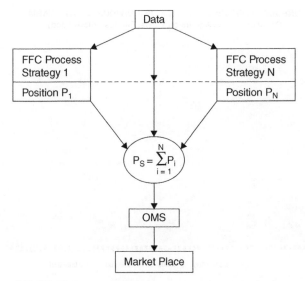

FIGURE 13.9 Diagram of the Linear Swarm

3. The thresholding of the fitnesses is performed and the swarm fit subset *SFS* is calculated. It is represented in the system as a synchronized list of indices of strategies whose fitnesses satisfy the criterion $\Phi > \phi^{ON}$.
4. All the desired positions of the *SFS* strategies are summed. This net sum is broadcast to the order management system, which acts as a recursive differentiator that aims at bringing this desired net position in line with the market position of the swarm system.

The last aggregation step is an important design feature that helps reduce transaction costs. Even if, following a recalculation event, the *SFS* has changed, it could still be that the total net position has not, and hence no trading event would occur.

13.4.1 Example of an Additive Swarm

Presented in Figure 13.10 is an example where the *SSS* consists only of one neighborhood *N* and one fitness function Φ. The swarm is run on minute-by-minute data of a continuously traded market, the *AUDCAD* exchange rate.

The family of parametric mean-reversion strategies $SWMR(\alpha, \beta, v, \tau)$ defined in Part One is used to build the neighborhood N_1. The dynamic parameters are α, which represents the minimal swing size multiplier

UNFOLDING FITNESSES IN TIME OF INDIVIDUALS IN A SWARM
(Time on X axis, Agents on Y axis, Fitness color-coded)

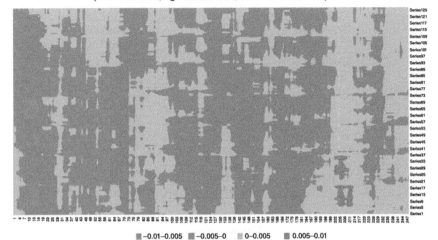

■ −0.01–0.005 ■ −0.005–0 ■ 0–0.005 ■ 0.005–0.01

Time Evolution of Additive Swarm Membership

■ In ■ Out

FIGURE 13.10   Example of Additive Swarm Run

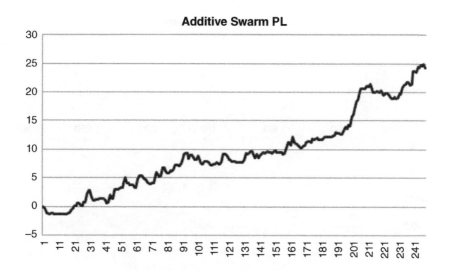

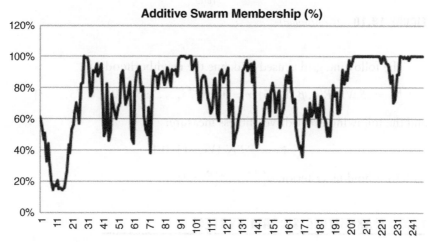

FIGURE 13.10 *(Continued)*

parameter, and β, which represents the trailing stop-loss multiplier parameter. Those parameters multiply a rolling volatility measure to ensure a minimal degree of scale invariance. The volatility is calculated by slicing the lookback period by time intervals of length $\tau = 15$ minutes. The lookback period $v = 1$ will be fixed to one trading day to remove intraday seasonality patterns.

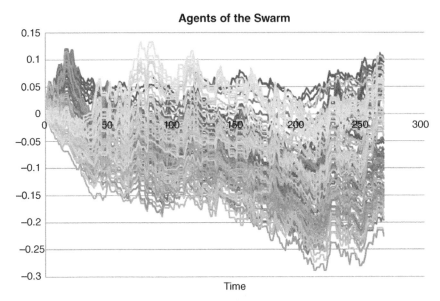

Agents of the Swarm

Time

FIGURE 13.10 *(Continued)*

The following grid is used to define the neighborhood N_1:

$$N_1 = \{SWMR(\alpha, \beta, 1, 15) | \alpha = 0.5, 0.75, \ldots 3; \beta = 0.5, 0.75, \ldots 3\}$$

and the following event-driven fitness measure:

$$\Phi_1 = RTNAV(2/11, 0.1)$$

with thresholding criterion $\phi_1^{OFF} = \phi_1^{ON} = 0$.

13.5 MAXIMIZING SWARM SYSTEM

The maximizing swarm is a strictly elitist choice mechanism, and only the top-performing model is allowed to participate in the market for each strategy type.

Definition 8. *Maximizing Swarm System.* Only members of the *STS* are participating in the trading process, so it is only at most one strategy per style neighborhood. The transitions between models are based on a switch mechanism discussed below and can entail substantial changes in the overall positioning.

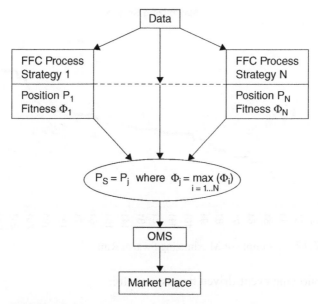

FIGURE 13.11 Diagram of the Maximizing Swarm

Figure 13.11 is the event-driven diagram of the maximizing swarm. Its algorithm is very similar to the earlier linear swarm and just differs by one item. Namely, after the *SFS* has been calculated in Step 4, the set of strategies of maximal fitness in each N_i is chosen, giving rise to the swarm top subset *STS*. The aggregation in Step 5 is then done on the *STS*, before the net desired position is sent to the OMS.

13.5.1   Example of a Maximizing Swarm

The example presented in Figure 13.12 takes two strategy neighborhoods, N_1 and N_2, where N_1 is the mean-reversion set chosen above. For N_2 a trend-following set is constructed from the $AMATR(\alpha, \beta)$ family from Part One. α represents the AMA's lookback period and β the width of the adaptive channel.

The following grid is used to define the neighborhood N_2:

$$N_2 = \left\{ AMATR(\alpha, \beta) | \alpha = \frac{2}{4+1}, \frac{2}{6+1}, \ldots, \frac{2}{20+1} \,\&\, \beta = 0.02, 0.03, \ldots, 0.10 \right\}$$

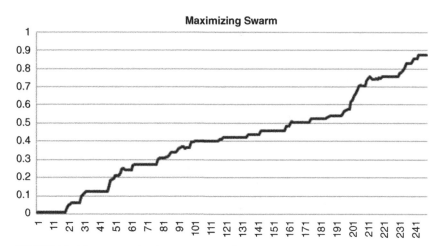

FIGURE 13.12   Example of Maximizing Swarm Run

and the following event-driven fitness measure:

$$\Phi_1 = RTNAV(2/11, 0.1)$$

with thresholding criterion $\phi_1^{OFF} = \phi_1^{ON} = 0$.

13.6 GLOBAL PERFORMANCE FEEDBACK CONTROL

Every model participating in a swarm system is usually endowed with its own stop-loss mechanism that is either a function of the PL on the current trade or on the history of recent trades. If the PL and hence the fitness falls below a certain threshold of acceptability, the FFC would remove the strategy from the *SFS* until its fitness recovers.

Usually the *SFS* would contain a series of neighborhoods of currently fit strategies traded in the swarm. It is very possible that, at any given moment, there is a concentration of positioning in such neighborhoods, meaning that the majority of the strategies would be either long or short. Figure 13.13, as an example, shows the time series of the overall exposure of the linear swarm discussed in the section above.

One sees that this exposure varies over time and sometimes creates a hot spot from a risk perspective—a concentration of risk and a potentially higher overall volatility of the PL of the swarm. When swarm systems are traded on several asset classes, those hot spots may be magnified even further.

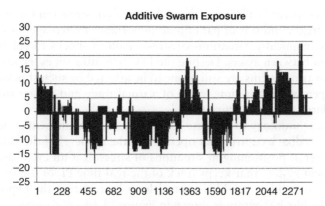

FIGURE 13.13 Example of Additive Swarm Exposure

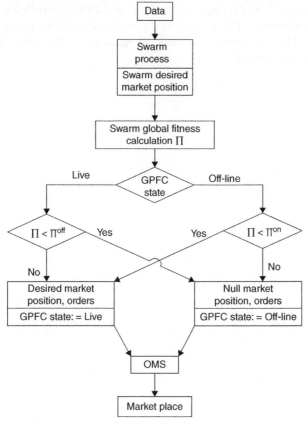

FIGURE 13.14 Global Performance Feedback Control (GPFC)

Markets periodically move through periods of stress (and sometimes of extreme stress), and it is of paramount importance to manage the exposure and risk dynamically. Situations of stress result in shocks to volatility and correlation between assets. Despite the FFC operating on every single component, swarm systems are still prone to be affected by such shocks, as they may happen within the time frame of a usual trade and trigger stop-losses across a large subset of active models.

One methodology to mitigate such shocks is to implement a global performance feedback control that operates on the top level of the swarm, and reduces overall positioning in situations of stress. It is an event-driven risk management system that keeps track of the real-time PL of the swarm and subsumes (overrides) the FFC control loop by resetting the exposure per strategy. Its block diagram is shown in Figure 13.14.

The risk-reducing methodology is based on calculating rolling volatility bands around the PL time series of a non–GPFC-controlled swarm that serves as a reference. The lower band provides the trigger to cut exposure completely. The exposure is put back on again when the noncontrolled PL reaches the upper band.

CHAPTER 14

Implementing Swarm Systems

From a collection of nonadaptive elementary trading strategies, the swarm methodology effectively creates a more complex and adaptive agent that participates in real trading.

The function of this aggregate swarm agent is to make a choice from a set of potential candidates based on the fitnesses of each individual. Two types of choices have been introduced, the purely elitist maximizing swarm and a fitness-thresholded additive swarm.

The individual strategies are all running in parallel but they are not participating in the market. It is only the aggregate swarm agent that is effectively trading.

All the building blocks for the programmatic treatment of swarms has already been introduced before. In fact, the representation of trading agents introduced in Part One has been a priori designed to naturally support swarm systems.

In order to set up and run the swarm simulation, one has to collect a set of individuals that constitute the swarm strategy set SSS.

For each event consumed by every member of SSS, the swarm fit subset SFS is determined via the computation of individual agents' fitness. This computation can be greatly optimized by running the agent **consume** processes in parallel (this works best for noncommunicating agents).

The aggregate swarm agent is defined as an instance of **AGGRE-GATEAGENT** class. This aggregate swarm agent takes SFS as set of its members. The **update** method on an aggregate agent then simply adds the individual positions and emits the resulting order into the market.

Finally the fitness relevant to the aggregate swarm agent itself is computed and stored.

The specific code pertaining to this process is described in the next sections.

14.1 SETTING UP THE SWARM STRATEGY SET

The first step is to set up the swarm strategy set, represented by the list
SSS. This list is composed of triples (A, Φ, ϕ) of the agent's class instance,
the fitness function that pertains to the FFC control of the agent, and the fitness threshold under which the FFC blocks the agent from trading.

For example, a two-dimensional family of swing breakout $SWBR(\alpha, \beta)$
agents is defined below:

```
(defparameter *SSS* NIL)

(defun create-SWBR-swarm (vollookback alphafactorlist
betafactorlist
                              &key (fitness-function #'LTDPL)
                                   (fitness-threshold 0))
  (dolist (alphafactor alphafactorlist)
    (dolist (betafactor betafactorlist)
      (let ((a (gensym)))
        (setf a (make-instance 'SWBR
                       :vollookback vollookback
                       :alphafactor alphafactor
                       :betafactor betafactor))
        (push (list a fitness-function fitness-threshold)
              *SSS*)))))
```

14.2 RUNNING THE SWARM

Before running the swarm, the aggregate ***SWARM-Agent*** needs to be set,
as well as data collection lists:

```
(defparameter *SWARM-Agent* (make-instance
                              'AGGREGATEAGENT
                              :name "SWARM-Agent"))
(defparameter *SWARM-Agent-fitnesses* NIL)
(defparameter *SWARM-Agent-LTDPLS* NIL)
```

In order to perform the simulation of the swarm on a list of events, one
needs to specify the fitness function measure that is appropriate for judging
the quality of the FFC control. The **swarm-ff** is that function and can be,
for example, the relative path-length fitness discussed in the last chapter.

The switch **swarm-type** chooses between the additive or the maximizing swarm.

```
(defun run-swarm (events swarm-ff &key (swarm-type :ADD))
  (dolist (e events)
    (mapcar #'(lambda (s) (consume (first s) e))
            *SSS*)
    (mapcar #'(lambda (s) (fitness (first s) (second s)))
            *SSS*)
    (setf *SFS* (remove-if #'(lambda (s)
                              (<= (first (fitnesses (first s)))
                                  (third s)))
                           *SSS*))
    (when (equal swarm-type :MAX)
      (setf *SFS*
            (max-list *SFS* #'(lambda (s)
                                (first (fitnesses (first s)))))))
    (push (if *SFS*
              (mapcar #'first
                      *SFS*)
              NIL)
          (members *SWARM-Agent*))
    (consume *SWARM-Agent* e)
    (format T "Update SWARM-Agent completed %")
    (fitness *SWARM-Agent* swarm-ff)
    (format T "Update Fitness SWARM-Agent completed %")
    (format T "SFS for event  A is  A %"
            e
            (mapcar #'(lambda (s) (name (first s)))
                    *SFS*))
    (format T "Fitness for FFC-Agent  A %"
            (car (fitnesses *SWARM-Agent*))))
  (push (funcall swarm-ff *SWARM-Agent*)
        *SWARM-Agent-fitnesses*)
  (push (LTDPL *SWARM-Agent*) *SWARM-Agent-LTDPLS*))
```

While the simulation is running, all the relevant position and PL data are automatically collected into the ***SWARM-Agent*** class in order to be analyzed at will. Finally, the specific fitness function pertaining to the efficiency of the swarm agent is computed. Examples of such runs have been discussed in the previous chapter.

CHAPTER **15**

Swarm Systems with Learning

The swarm systems presented in the last chapter are a particular way to look at adaptation. The mechanism of adaptation was essentially the systematic choice of the fittest strategies among an a priori defined variety in the swarm set. The strategies themselves were simple and the complexity was concentrated in the design of the FFC-driven switch mechanism between strategies at the top level. In analogy with robotics, the fitnesses computed on all individual strategies were the agents' sensors that helped to gauge the likely state of the market. The control mechanism was the choice of the SFS or STS sets given by the FFC switch and subsumed at a higher level by the GPFC. The actuator was the OMS reacting to an aggregated position signal.

The adaptation that a simple swarm system achieves presupposes knowing a range of market regimes and strategies that are able to exploit such regimes. This collection of nonadaptive strategies is the set of the swarm aggregate agent's potential behaviors. The swarm agent derives its own action plan from this set of potentials either by averaging (additive swarm) or by elitism (maximizing swarm).

The persistence and change of market regimes is reflected in the performance and decay of potential behaviors. The rate at which the performance decay happens dictates the probability with which a particular behavior will be abandoned by the swarm.

The GPFC gives an additional stopgap in the situation where the regime changes suddenly to an unknown one. Then the system automatically trades out of the market until a known regime is found again. But the system does not learn anything nor does it have the ability to adapt to new facts.

This chapter presents ideas on how to make the mechanism of choice for the swarm more flexible and endow it with a certain amount of learning and exploration. The learning element is achieved by reinforcement from rewards gained from choosing appropriate control parameters while the swarm is going through a cycle of market regimes. The exploration element is an area of active research for me.

15.1 REINFORCEMENT LEARNING

Learning is a very broad topic that permeates and brings closer many facets of science. It is studied in neurosciences, psychology, control theory, artificial intelligence, and artificial life. There are many learning techniques but their goals fall mostly in two broad categories: recognition of perceptive patterns and learning of behaviors.

Perception and pattern matching are usually implemented via supervised learning techniques in which the system is presented with a series of examples of the pattern to learn. It implicitly supposes a teacher who shows the system different images of the same pattern and also images of other patterns that do not belong to the type. For each image, it mentions right then whether that pattern is of the sought type or not.

The learning of behaviors is a more involved matter. Behaviors unfold in time, and it is only after the fact that one can judge whether one had done the right thing or not. Like a child, the system either gets told off or gets a reward. On the next time period, one changes the behavior so as to increase the probability of being rewarded at the end of it. In order to do so, the system gauges whether to use a previous behavior for which it got rewarded or to explore a new one for which it may or may not get an even higher reward. This delayed reward mechanism combined with a degree of exploration versus exploitation constitutes the essence of reinforcement learning.

15.2 SWARM EFFICIENCY

In Chapter 12, "Feedback and Control," a statistical measure of efficiency of control was introduced. For a given control triple $\Psi = (\Phi, \phi^{ON}, \phi^{OFF})$ and strategy S, the efficiency measure $Eff(S, \Psi)$ is the difference between the robustness $R(S)$ of the uncontrolled strategy with the robustness $R(FFC(S, \Psi))$ of the FFC-controlled strategy.

For a particular strategy s, the robustness measure $R(s)$ is determined by comparing the masses of the left and right distributions of the relative path-length fitness $RPLF(s)$ computed on a symmetric set of past or forward-generated market paths. The $RPLF$ measures how well the strategy s performs relative to the best static strategy (either long or short) on a certain market path $P_i(t)$ on the interval of length T.

The FFC is implemented by computing the rolling trade NAV $\Phi(s) = RTNAV(s, \lambda, \alpha)$ on the trade-by-trade time series of the strategy. When $\Phi < \phi^{OFF}$ the strategy falls out of the swarm fit subset SFS and becomes a member again when $\Phi > \phi^{ON}$.

In order to judge the overall efficiency of the FFC independently of the type of swarm mechanism chosen, a measure $Eff(FFC(\Psi))$ is computed by averaging $Eff(FFC(s, \Psi))$ on a wide set of strategies s. This gives a measure of universality to the control mechanism over a diversified set of strategies and time frames. As mentioned previously, it is thanks to this universality that a swarm system composed of various styles of models can be implemented using just one control triplet Ψ across all strategies $s \in SSS$.

For swarm systems, the efficiency measure can be refined further. Call $SWARM(\Psi)$ the aggregate trading agent resulting from the application of the swarm process. Then one can compute

$$Eff(SWARM(\Psi)) = R(SWARM(\Psi)) - \sum_{s \in SSS} R(s)$$

for an additive swarm and

$$Eff(SWARM(\Psi)) = R(SWARM(\Psi)) - Average_{s \in SSS}(R(s))$$

for a maximizing swarm. This compares the robustness of the swarm agent to either the sum or the average robustness of strategies in the swarm strategy set.

To compute those measures, it either supposes running the swarm for a long time, so that enough different sub-paths can be experienced by every single strategy, or alternatively by backward or forward simulation. The question arises as to what the optimal parameters $(\lambda, \alpha, \phi^{ON}, \phi^{OFF})$ are that maximize the efficiency of the swarm control mechanism.

Simulation is good as a starting point for discovering the optimal parameters; however, the risks of over-fitting associated with both backward and forward simulations have been pointed out. A more dynamic approach is warranted and is based on reinforcement learning.

15.3 BEHAVIOR EXPLOITATION BY THE SWARM

Assume that a simulation has been performed on the collection of individual strategies and helped determine the range of efficient enough parameters for the FFC. This means that a neighborhood N has been found for the parameter set $\pi = (\lambda, \alpha, \phi^{ON}, \phi^{OFF})$ where on average $Eff(FFC(s, \Psi(\pi))) > 0$ for the collection of strategies $s \in SSS$.

In order to optimize the search for FFC parameters as the market data unfolds, it is possible to implement search strategies inspired from reinforcement learning. The following steps are an example:

1. Initialize the parameters by choosing a point $\pi_0 \in N$.
2. Run the swarm with control triplet $\Psi(\pi_0)$ on an interval $[0, T]$ so that enough statistics are gathered for every strategy $s \in SSS$.
3. Compute fitness measures $RPLF(s)$ and $RPLF(SWARM(\Psi))$ and determine the realized incremental rewards on $[0, T]$

$$K(SWARM(\Psi(\pi_0))) = RPLF(SWARM(\Psi(\pi_0))) - \sum_{s \in SSS} RPLF(s)$$

   for an additive swarm and

$$K(SWARM(\Psi(\pi_0))) = R(SWARM(\Psi(\pi_0))) - Average_{s \in SSS}(RPLF(s))$$

   for a maximizing swarm.
4. Determine the optimal parameter $\pi_0{}^*$ on the interval $[0, T]$ that, in back-test over that interval, maximizes $K(SWARM(\Psi(\pi_0^*)))$. For this the fitnesses of the individual strategies need not be recomputed, only the $RPLF$ of the swarm on a grid of parameters from N. The optimal reward corresponding to that parameter is K^*.
5. For the next run on $[T, 2T]$, choose the parameter $\pi_1 = \pi_0^*$ with probability $1 - \epsilon$ and a random parameter set from N with probability ϵ.
6. Go to Step 3 and run the swarm using the interval $[T, 2T]$ with control triplet $\Psi(\pi_1)$. This is an ϵ-greedy algorithm and the probability ϵ is a sigmoid function of $\| K - K^* \|$.

The above search algorithm assumes that the optimal parameter set for the next computational episode $[T, 2T]$ is, with high probability, the back-tested optimal parameter set for the episode $[0, T]$. However, it contains an element of exploration by allowing the choice to be elsewhere in the set N with a small probability ϵ, that is proportional to the deviation between the observed reward K and the optimal reward K^*.

Other variations on this theme can be tested. For example, rather than doing a grid search at Step 4, one could implement a genetic algorithm, given that even in this relatively simple case, the search space is already four-dimensional.

One could also use increasingly long episodes, so that instead of $[T, 2T]$ the interval $[0, 2T]$ could be used at Step 5. The effect of this would be a gradual averaging of optimal behaviors on longer and longer histories.

15.4 EXPLORING NEW BEHAVIORS

The ϵ-greedy search strategy described above contains a certain element of exploration. It explores the viability of a new parameter with a certain probability and sticks to what is known to have worked the best with some other (larger) probability.

This exploration is confined to the set of parameters of the same class of strategies. It does not contain any fundamental element of innovation.

Innovation is a tricky part in any endeavor and is the crux for long-term progress. A true exploration should contain true innovation, not just a parameter search.

The first avenue toward innovation for the trading busienss is the invention of new trading strategies by the symbiotic interaction of researchers and traders. As soon as new strategies are found they can be added to the swarm as new elements of SSS. The swarm then can decide how much risk to allocate to them based on their rolling performance metrics.

Innovation can also be applied to the FFC mechanism. The choice of the functional form of the FFC fitness Φ is the primary driver of the universality of the method. Although some ideas have been presented in this book, they should be seen as a starting point for an open field of research.

There have been attempts to use genetic programming techniques for evolving decision-making strategies, and one hopes that such an approach may at some point bear fruit for both the underlying strategies and the control system.

However, at the date of this writing, not much actual result has been achieved, despite a resounding success of such techniques in other fields. It may be that the problem at hand is too cumbersome in the way it was posed, and the raw application of GP never converged to any stable set of behaviors. I am attempting to evolve finite-state-machine agents, so this is work in progress.

In any event, the swarm paradigm provides a test-bed for a coevolution of a robust trading framework with either the human or machine-generated innovation process of potential new behaviors.

15.5 LAMARK AMONG THE MACHINES

Since the start of evolutionary thinking, there have been two major schools of thought. The dominant Darwinian ideas of blind nondirected selection via survival of the fittest over generations have dominated scientific thinking for a long period.

On the other hand, Lamarkian ideas of inheritance of learned traits have been largely criticized and research into those possibilities has not progressed until the arrival of ideas from computer science, namely artificial life.

However, new discoveries in biology and also in the study of complexity are chipping away at the reductionistic Darwinian dogma that is centered on the genotype, and presents the phenotype (i.e., the organism itself) as a means to an end to carry its genotype forward in time (e.g., see *The Selfish Gene* by Richard Dawkins). Subtle feedbacks have been discovered where the phenotype, via its biochemistry or knowledge, can influence the genotype going forward, and also influence the phenotype of its progeny (e.g., see *Evolution in Four Dimensions* by Lamb and Jablonka 1996 and *Artificial Life* by Langton, etc.).

Hence it is not clear whether the Darwinian ideas apply to intelligent animals to the same extent that they do indeed apply to simple organisms. Lamarkian ideas that put forth elements of memory, learning, and behavior are coming back to the fore again.

In this book, the main emphasis is on creating a framework that allows one to think of trading strategies as autonomous agents. The introduction of swarm systems allows extension of this idea to adaptive agents. In the last section, some rudimentary elements of learning were introduced to make the adaptive agents enhance their adaptation over time. In a nutshell, the goal of this part of the book is to introduce ideas to make agents smarter by making them learn to adapt better. It is an active area of research for me in the higher frequency domain.

The beauty of the concept of artificial life systems is that one is free to explore a whole universe of ideas and methodologies while designing them. Learning to adapt and passing that knowledge on to the progeny is one of them. Had Lamark been among the modern machines, he would have seen the application of his ideas straight away!

Three

Optimizing Execution

P art Three is an important stepping stone for a market-operational implementation of the type of trading strategies discussed in the first half of
this book. The research presented in Parts One and Two is only the starting
point and it has to be embodied into a trading business that operates in the
real world.

The practical work of making the transition from the cozy lab to the big
bad world starts here and concludes in Part Four. The nemesis to all free
movement is friction. Friction generates heat, especially when nice models that back-test to beautiful results start losing money as soon as they
are traded.

This part deals with how to address the biggest sources of friction in
the marketplace that translate into high trading costs. Those are liquidity and market impact costs. These costs can be mitigated via two main
angles of attack—the algorithmic execution method used and the trading
model itself.

Before proceeding, it is important to make a conceptual distinction between a trading strategy (or just strategy, or model) and an algorithmic execution methodology (or execution algo or just algo). In essence, the trading
strategy gives the trader the desired position in the market and the algorithmic execution methodology provides the way to get that position on the
trader's book. This book uses algorithmic execution methodology instead of
the commonly misused algorithmic trading strategy to make this distinction
very clear.

This part starts with analyzing the variability in liquidity in the markets and giving examples of intraday seasonality. Then time-series data of the full trading book is used to derive information on the impact of transactions on the book.

It is argued that algo execution methodologies should be adapted, or at least compatible with the trading strategies they serve. The agent-based paradigm from Parts One and Two is applied to the testing of algorithmic execution methodologies and the joint testing of trading strategies and algorithmic execution methodologies.

The part concludes with a discussion of some of the basic algorithmic execution strategies.

CHAPTER 16

Analysis of Trading Costs

16.1 NO FREE LUNCH

The arithmetic of the impact of trading costs on performance is straightforward. If each trade costs you $10 and you make 100 trades, at the end of it you would need to be in profit by more than $1,000 to break even. Otherwise all the hard work will result in a loss. It is of course paramount in the arena of high-frequency trading where expected profits per trade are commensurate with transaction costs.

The total cost to perform a trade comes from the sum of various components. The components can be grouped into two main categories:

1. *Deterministic Costs:* exchange fees, brokerage fees, clearing fees, give-up fees
2. *Nondeterministic Costs:* liquidity costs (bid-offer spreads), market impact (impact of own order on change in price and volume of the security), latency costs (missing trades because of delays in communication of orders), business interruption costs (missing trades because of system problems at the exchange, broker, or own firm)

The nondeterministic costs are not invoiced directly to the trader but they show up in different sneaky ways. They usually add up to much more than the sum of deterministic costs and are therefore very important to control.

For example, costs associated with latency can be substantial. Some trading activities like electronic market-making cannot survive if not implemented within a very low latency infrastructure. This is because a market-making engine that cannot respond quickly enough to changes in the order book will be last in the queue to place its orders. This will imply that it will not be executed on all the size it needs and hence will be forced to carry unwanted inventory. That inventory can present a substantial market risk and make the whole business proposition uneconomic. Part Four provides guidelines and design patterns to help minimize as much as possible the latency and business interruption costs.

The focus of this part of the book is on the minimization of liquidity and market impact costs, and some of the algorithmic execution methodologies presented here are specifically designed to address these problems.

16.2 SLIPPAGE

Before starting to delve into details, it is important to define a term that will be used throughout: slippage. Liquidity and market impact costs are often clumped into the unifying word slippage in the systematic trading world. This is actually a bit misleading and a concrete definition is needed.

Definition 9. Price slippage is defined as the difference between the average execution price and the model target execution price for a given trade size. Size slippage is defined as the difference between the target execution size and the realized execution at a given trade price. The slippage cost is defined as the difference between the PL on an executed completed trade in the market versus the PL on a completed trade at target model prices. Here a completed trade means an entry followed by a complete exit.

Slippage is hence a two-dimensional opportunity cost. Seen in this light, slippage becomes a relative concept that puts equal emphasis on model and execution. The value of the slippage cost is either positive or negative but, of course, it is unfortunately negative most times. To minimize slippage costs, one has to focus both on the model and on the execution of the model. This means that:

- A model should take into account various factors that may impact its good execution. For example, if the goal is to trade at certain frequencies, the times at which the execution occurs should correspond to periods of biggest expected liquidity in the relevant markets. If the goal is to generate revenue by providing liquidity to the market then periods of lowest expected liquidity are more relevant.
- An execution methodology should be compatible with various implicit and explicit constraints imposed by the model. For example a daily VWAP execution algo cannot be applied to a strategy that may generate trading signals based on entry points that are less than an average daily price range away from each other.

Slippage is intimately related to liquidity and minimization of slippage cannot be seen separately from studying liquidity patterns in the marketplace.

16.3 INTRADAY SEASONALITY OF LIQUIDITY

Liquidity reflects the potential for market transactions in an asset. It is driven by the availability of market-makers and other market participants at a given time. It is not a measure of supply or demand for an asset but of the actual supply of participants willing to post two-way prices at a given spread.

Hence a quantitative measure of liquidity should have the following features: (1) increasing function of tradable volume posted, (2) decreasing function of bid-offer, and (3) decreasing function of book imbalance (volume-weighted offer minus volume-weighted bid). The liquidity indicator $L(t)$ is defined as follows.

Definition 10. Let $B(t) = \{(b_i, V_i), (a_j, V_j)\}$ the order book for a security at time t. Let V_T be the total outstanding issued volume of the security and τ the minimal price increment (tick). Let $V_b = \sum V_i$, $V_a = \sum V_j$ the total bid and ask volumes, $B = \sum b_i V_i / V_b$ and $A = \sum a_j V_j / V_a$ the volume-weighted bid and ask prices. Then let us define the bid, offer, total liquidity, and price pressure as

$$L_b(t) = \left(\frac{V_b}{V_T}\right) * \left(\frac{\tau}{A - B}\right)$$

$$L_a(t) = \left(\frac{V_a}{V_T}\right) * \left(\frac{\tau}{A - B}\right)$$

$$L(t) = Min(L_b, L_a)$$

$$PP(t) = L_b - L_a$$

Figure 16.1 shows by way of example $L(t)$ and the bid-ask spread for five minute intervals during two days of trading for the front month Comex copper future. As expected, the liquidity is low in the overnight session and is the highest in the U.S. morning then after lunch into the close.

The foreign exchange (FX) markets exhibit also intraday seasonal patterns of liquidity. This has been discussed in Chapter 7 in the context of opening range breakout models (See Figure 7.11). The various FX rates can be clustered into roughly seven different behavior patterns. For example,

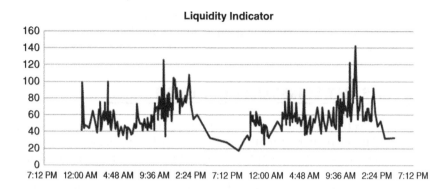

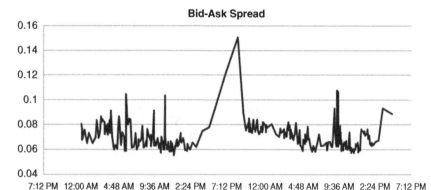

FIGURE 16.1 Liquidity and Bid-Ask spread over Two trading days for copper futures

Asian currencies are mostly active in Asian business hours, and the Canadian dollar in the American time zone.

The above clustering is partly due to the lack of enough market-makers in certain crosses in certain time zones, but also to the segmented end-user communities. These patterns present potential opportunities to exploit, and the opening range breakout strategy applied to different time zones is one example.

16.4 MODELS OF MARKET IMPACT

Both aggressive and passive orders have an impact. Someone who needs immediate liquidity pays a price because that liquidity is not a priori immediately present at a desired price. On the other hand, someone who provides liquidity shows its hand and by doing so reduces the probability of transacting at the announced price.

Understanding and figuring out ways to measure those two opposing forces is an important matter for building both execution algos and market-making strategies.

16.4.1 Reaction to Aggression

The aggressive market impact measure $AMI(V)$ is the quantification of the change in price P of a security induced by an aggressive trade of a certain size V. It is an important factor to take into account for the design of algos that generally aim at splitting a large order so as to minimize the full impact.

In its most general form the impact of an aggressive trade can be conceptually decomposed into

$$AMI = SI + MI + PI$$

where SI is the impact of the bid-offer spread, MI is the momentary impact that is felt short term, and PI is the permanent impact that presents the information element. This model in general assumes that SI is proportional to the bid-offer spread, MI to the volatility of the underlying security, and PI to the ratio of V to the average daily traded volume.

There are several parametric models that have been developed to disentangle and measure these three components [see DB, Almgren, Bloomberg etc]. Those models are fit with transaction data that ideally contain all of the order book information.

One of the most promising avenues in understanding AMI is the zero-intelligence model of the double-continous auction by Farmer, Petelli, and Zovko. There are no assumptions on intelligence or rationality of agents, and all that is assumed is that they place orders into the limit order book randomly, with different arrival frequencies for passive and aggressive orders, as well as cancellations of passive orders.

A nontrivial dynamic results from it, and the model predicts with a high degree of accuracy both the distributional characteristics of the prices as well as the aggressive market impact functions observed in real life.

This model, which uses zero intelligence as a benchmark, provides itself an interesting benchmark to disentangle true information from noise.

16.4.2 Limits to Openness

Trading, like dating, is a frustrating business. If you show your willingness too much, you are at risk of being snubbed. There is a higher probability that your prospective partner will make the first move and come and get you, if you don't act too eagerly. On the other hand, if you wait too long, someone else will come and steal your partner. After all, there is a market out there.

Placing limit orders into the market is no different. If the order size is too big then the market participants needing liquidity will have the "come and get me" attitude. Large limit orders have the repellent effect on potential liquidity takers, who are then happy to wait and suddenly become more passive. This morphing of one behavior into another is another reason why there is so much complexity in the markets.

Several studies attempted at estimating the impact of the size of the limit order on the probability of its being executed, and also the expected time to execution. As per common intuition, these studies have found that the probability of execution depends somewhat on the state of the order book, market volatility, distance of the order from the mid-price and the size of the order. However, the predictive power of any modeling that only uses the trade and visible book information is inherently impeded by the presence of stealth algos (like icebergs for example). Finding ways of hiding your intentions in the modern electronic world is no different from the tactics of the large and successful traders of the past and present. Some traders would hide and spread their size among many brokers, and while appearing to be "buying" to the trading crowd, in reality they are selling out of their large positions via the brokers. In this way they are trying to keep the cooperative accumulation game going while trying to get out of their positions. The information advantage is money, and like money it is easy to lose. Hence it is only natural that with all the transparency in the world people will still try to hide their hand as much as possible within the regulatory constraints. Hence in my opinion, while many of those studies are interesting from a theoretical viewpoint, they do not necessarily help to increase profitability.

CHAPTER 17

Estimating Algorithmic Execution Tools

This chapter extends the agent-based methodology to the simulation and optimization of algorithmic execution tools. It starts with a brief overview of commonly used types of algos.

17.1 BASIC ALGORITHMIC EXECUTION TOOLS

From the outset, it is important to note that some ECNs only support limit order placement. This is because exchanges and ECNs have at their heart an order book that accumulates resting limit orders. Trades are consummated when buy limit orders are placed above sell limit orders and the matching engine is then responsible for routing executions to the owners of those orders.

Hence all other order types, including algos, may need to be implemented at the trading node level. Sponsoring brokers who give access to the ECN usually provide an algo layer that can be utilized by the client, and in most cases such functionality may be sufficient. However for control and speed efficiency it may sometimes be better to reimplement even the most basic order types.

Market and Stop-Loss Orders   Market (MKT) and stop-loss (STP) orders are designed to take liquidity out of the order book for immediate execution. The **AGRESSOR** algo presented in Part One is an example of such order type that sweeps the book to fill its liquidity need.

To avoid inducing large price swings when liquidity is insufficient, the MKT and STP orders usually come with limit prices beyond which the execution is precluded.

One has to be very careful when using MKT and STP orders in an automated trading environment as most overtrading mistakes come from it. The worst price spikes and losses have been induced historically by aggressive orders emanating either from a human fat finger or an electronic race condition. The fat finger situations occur when human traders put in the wrong sizing or mistake economic value for number of contracts. Race condition situations may happen in a multithreaded environment where one process inadvertently keeps blocking another while aggressive orders are being generated. If those aggressive orders are not getting the relevant fill feedback from the ECN because of the blocking then a trading or execution system may inadvertantly emit masses of such orders with potentially very expensive consequences. Part Four discusses some of those points.

Icebergs Iceberg orders are designed to hide the full size of a large limit order. The iceberg would break the original order in several smaller components of random size in order to avoid showing any patterns. As soon as a small portion is done the iceberg would initiate the next order either at the original price or better.

As an iceberg is usually executed with limit orders, there is no guarantee that it will complete.

VWAP Given the intraday history of traded prices and volumes associated with those prices, the volume-weighted average price for the day is defined as:

$$VWAP = \sum v_j P_j / \sum v_j$$

It is the execution benchmark for institutional equity trading, which is the main reason why it has attracted so much research and attention.

A VWAP algo tries to execute a large order that can be expressed as a percentage α of the daily expected volume V as close to the day's $VWAP$ as possible.

Of course, it is impossible to predict both the daily volume and the associated $VWAP$ so there is no guarantee on outperforming the VWAP price on any particular day. If the volume pattern $v(t)$ for the day were known with certainty in advance, then the VWAP algo would just execute $\alpha dv(t)$ at the prevailing market price $P(t)$ in the interval $[t, t + dt]$.

Because the volume is not predictable, then the VWAP algo should be set up so that it outperforms on average, meaning that its expected execution average price over the history of previous volume paths is better than the historic VWAPs. One way of doing this is to study the average intraday volume patterns $v_{avg}(t)$ and execute $\alpha dv_{avg}(t)$ in $[t, t + dt]$.

A way of improving a VWAP algo is to make a simple procedure based on the average volume pattern communicate with a trend-following agent. The idea is to decrease the relative execution volume into downtrends and increase it into uptrends, for long VWAP orders. This is explained later in this chapter.

TWAP Time-weighted average price is just the average price throughout a defined time interval $[t, t + T]$. The TWAP algo slices the order into N equal suborders and executes each portion on the subinterval $[t + iT/N, t + (i + 1)T/N]$.

Execution of Spreads and Portfolios Clean execution of spread or more generally portfolio trades is very important for the risk management of such portfolios while execution is under way. Basically the key is to avoid legging the trades unless such legging is within certain acceptable risk bounds.

As a simple example, a calendar futures spread (a roll) has to be managed so as to avoid price exposure to the underlying. This means that the spread algorithm should not allow situations where the naked net exposure is more than a certain number of contracts (or certain percentage of total volume to be executed).

Spreads can be seen as securities that have their own bid and offer. For example, if security A trades at a market (BID^A, ASK^A) and security B at (BID^B, ASK^B) then the spread $A - B$ would trade at the market $(BID^A - ASK^B, ASK^A - BID^B)$. At that worst market, the trader would achieve immediate execution of either buying or selling the spread. The goal of the spread algos is to execute as much as possible inside that interval by taking advantage of the trading noise by placing half of the spread order (one leg) at a limit price and aggressively executing the other side when the limit price is filled.

The main reason why it is important to control the net exposure at all times is to reduce market risk in situations of disconnect and other faults that may preclude timely processing of fill information.

Inter-market spreads present the next level of complexity. The spreads need to be treated in a more subtle way because the sizing of each leg is a function of the nature of the trade. For example, legs may be sized by economic value or beta for a long-short equity spread, or interest rate or credit dv01 in fixed income.

If the components of a spread are traded on two different ECNs, another source of complexity comes from different latencies between ECNs and the trading node. Some brokers have introduced worldwide networks that mitigate those latency differentials by warehousing or throttling the fastest connections in order to put all ECN accesses on the same synchronized internal clock.

17.2 ESTIMATION OF ALGORITHMIC EXECUTION METHODOLOGIES

As discussed in the previous chapter, it is best to tailor the execution algos to the models. To estimate and back-test a model to the highest degree of realism one has to take into account potential execution times and volumes so that some degree of probability could be assigned to missed or partially executed signals.

To take into account the execution shortfall, one can adopt two approaches. One can either jointly test a model and an algo on tick data or one can derive an average measure of the efficiency of the algo and introduce a probabilistic slippage factor into a model.

The choice between these two approaches depends on the nature of the model as this dictates how much data is needed. The relevant data may simply not exist. To give an extreme example, it is probably unwise to perform a full joint back-test of a long-term trend-following model and a VWAP algo. That estimation would need data from years ago when no intraday data was ever collected.

On the other hand testing an intraday opening range breakout model with an aggressive time-limit execution algo may be much better than to assume average slippage on all trades. This is because market breakout behavior is correlated with volatility spikes that themselves are correlated with liquidity clumps. Average slippage resulting from average efficiency of a time-limit aggressive algo may underestimate the transaction costs for such a model.

This chapter starts by discussing the algo back-test engine. The engine can be used to estimate the algo efficiency and derive measures of expected shortfall versus the objective function of the algo. This gives a method to estimate stand-alone algos and is useful for brokers and electronic market access providers.

Once an algo has been chosen for a model, the algo's efficiency measure can be incorporated to derive the model's expected performance under an average transaction process. Price slippage can be incorporated directly into the test.

17.2.1 A Simulation Engine for Algos

The simulation engine for an algo does not differ from the one described for a trading strategy in Part One.

An execution algo is represented by an agent or sets of communicating agents consuming either **PRC** or **BOOK** events. This agent usually slices a large order into a series of smaller suborders that it places into the market according to its particular strategy.

These suborders can be either limit orders or aggressive orders. In order to simulate the impact of the suborders on the market, the algo agent uses itself as an instance of the **ALGO** class to model the placement and execution those suborders. This particular class instance of **ALGO** uses the slippage estimation and market impact modeling from the previous chapter in order to realistically reflect the influence that the suborders exercise on the market. So in the design presented in this book, the algo agent uses its own very localized **ALGO** class to simulate its slippage.

The real goal of the simulation is to test the agent's performance against an a priori performance metric and optimize the parameters of its FSM accordingly.

The performance measures are a function of the algo agent itself. The next chapter presents some classic algos and their objective functions. In general, these objective functions embed a measure of shortfall of either the executed price or size relative to the a priori stated goal.

In a VWAP scenario, for example, the objective is to minimize

$$F(A, M) = VWAP(A)/VWAP(M) = \frac{(\sum(w_i(A)P_i(A))/\sum w_i(A))}{(\sum(v_j P_j)/\sum v_j)}$$

where $w_i(A)$ are the realized trade sizes by the agent at prices $P_i(A)$ and v_j are the realized total traded market volumes at prices P_j during the same period. The closer that ratio is to 1, the better the quality is of the VWAP algo.

17.2.2   Using Execution Algo Results in Model Estimation

Once the parameters of an appropriate execution algo have been estimated, the algo's average performance can be used for the estimation of trading costs of any trading agents that use this execution method. In order to incorporate those results, a new instance of the **ALGO** class is written that takes as a parameter the average slippage information from the newly estimated execution algo.

For the purpose of this exercise, it has to be re-emphasized that the expected completion time on the algo should be an order of magnitude lower than the expected time between the repositionings of the trading agent to avoid the intermeshing of the two. The agent needs to be done with the previous signal before tackling a new one.

17.2.3   Joint Testing of Models and Algos

It has been shown previously that the overlay of longer-term strategies can be useful to improve the quality of market-making strategies. It is also the case that such types of overlay can also be beneficial for improving execution algos.

When a breakout strategy detects a signal, it could be useful for an execution algo to throttle up its order placing in case the price is moving in the wrong direction. Vice versa, it may want to wait for better prices if the breakout move happens to be beneficial to the algo.

In the framework presented here, the inter-agent communication paradigm is the appropriate flexible tool. A set of longer-term strategies may be run in simulation mode while broadcasting to the algo their state information.

The joint testing framework is hence naturally available under the agent-based strategy design paradigm and is an extension to the simulation engine presented in Part One.

As an example, here is an FSM represenation of a smart VWAP agent that communicates with an intraday trend-following model TF. The TF model has three states, $FLAT, LONG, SHORT$.

Let $V(t)$ be the average volume traded at the time of day t, averaged over many days. It represents the expected intraday seasonality of liquidity.

Assume that the VWAP's task is to buy a size S at the daily's VWAP. Let $\alpha = S/W$ be the proportion of the order to the expected total daily traded volume $W = \int V(t)dt$. Normally a dumb VWAP agent would be attempting to buy $U(t) = \alpha V(t)$ units at time t until it is done. If it is not done within a certain cut-off time before the market closes, it will start gobbling up more volume to get the size shortfall done in that remaining time.

Intuitively, if the market is rising at time t, it is safer to buy more than the prescribed $U(t)$, and if it is falling it is better to buy less and wait for a better price.

The FSM for the "simple" VWAP agent is presented in Figure 17.1 and contains three states: $INIT, NORMAL, CONCLUDE$.

The FSM for the smart VWAP agent that communicates with TF is presented in Figure 17.2 and contains five states: $INIT, SLOWER, NORMAL, FASTER, CONCLUDE$.

In the $SLOWER$ state that occurs when TF is in the $SHORT$ state, the VWAP agent buys at a rate of $(1/k)U(t)$ where $k > 1$. In the $FASTER$ state that occurs when TF is in the $LONG$ state, the agent buys at a rate $kU(t)$.

Simple VWAP Agent			
Shortfall is the remaining absolute value of original order size			
T_O is market opening time			
T_C is a certain time before market close			
	Init	Normal	Conclude
Init	T < T_O OR Shortfall = 0	T > T_O Shortfall > 0	NIL
Normal	Shortfall = 0	T < T_C Shortfall > 0	T > T_C Shortfall > 0
Conclude	Shortfall = 0	NIL	T > T_C Shortfall > 0

FIGURE 17.1   Simple VWAP Agent FSM

Communicating VWAP BUY Agent					
Shortfall is the remaining value of original BUY order size					
SELL agent is obtained by swapping sign of shortfall and faster, slower states					
	Init	Normal	Faster	Slower	Conclude
Init	T < T_O OR Shortfall = 0	T > T_O Shortfall > 0 AMATR = FLAT	T > T_O Shortfall > 0 AMATR = LONG	T > T_O Shortfall > 0 AMATR = SHORT	NIL
Normal	Shortfall = 0	T < T_C Shortfall > 0 AMATR = FLAT	T < T_C Shortfall > 0 AMATR = LONG	T < T_C Shortfall > 0 AMATR = SHORT	T > T_C Shortfall > 0
Faster	Shortfall = 0	T < T_C Shortfall > 0 AMATR = FLAT	T < T_C Shortfall > 0 AMATR = LONG	T < T_C Shortfall > 0 AMATR = SHORT	T > T_C Shortfall > 0
Slower	Shortfall = 0	T < T_C Shortfall > 0 AMATR = FLAT	T < T_C Shortfall > 0 AMATR = LONG	T < T_C Shortfall > 0 AMATR = SHORT	T > T_C Shortfall > 0
Conclude	Shortfall = 0	NIL	NIL	NIL	T > T_C Shortfall > 0

FIGURE 17.2   Smart VWAP Agent FSM

Finally, when TF is in $FLAT$ state, the VWAP agent proceeds at the normal pace $U(t)$.

The fitness function for each VWAP agent is computed at the end of each day and is the $F(A, M)$ ratio described above. The goal is, over time, to reach an average fitness as close to 1 as possible, where averaging is done over all the daily simulation runs.

Practical Implementation

This part presents a practical discussion of a real-time low-latency automated trading infrastructure designed to support a swarm of trading agents operating on a collection of ECNs.

The focus here is mostly on design patterns rather than on the concrete implementation in a particular language. The implementation of the core of the trading engine, namely the swarm of trading agents, has been presented in detail in LISP and the Common Lisp Object System (CLOS). The choice of LISP has been driven by its extreme flexibility and parsimony as well as its dual interpreted and compiled nature. The external communication, persistence, and human interface layers of the trading architecture, however, can be implemented in any other languages that are the most optimally adapted to the tasks at hand and are dependent also on the chosen hardware. Communications between the core engine and the external layers are achieved via foreign function interfaces. Communications between the external layers can be achieved via object marshalling techniques.

It is important to keep the big picture in mind at all times. Namely, that the whole trading architecture needs to be designed with the maximal set of controls possible. The two main types of controls are:

1. Performance Controls: The core trading engine needs to take care of strategy choice according to their performance and other measures. The risk management module that operates at the top level of the trading architecture needs to take care of the aggregate exposure so as to stabilize overall PL.

2. Operational Controls: The order management system needs to ensure that the orders have been received by the ECN before allowing any other event processing and that all fills have been communicated to relevant agents. The persistence layer needs to ensure that all the market update and communication events can be replayed to the agents in case of system downtime and ECN disconnects and must be able to switch to another clone of the whole trading system in extreme cases.

The swarm-based design of the core trading engine goes a long way toward addressing the robustness of the performance controls and the reader is encouraged to fully utilize the power of those concepts in conjunction with personal intuition and research on tradable patterns.

This part focuses mostly on the operational controls and guides the reader toward a necessary and sufficient design for an automated trading architecture that embeds them. The efficient design of such controls is paramount for the survival of the automated trading architecture as a long-term profitable business.

CHAPTER **18**

Overview
of a Scalable Architecture

A top-level view of the architecture for the automated trading front office infrastructure is shown in Figure 18.1. The trading infrastructure is a concurrent set of trading nodes that operate independently of each other. In each node a particular set of trading agents consumes a particular subset of market events.

The architecture of a trading node is shown in Figure 18.2. It is composed of several layers. It is easiest to explain the layers and the flow of information between them by following the arrows starting at the very top of the diagram.

18.1 ECNs AND TRANSLATION

The flow of information starts in the external world, epitomized by the ECN layer. This is just a collection of connections to various electronic exchange networks and real-time market data sources. The ECN layer broadcasts three types of information:

1. Information pertaining to exchange conectivity: heartbeats, sequence numbers, etc.
2. Market update events: trades, volumes, and order book updates (collectively called ticks)
3. Communications specific to the trading node: acknowledgment of orders sent, rejects, acknowledgments of fills (partial or total)

Usually the ECNs communicate with the world via either the FIX protocol or their own specific protocol that is less verbose and more efficient than FIX. Either way, the messages coming from the ECNs need to be translated

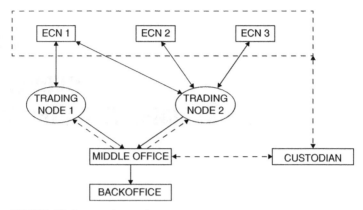

FIGURE 18.1   Trading Infrastructure

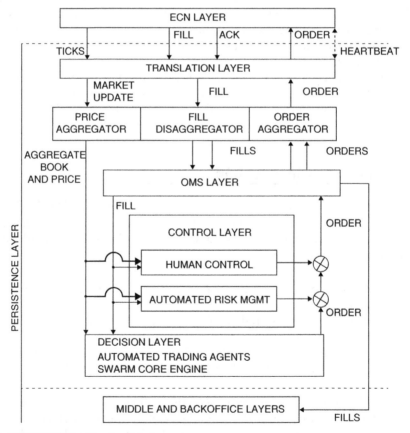

FIGURE 18.2   Trading Node

into objects that the trading node can interpret and act upon. Symmetrically, the communications of the trading node to the ECNs need to be encoded into FIX or the specific protocol. The translation layer is responsible for this two-way traffic.

As the gateway to the ECN, the translation layer also handles the basic heartbeat and connectivity logic of the whole trading node to the ECNs.

There are many commercial FIX engines available and some ECNs provide direct APIs that bypass FIX. Several of those are written in C++ or Java. In the case that, as presented in this book, the core of the trading node is written in LISP, the translation layer also contains the foreign function interface between LISP and Java or C++. That interfacing is light weight and the only data passed are lists of numbers or strings. Remember that the **PRC**, **DELTA**, and **BOOK** classes have lists (or pairs of lists) in their **value** fields.

Once the ECN data is translated into an event object, that object enters the trading node's internal world. The whole internal world constitutes the persistence layer and is implemented as a distributed memory cache that periodically flushes data to an external physical database. That database is crucial for the recovery layer and contains the history of market update events, orders sent, fills received, and the copies of the trading agent classes that themselves contain histories of states, PLs, trades, and statistics.

18.2 AGGREGATION AND DISAGGREGATION

When the event enters the internal world, it comes directly into the aggregation/disaggregation layer. The way that the event is dealt with by that layer depends on its nature:

- Market update event: If it is a traded quote recap **PRC** it is directly passed to the next level—the OMS. If it is a **DELTA** or a **BOOK** event for a security S and ECN E it aggregates that information into the full book for security S across all the ECNs that support that security. This is particularly relevant for accessing liquidity across various FX market-makers as well as equity dark pools.
- Fill update: If the ECN sends back a fill (or a list of partial fills), that information needs to be potentially disaggregated among agents. This happens because aggressive orders in a particular security are netted out across agents and only the net order is sent to the ECNs to reduce transaction costs. The disaggregator takes the (potentially partial) fill received from the ECN and apportions it to the set of agents that emitted it.
- Acknowledgments and rejects: ECN responses to orders or cancel/replaces sent by the OMS are passed back directly to the OMS Layer.

18.3 ORDER MANAGEMENT

The order management system layer contains the principal logic to deal with potential latency and reject problems that can occur while communicating with the ECN. The way that the OMS deals with *incoming* information is as follows:

- Fill updates are passed directly to the control system layer.
- Market update events are passed to the control system layer unless the OMS is waiting for an acknowledgment or a reject of an order it had sent previously, in which case those market updates are queued.
- If an acknowledgment is received, the market update channel is reopened.
- If a reject is received, either the market update channel stays closed and the OMS tries to place the order again, or it is reopened and the OMS passes the reject to the agents that emitted the order, depending on the nature of the agents.

It is of paramount importance for the stability of the whole trading architecture to adequately set up the behavior of the OMS in the way it is to deal with acks and rejects. It is this exact area where the precise coupling between the OMS and the trading agent needs to be defined. That coupling depends intimately of the nature of the trading agent.

18.4 CONTROLS

Finally, events reach the control layer that is itself composed of the human control, the automated risk management, and the automated trading agents layer.

The human control layer contains all the visual representations of the state of the trading node (markets view, order and trade recap, agents' PL monitor, risk monitor) as well as essential controls. The controls are the panic button that allows all net positions to flatten as quickly as possible, a dashboard to set the agents' sizes (for a potential participation in the swarm), and a scheduler to shut down and restart the trading activity. The human control is designed to monitor activity and to deal with unexpected situations. While the OMS is waiting for an ack on a particular order, the human control layer flags that order as being in an undefined state. If the order is rejected and not resubmitted, a clear message would appear. Thus the human control layer can be designed to visually monitor the state of the OMS, and it consumes and rebroadcasts downstream all the events that the OMS is sending.

The automated risk management layer aggregates positions and PLs across all active agents and securities. It monitors adverse changes in the aggregate PL that may be due to correlation and liquidity shocks across markets. It is designed to reduce the overall position in the subset of money-losing agents more quickly than the individual or swarm control systems would. In a multi-security multi-agent trading environment this global risk control mechanism is very important. The automated risk management layer consumes and rebroadcasts downstream market update events.

The human control layer subsumes the automated risk management layer with the help of the panic button. In turn, the automated risk management layer subsumes the automated trading agents layer via the overall risk reduction on a subset of agents.

This is how the basic subsumption architecture works within the control layers. First of all a fill event (actually a set of disaggregated fills) is communicated directly to the automated trading agents layer so that every agent adjusts its **trades** fields accordingly. If the OMS is not waiting on an ack, and no action is taken by the human supervisor nor the risk management system, the next market update event is finally passed to the automated trading agents layer. This layer can be organized into a set of swarms with their own meta-methods that automatically choose the subsets of fit strategies.

18.5 DECISIONS

The consumption of the market update event finally occurs according to the machinery described in Parts One to Three. The agents (and/or the aggregate agents representing the swarms) each potentially emits to the OMS layer a list of passive orders and an aggressive order along with the information on what algo to use to place those orders. The algo can be internal to the trading node or external (for example, when the connectivity to an ECN is done via a broker, who can embed further functionality on the order management).

In turn, the OMS layer aggregates all the aggressive orders by security, and sends the net order along with disaggregation instructions to the aggregator/disaggregator layer. The net aggressive order along with the list of passive orders (potentially containing external algo information) are then passed to the translation layer and sent off to the ECN. This completes the data flow cycle through the trading node.

18.6 MIDDLE AND BACK OFFICE

The OMS layer is connected to a persistent messaging bus that channels fills and certain price information to the middle and back office systems. Those systems are physically separate from the trading node and should be run on a separate server. This helps to optimize the computational efficiency of the trading node. It is also advisable in some cases to separate the human control layer onto a different server and use the messaging bus to pass the price and control information in and out of the trading node. However, the automated risk management and the trading agents layers should be designed to be in the same CPU neighborhood so as to minimize event-passing latency.

There are a variety of third-party middle and back office systems available, so it is important to research them first before attempting to reinvent the wheel in that space. Many fund administrators have teamed up with such service providers and offer the technology as a white-label and part of the package. Most middle office systems have FIX APIs and can automatically connect to brokers and custodians to perform reconciliations. This book's emphasis is on the design of a scalable front office architecture so the back office issues fall mainly outside of its scope.

18.7 RECOVERY

Periodically all classes of the persistance layer are saved into physical databases connected to the distributed memory cache. The databases contain crucial recovery information in case of system or network downtimes. The recovery layer contains the most up-to-date information necessary for complete cloning of the trading node on any machine connected to the distributed memory cache.

The steps to recovery of data and re-instantiation of the computational process depend on the type of fault that occurred. The faults fall into two main categories—caused by either internal or external issues. A subsequent chapter is dedicated to some of the intricacies of setting up efficient recovery mechanisms.

CHAPTER 19

Principal Design Patterns

This chapter elucidates the principal features of an efficient and robust design of the automated trading infrastructure. Various options are discussed for the major computational and architectural features of the components of the node. The ultimate goal of the design guidelines is to ensure that

- The trading infrastructure be scalable via a concurrent clustering of trading nodes.
- Each trading node be designed in a modular way, so that components can be written and re-used easily.
- The whole infrastructure be designed in a way that recovery is fast.

This chapter deals with the modularity aspect and the next chapter with recovery.

19.1 LANGUAGE-AGNOSTIC DOMAIN MODEL

The trading node is a layered computational process that uses a set of objects, methods, and functions to perform its operation. Each layer takes certain objects as inputs and outputs another set of objects to be consumed by the next layer.

A domain model for a process defines the collection of objects and functional relationships between objects that the process uses. It is designed to be language-agnostic so that the implementation could be performad in any set of languages.

The set of five object categories necessary and sufficient to design the trading node consists of:

1. Market updates. The ECNs send various transaction and order book updates to the trading node. These are respectively translated into the

PRC and **DELTA** classes for individual securities. The order book updates are aggregated by the aggregation layer into the full **BOOK** class for a security and transmitted to the control layer.

2. Order updates. The control layer emits orders that are communicated to the order management system. The OMS may aggregate aggressive orders across agents in one security to reduce transaction costs. The **ORDER** and **AGGREGATEORDER** classes represent the necessary and sufficient information.

3. Order status updates. When orders are sent to the ECNs, their status is communicated back to the OMS. They may be accepted (acknowledged) or rejected. The information is translated into the **ACK** class. This information may or may not be passed directly to the Control Layer depending on the nature of the agent that generated the original order.

4. Fill updates. When the ECNs send trade executions back to the trading node they are translated into the **AGGREGATETRADE** class. The OMS disaggregates it into the **TRADE** classes that are sent to the relevant agents.

5. Agents. Agents contain all the up-to-date historic information on positions, orders outstanding, performance, and state. The **AGENT** class has been discussed at length in the previous parts. All the information pertaining to agents can be confined to the control and OMS layers. For certain strategies, only the control layer deals explicitly with agents. Agents receive aggregated market update events and generate potentially aggregated orders.

The flow of information exchange is described in Figure 19.1.

19.2 SOLVING TASKS IN ADAPTED LANGUAGES

In my opinion, it is preferable to write certain layers in certain languages and use the domain model to pass objects between those layers. However, care should be taken to optimize those language choices while balancing the complexity associated with inter-language communication. The key is to make sure that the objects that are passed between layers are simple so that the marshalling time is minimal. This is the case with the classes described above.

Some languages are naturally more adapted to certain tasks. For example it is easy to manipulate matrices in Matlab (the *Mat* part of the name stands for *matrix*). It is easy to perform all kind of statistics in R. It is easy to design FSM agents in LISP.

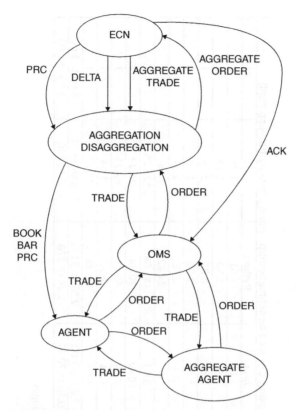

FIGURE 19.1 Trading Node Information Flow

Some languages have unfortunate inherent limitations in their design. Java and C++ do not have multiple inheritance while LISP does. Multiple inheritance is a very natural concept and as long as there is a clear method combination procedure there is no risk of aliasing or circular references. Java and C++ do not have closures nor continuations, while LISP and Scheme do. Java has a serialization procedure whereas LISP needs MemCached or AllegroCache to perform similar tasks.

Of course, despite inherent design limitations, every advanced language can theoretically perform any task that another language performs more naturally. This is because every advanced language is a universal Turing machine (when memory is unlimited, of course). Hence some people have spent time trying to emulate one language in another, and many weird hybrids have emerged. It is not clear at this point whether those hybrids will survive or will be relegated to the shelf of digital curiosities, Esperanto-style.

Comparison of Language Efficiency, taking C++ as a benchmark (http://norvig.com/python-lisp.html)

	Lisp	Java	Python	Perl	C++
hash access	1.06	3.23	4.01	1.85	1
exception handling	0.01	0.9	1.54	1.73	1
sum numbers from file	7.54	2.63	8.34	2.49	1
reverse lines	1.61	1.22	1.38	1.25	1
matrix multiplication	3.3	8.9	278	226	1
heapsort	1.67	7	84.42	75.67	1
array access	1.75	6.83	141.08	127.25	1
list processing	0.93	20.47	20.33	11.27	1
object instantiation	1.32	2.39	49.11	89.21	1
word count	0.73	4.61	2.57	1.64	1
Median	1.67	4.61	20.33	11.27	1
25% to 75%	0.93 to 1.67	2.63 to 7.00	2.57 to 84.42	1.73 to 89.21	1.00 to 1.00
Range	0.01 to 7.54	0.90 to 20.47	1.38 to 278	1.25 to 226	1.00 to 1.00

FIGURE 19.2 Comparative Performance of Languages

My experience in implementing trading nodes points to maximizing the efficiency of certain tasks in particular languages and focusing on lightweight interfaces between them to glue the information together. LISP has always been my primary choice for designing agents because it is a language that allows for a lot of experimentation without many burdens that strongly typed compiled languages, like C++ or Java, present. It is a language that fosters research and development.

Hence, in one of the implementations performed by me and my team, the core engine and risk management layers were written in LISP and the human control layer, the OMS, the aggregation/disaggregation, and the translation layers in Java. In another implementation, the human control layer was written in .NET, the risk management layer in SQL, and everything else was in Java.

Figure 19.2 shows the difference in computing time of a selection of standard algorithms, compared in 5 languages and where C++ is the benchmark, from the comparative study taken from http://norvig.com/python-lisp.html.

It shows that C++ is generally ahead of the pack with LISP in second place then Java. This is an important comparison table that puts LISP back to where it ought to be—among the top three languages.

When choosing languages to solve a task, one has to balance, like in reinforcement learning, exploration versus exploitation. One has to be able to invent the wheel where it needs to be invented and not reinvent it where it had already been invented. Java, for example, is a very useful language because many APIs to software and hardware applications have already been written by a generation of excellent programmers. This means that one can benefit from an accumulated expertise and, most important, from a lengthy debugging process. On the other hand, writing a genetic programming algorithm on the agents' finite state machines is much better done in LISP.

19.3 COMMUNICATING BETWEEN COMPONENTS

In order to communicate effectively between languages and layers, several techniques can be used. One technique is to pass reasonably simple serialized data between languages with a message-passing protocol. Another technique is invoking foreign functions and remote procedure calls.

In general, whatever approach is used, the idea is to minimize the complexity and size of objects transmitted between processes in order to reduce the time of marshalling and unmarshalling.

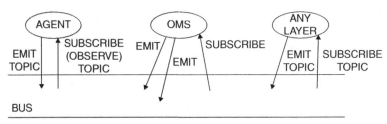

FIGURE 19.3   Messaging Bus Architecture

19.3.1   Messaging Bus

The most universal, albeit not necessarily the most efficient, technique is to embed the whole trading node into a messaging bus environment as per Figure 19.3.

This enables the layers to be both emitters and receivers of a range of topics. Every topic is defined a priori and every layer may subscribe or not to that topic (the specialization of the method **observe** to a particular agent is a model of such topic filtering). For example, the aggregation/disaggregation layer subscribes to the price and order book updates coming from the translation layer. It also subscribes to the orders and the associated agent aggregation information coming from the OMS. It emits on the topic of partial fills that is listened to by the OMS.

Several open source and commercial entities provide messaging bus infrastructures. These infrastructures would usually contain language APIs to connect to the bus. Commercial entities also provide the routing hardware itself that is composed of very fast network switches. The messaging buses are used extensively by exchanges and brokerages to route a large volume of market update data.

The messaging bus can be seen as providing the glue between the various computational entities (layers or components of the trading node). It translates the information passed between components into a defined format.

The formats and their handling constitute part of the communication protocol of the bus. The other part of the protocol deals with message passing itself. Usually buses are designed to queue messages at each receiver level, so that no information is lost however slow the receiver's speed of processing. The receiver can then decide whether to process the entire queue or the last incoming element.

The act of translating an object from a computer language to the transmission format of the bus is called *marshalling* and the reverse is called *unmarshalling*. In the object-oriented world that we live in, there is a natural tendency to pass objects between processes. Objects not only have data but methods attached to them. Hence marshalling is not just aiming at translating data but also at providing functionality embedded in the methods.

There are standard communication protocols that are used to implement the messaging bus. One of the original ones was SOAP (simple object access protocol) that is based on encoding and decoding objects into XML messages. XML, although human readable, is very verbose and not very efficient. For example, Apache ActiveMQ is a widely used open source bus software that is based on SOAP. Another implementation, ICE (Internet communications engine) uses a binary encoding of objects that is more time and bandwidth efficient.

Messaging buses are essentially media that implement a flow of asynchronous message passing between components that may or may not queue them. Components can be written in any language as long as they have receivers and transmitters of standardized format messages.

19.3.2 Remote Procedure Calls

The second technique is to use remote procedure calls (RPC) where a client process invokes a calculation on a host (a.k.a. server) process. The processes may be running either on the same computer or across a network via sockets. Usually the RPC call itself is single-threaded and the client process blocks until it receives the answer from the result of running the procedure on the host. RPCs over a network are usually implemented via socket connections.

The subtleties surrounding the efficient use of RPCs are numerous and range from the design of the information to be passed in the call to the control of garbage collection on the host.

One important consideration is which process should be the host and which should be the client. The client process is the one that invokes foreign functions that run on the host process.

The trading node's computational process is at the outset driven by events received from the ECNs. The top level of control is performed by the translation node that sends a market update or an order management event downstream and needs to receive a response to it from the control layer before sending another event. That response could be the resulting set of orders or just the indication that the control and the OMS layers have stopped processing the information and are passing the thread of control back to the translation layer.

As mentioned previously, there are several open source and commercial applications written in Java and C++ that perform the function of the translation layer, via the implementation of a FIX engine, and also often integrate elements of an OMS. This FIX engine should be seen as the client process that would be calling the control layer process as host. If the control layer is written in another language like LISP, this is where the RPCs are invoked at the client level.

Foreign Functions   Foreign function interfaces (FFI) are examples of RPC handling for functional languages. For example, LISP provides several FFIs, such as CFFI or Allegro's JLinker library, that allow calls to C and Java functions from within LISP programs and vice versa.

As an example assume that the translation layer is designed in Java on one machine. One would have a Java virtual machine (VM) running on that machine invoking the control layer via an FFI call to a LISP process running either on the same machine or remotely. The control layer LISP process can be packaged as a Java Bean via JLinker.

Object-Oriented Middleware   With the current dominance of the object-oriented paradigm, efforts have been ongoing to standardize the way objects and methods are presented to the outside by the various object-oriented languages.

An ambitious distributed-object protocol is the CORBA project that stands for Common Object Request Broker Architecture and aims to create a universal middleware between object-oriented languages. This means that a process written in one language can invoke a method that operates on another process and that is written in a different language.

In CORBA each object and method have an interface that is exposed to the outside world via an interface definition language. CORBA provides the interpretation of that interface in each particular computer language as well as an automatically generated object request broker (ORB) process that manages the load on method calls at the host level.

CORBA's way of remote method invokation is also basically an RPC but has a wider set of communication protocols. Alongside the synchronous two-way protocol used by RPCs, it also has the ability to not lock the client while waiting for the host's response (either by not locking or by callback after a certain time or more complicated mediation methodologies). The communication between client and host is based on binary encoding via the Internet Inter-ORB Protocol (IIOP) and is faster than XML-based message passing of SOAP.

19.4   DISTRIBUTED COMPUTING AND MODULARITY

The combination of the standardization provided by the domain model with the permeability provided by the messaging bus allows for a flexible, distributed computing architecture. The various layers can be run concurrently on separate machines and address spaces.

Distributed computing presents several advantages but could also come with some dangers if not architectured properly. For example, in the message bus scenario, the dangers come from the fact that the message passing is asynchronous. Once the message has been broadcast, the bus simply controls the queuing of that message for each receiver, and if a receiver is stuck, the message can be waiting forever to be processed. There is no natural blocking of new messages if one of them has not been processed. Hence one needs to think carefully about which elements of the trading node can be distributed and which cannot be.

Starting at the top level, the appropriate distributed computing architecture is a function of the nature of the agents. If each agent only consumes market update events for one security, then it is best to clone, on an asynchronous basis, as many trading nodes as there are securities. If, on the other hand, a subset of agents process a subset of securities (e.g., a pairs-trading strategy or a roll execution algorithm) then that subset of agents should constitute the core of a trading node. This is shown in Figure 19.4.

Each trading node will have its independent translation, aggregator, OMS, and control layers. However, they can all share the database and recovery layers because all this information is less time sensitive and mission critical.

Also, an overall risk management layer that aggregates PL data across agents can be designed as an asynchronous process from the trading core. Its primary function is, on very rare occasions, to short-circuit and potentially flatten positions for the whole trading operation. The states of the world in which that eventuality may arise, however, would be such that what matters is overall survival rather than optimization of execution.

Processes that require synchronization have to be run in a single layer (and sometimes in a single thread). In general it is better to design the core

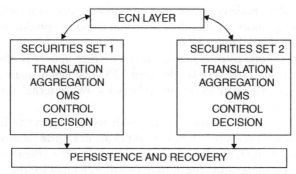

FIGURE 19.4 Distributed Trading Nodes

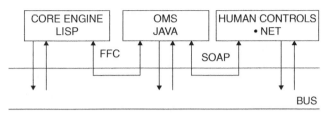

FIGURE 19.5 Distributed Trading Architecture

engine and the OMS to be run in a single thread of control for each security so that the relationship between the states of the agent and the states of the OMS is unambiguous.

An example of a distributed trading architecture that uses both the messaging bus and the remote procedure calls between layers is shown in Figure 19.5.

19.5 PARALLEL PROCESSING

A matter related to distributed computing is parallel processing. However, despite sounding similar, their goals in the context of the trading node are different.

The distributed computing architecture aims at removing as much load as possible from the core layer, by treating as asynchronous any component of the node that is not mission- and latency-critical.

The parallel processing architecture, on the other hand, is designed to optimize the computation within the core layer.

The agent-based design of the core layer presented in this book naturally fits into a parallel processing architecture.

For purposes of illustration, assume that the overall architecture is such that every trading node is a consumer of market updates for only one security. The trading nodes are therefore distributed and run on different process clusters, as shown in Figure 19.5.

Focusing on one trading node, when a market update is observed, the event is then passed to every single agent's FSM. When a single agent consumes the market update event, it updates its own internal state, desired position, and orders.

Instead of passing the event consecutively to the ***agents*** list, one can pass it in parallel, spawning a new thread per agent's **update** method. Once every agent is updated, the threads join and a single thread then continues the computation by aggregating the desired position changes for the usage of the

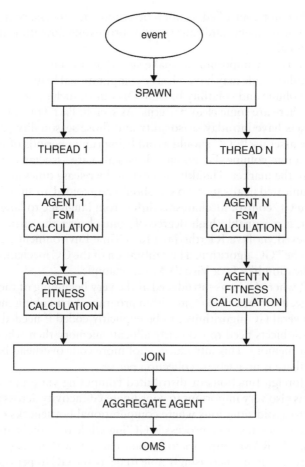

FIGURE 19.6 Parallel Processing within the Trading Node

aggregation and OMS layers. Figure 19.6 shows the diagram of information flow and the pseudocode.

19.6 GARBAGE COLLECTION AND MEMORY CONTROL

An important efficiency consideration is the fine-tuning of the Garbage Collection (GC). Unless one uses a very sizable RAM that allows one to run the trading node uninterrupted for days on end, GC will invariably be occuring.

GC, when not controlled, is not a deterministic process, so it can occur at inopportune moments and cause serious processing downtime that can be business-critical.

Hence it is very important to make sure that it is not occuring at times when the trading node may have a heavy computational load (e.g., periods of high quote volume and volatility bursts). Of course, such periods are hard to predict but there are some clear patterns. As seen in Part Three, trading volume for assets have intraday seasonality and those seasonality patterns depend on the asset itself. GC should avoid being run in periods of high transaction and quote volume. Economic releases also are associated with bursts of activity in the market. Thankfully most of the release times are scheduled and communicated in advance. So GC should be avoided around those times as well. The GC control mechanisms differ from language to language.

In Java, a reasonably high degree of control over the virtual machine can be achieved via Java RT (the Java Real Time Environment), which uses a "metronome" GC algorithm. The calibration of the GC mechanism is done via an application like Java VisualVM for example.

In LISP, where GC was introduced at the very beginning of the design of the language, it can be called from within programs by invoking the function (gc), so several GC algorithms can be explicitly coded if needed.

In C++, objects need to explicitly allocate memory then when destructed, to clear memory. This introduces a lot more code overhead but is more precise, so there is no garbage collection per se.

When foreign functions or distributed computing via a messaging bus are used, it is also very important to coordinate GC activity across processes. One needs to avoid situations where computational bottlenecks or message queuing occurs because one process is GC'ing while the others are not.

Fortunately, RAM continues to become cheaper with time, so hardware solutions are becoming increasingly able to delay the GC to periods that can be controlled explicitly and where computational downtime presents less business risk.

An interesting application of the cached memory infrastructure discussed in the next chapter is its usage to avoid untimely GC'ing. Some open source and commercial products currently offer up to one terabyte of cached memory.

CHAPTER 20

Data Persistence

T here are several important goals of persisting data, namely for the back office and reconciliation with trading counterparties and custodians, building databases for research and development, and for recovery from system and communication downtimes.

In the design of the automated trading infrastructure some serious consideration needs to be given to selecting what database technologies to use for what purpose.

Data persistence is about saving all the important information. There are two ways to save, on-the-go caching and physical storage. The best way to ensure robustness and computational efficiency is to combine the two.

20.1 BUSINESS-CRITICAL DATA

In order to figure out what to save, one needs to decide which data is critical for the operation of business. There are, conceptually, two types of information that need to be recoverable at will. If one thinks of the trading infrastructure as a finite-state machine interacting with the external world, at every point in time one should be able to reconstruct the internal and the external states of the machine. Then it would continue operating as if nothing happened.

Preserving External State   The external state is how the trading business is seen by its trading counterparties: ECNs, prime brokers, custodian, and administrator.

The ECN sees the history of all the communication traffic (FIX messages). This consists of orders, acknowledgments, rejects, fills, sequence number resets, and so on.

The prime brokers see the executed disaggregated trades reflected in the various subaccounts that the trading business holds with them.

The custodian and administrator see the aggregate data from prime brokers potentially disaggregated in a set of subaccounts.

From a practical standpoint, the business-critical data needed to preserve external state is the history of executed trades and the current outstanding orders. One does not usually need to keep explicit tab on the history of FIX messaging although sometimes it is handy for debugging.

Preserving Internal State The internal state of the trading business is intimately related to the internal states of every one of its trading agents. The FSM paradigm for trading agents comes in very handy because it defines the minimal amount of data that needs to be kept to preserve the overall internal state.

Indeed, as per the discussions in the previous parts, every trading agent recomputes its FSM as new data comes in (be it from market updates, fill updates, or from other agents' communications). The FSM is computed via a series of indicators that are based on event histories. Agents need to preserve these indicators in such a way that at recovery, the state of each agent is exactly the same as before the power-down.

Let us reiterate that the operation of each agent is path-dependent on the history of events and potentially on the operations of other agents. This is where recursion comes into play, because computing indicators recursively helps greatly to reduce the amount of data that needs to be saved and retrieved for each agent at recovery.

Hence agents need to be preserved with their whole class structure for efficient recovery. They are crucial data items to be persisted and contain in themselves sufficient information for their own individual recovery. By this method the agents preserve the history of their individual fitnesses, positions, trades, and orders.

The swarm also needs to be preserved in its entirety, that is, the histories of members of the SSS and SFS sets, along with all the global fitness historical data and the histories of aggregate swarm orders, trades, and positions.

At the level of the OMS and the aggregation/disaggregation layers, it is crucial to preserve the entirety of current orders outstanding with the disaggregation data.

Finally, at the level of the translation layer, the current sequence numbers need to be preserved for each ECN.

Ancillary Data The ancillary data that should be preserved in a different database consists of ECN market update histories. Those could be either raw data or aggregated synchronized data by the aggregation layer. The aggregated data is most relevant for FX because many ECNs and banks publish different streams and the trading business should be aggregating that data in its own private stream.

This time series tick and book data is very valuable for strategy testing. It is, however, very bulky and should ideally be saved in another database (and format) from the business-critical data needed for state preservation and recovery.

20.2 OBJECT PERSISTENCE AND CACHED MEMORY

As soon as raw ECN data gets translated by the translation layer into the trading node, it enters the persistence layer that encompasses the majority of the node. Every component of the persistence layer is connected to a distributed memory cache. The memory cache itself is connected to a set of physical databases discussed in the next section.

Distributed cached memory (or network cached memory) is a shared RAM resource across a network for short-term persistence and data sharing between concurrent processes. Every object that ultimately needs to be written into a physical database would live in the cache until the moment it is actually written.

If one of the nodes (computers) that supports the cached memory goes down then data is not lost as it is replicated in the other nodes and in the database. Another very important feature is that caching improves computation speed because the database writes are asynchronous (and queued). Those two features make the memory cache an essential feature in the operation of the trading node. Figure 20.1 shows the salient features of a distributed cache architecture.

Several commercial and open source caching technologies are built around some design principles introduced by MemCached, an open source project.

As discussed at length in the book, the most convenient way of designing the trading node's layers and components is via an object-oriented methodology where a set of objects interacts via a set of generic functions and methods. These objects may live on different machines and communicate between each other via bus messaging or remote procedure calls. Some memory caches have been designed specifically for object-oriented environments, like AllegroCache for LISP and Terracotta for Java.

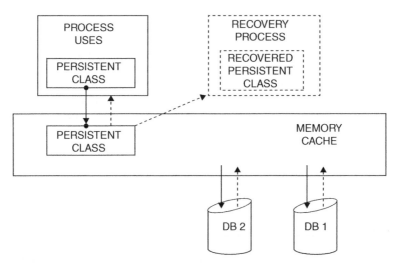

FIGURE 20.1   Memory Cache Architecture

In those object-oriented caches, all objects that need to be persisted would inherit from a persistant class that automatically manages the writes into the physical database cluster to which the cache is attached.

In AllegroCache, when a class is specified to be persistent, it will be automatically storable and retrievable via an indexing system that can be set in advance. The AllegroCache database has all the features (and more) of relational databases like Oracle or MySQL. For example to make the **EVENT** class persistent one would simply write the following definition:

```
(defclass EVENT ()
  ((timestamp
    :initarg :timestamp
    :accessor timestamp
    :index :any)
   (value
    :initarg :value
    :accessor value))
  (:metaclass persistent-class))
```

Here the only differences from the definition given in Part One are the last line that specifies that the class is persistent and the **:index :any** addition to the **timestamp** slot. This last feature creates an index that would allow the retrieval from the database of all **EVENT** objects that have a certain timestamp.

In Java one of the popular and efficient open source distributed caches is Terracotta. Terracotta has been developed for clustering of Java virtual machines. It allows sharing of cached objects and multithreading across JVMs. Terracotta is connected to a database cluster.

When setting up Terracotta, one needs to specify the clustering configuration of the Java processes. By that one defines a priori what objects are to be shared by the cluster of JVMs and their concurrency characteristics. Those constitute the shared object graph. That graph is defined a priori via an XML specification of the root objects, instrumented classes, and locks. The child classes derived from root objects are the shared classes accessible from any JVM on the cluster (they are cached). Instrumentation is the process by which Terracotta sets up the persistence and clustering characteristics when the classes are loaded into the JVMs. Every bytecode of an instrumented class is modified to include the Terracotta-specific fields and methods that connect the class to the cache. Locks are specified on the methods and the relevant bytecode is modified at load time in order to ensure cluster concurrency.

Terracotta does not require any modification to the native code, unlike the example given previously for making the **EVENT** class persistent in AllegroCache. It requires instead the setting up of a series of XML files that control the whole instrumentation process.

In addition to the memory caching, Terracotta allows, by its design, for distributing calculations across JVMs. Assume, for example, that the trading infrastructure is composed of several trading nodes and that two of those trading nodes share the market event updates for one security S. The trading agents in both clusters use S's price updates (along with other security price updates that are different between the two clusters). The trading nodes can be configured in a way that when S is communicated by the translation layer, the aggregation/disaggregation level implements a master-worker pattern to distribute the work between the two control layers and gather the information on the aggregate desired position change and set of orders pertaining to S. This design would only make sense if the two nodes are not required to receive synchronous sets of price updates of other securities along with S.

20.3 DATABASES AND THEIR USAGE

The cached memory is connected to a set of physical databases into which periodic asynchronous writes are performed. The way data is represented in the database depends on the nature of the database and the query language associated with it.

Types of Databases All useful databases need to meet the ACID (atomicity, consistency, isolation, durability) tests that ensure referential integrity of data and mechanisms that prevent multiple concurrent users from committing data inconsistently. Also, databases should be endowed with efficient bulk loading mechanisms into the cache as well as the logging of transactions that help in restoring data in case the system crashes while writing from the cache.

There are basically two broad types of database design, the RDBMS and the NoSQL databases, and they differ by how data is reflected in them.

The relational database management system (RDBMS) requires a schema that rigidly defines the format and types of stored data and the relationships between data. The data in the database is represented by tables, and relationships between data are defined by tables as well. These databases are most widely used by the business community, and are usually set up and queried by the structured query language (SQL). Examples of such databases are the stand-alone MySQL and the clustered version provided by Oracle.

The NoSQL databases are a response to the challenge posed by the constraints that the overly structured RDBMS design imposes on real-world data. For example, experimental data (representations of large time series of visual data or biological data) do not fit the structured table representation well, as the structure of the data may change in time or depend on context. The acute need for representing data within its context is found in the Semantic Web effort. The idea is to design a data representation endowed with local knowledge on how to interpret it, not just a table of numbers and strings that can be interpreted only by unchanging global semantics.

For example, Google and Amazon do not use the standard RDBMS architecture but have designed their own database technologies to address their business needs. The scientific and defense communities have designed the Hierarchical Data Format (currently HDF5) to deal with large sets of unstructured observational data. The data representation of HDF5 is a directed graph of simpler components. AllegroGraph is another example of a database that uses graph representation of data and a Prolog-based query language.

Long high-frequency time series of even simple data (like ticks) present another challenge to the RDBMS model because of bottlenecks associated with speed of loading and writing. Some proprietary technologies, like Xenomorph, have emerged to help deal with such problems. One approach is by storing time series as binary vectors and by bulk loading them directly into RAM or cache. The Matlab and Mathematica analysis software use HDF5 for time series representation of data.

AllegroCache is a NoSQL database that stores objects and relations between them as "b-trees." This is particularly handy for LISP objects as they are represented as lists (trees).

Back Office Reporting and Give-Ups A copy of the set of executed trades and their allocations between the trading agents persists independently of the copy held by the trading node. This database can be an instance of the RDBMS as the schema for the data is simple.

This middle-office database performs the external reconciliation and give-ups function. The reconciliation is in two parts, ECN and give-up to the custodian. Unless errors occur at the ECN (busted trades) or give-up errors occur between the ECN and the prime broker, the execution data is then deemed clean and passed to the back office database and external administrator.

If errors occur then a roll-back mechanism needs to be in place between the middle office and the trading node; this is dicussed below.

State Persistence The database for recovery purposes needs to contain the minimal information for internal and external state reconciliation. As mentioned above, the object-oriented agent-based paradigm adopted in this book calls for efficient storage of agents as objects, as well as other business objects like the OMS and the aggregation/disaggregation-related objects. Those objects contain the accumulated data histories and procedures needed to recover the range of functionalities.

It is of course possible to use RDBMS again for such purpose but a NoSQL database of the AllegroCache type is more useful and user friendly, as it can be reloaded and queried by the same LISP code. The AllegroCache would restore the whole of the LISP environment as it was before power-down, so no marshalling and unmarshalling of objects into tables would be involved.

Research and Development As mentioned above, it is very valuable to preserve the market update data, either in raw form as it comes from ECNs or in the aggregated in-house format coming from the aggregation/disaggregation layer.

High frequency tick data can become very bulky (petabytes of data), so efficient storage and retrieval methods need to be used. It becomes a Big Data problem that requires big solutions. Data is expensive and all efforts should be made to preserve it for future research purposes, if it makes sense from a business prospective.

An assessment needs to be made whether to build your own big data server or use third-party vendors. The third-party vendors are certainly not cheap, but they provide many advantages, and may end up costing less in the long term. Several companies have developed "ticker plants" that solve the in-house filtering, representation, and storage issues.

For example, Thomson's Velocity Analytics platform not only provides historical data but also allows the client to contribute its own aggregated data. Nanex's NxCore is another example of a very efficiently compressed data plant, whose visualization and analytic tools have helped to shed light on the events during the Flash Crash (see Nanex website).

The main point to make sure of is that such third-party platforms integrate seamlessly with the trading infrastructure.

Unlike the necessary focus on the in-house development of the trading node's core layer, in my opinion it is better not to reinvent the wheel in increasingly commoditized services like historical data storage and retrieval.

CHAPTER 21

Fault Tolerance and Recovery Mechanisms

F ast recovery from systems or communications downtime is a very crucial aspect of the architectural design for the trading infrastructure. Loss of data and loss of time can yield a catastrophic failure of the whole trading and risk-management process, with consequences on the future survival of the business.

21.1 SITUATIONS OF STRESS

There are several types of situations where a complete or partial recovery is warranted for the trading infrastructure. This is a complex topic and depends on the nature of the downtime. The main types of situations are described below and fall into the external and internal categories.

21.1.1 Communication Breakdown

Communication breakdowns are the most common of all problems. Whether a disconnect in communications happens because of problems at the ECN, problems on the network, or problems at the trading business makes no difference to the problem.

What matters is which data is not being received. There are several ways communications can break down: one can be disconnected from the ECN's price source or order routing or fill updates or a combination thereof.

Suppose that a full communications breakdown occured at T_{-1} and no prices or fills have been received since then. However, an alternate price source exists (e.g., Bloomberg or Reuters) that can be queried to fill a gap of price history. Assume that the alternate price source also got disconnected for a while. It is now T_0 and both the historical prices and the ECN are reconnected. In order to recover from this situation one needs to implement a process of the following kind:

- Restart trading node off-line now at time T_0 and start receiving and caching all ECN updates. The ECN will send the new sequence numbers and re-send the fill updates that were lost during disconnect.
- Load from the historical price source all the price data from T_{-1} into an event queue and keep adding the real-time ECN updates to that queue as they come in.
- Also load the time-stamped ECN fill and order updates into the event queue, respecting the time ordering.
- Re-simulate the whole trading process from T_{-1} by popping data from the event queue.
- At some point T_1, the queue will be empty because the simulation process is faster than the real trading process. That means that the simulation has finally converged back to reality.
- At T_1 bring the trading node back online and restart consuming the real-time market update events as they come. The trading node will have to reposition itself according to its new correct state as well as replace some outstanding orders. This is achieved by comparing the existing market position to the desired market position and the existing orders to the desired orders.

The above sounds easy, but in reality it is quite complicated. The main issue is the fact that simulation cannot achieve a waterproof representation of reality, especially in situations of nonlinear market impact and dealing with uncertainty of the execution of limit orders.

21.1.2 External Systems Breakdown

External failures and breakdowns do happen—ECNs and broker systems are not foolproof and have downtimes. This may consist of power-downs and system failures at the ECN.

It is important for the trading business to continuously save its external state, that is, the set of positions and outstanding orders at the trading venues.

The trading node always keeps its own record of these in the memory cache and on disk. If there is an external breakdown, then a reconciliation can be accomplished with the trading venue by requesting a comparison of trades confirmed and orders sent.

When situations like this happen, there are usually no market updates coming from the stopped trading venue, so no issues would arise with back-filling gaps in data, as those are real gaps with no data. This means that during those downtime periods, the agents would not change state and would not emit any orders.

21.1.3 Trades Busted at the ECN Level

ECNs can bust trades in certain situations (e.g., Flash Crash in 2010, Knight's overtrading in 2012, etc.) so a confirmed trade from the ECN is not necessarily the final word. Usually the decision to bust is based on the concept of "clearly erroneous execution," where the price or quantity traded is inconsistent with the current trading pattern for the security (e.g., see NYSE Arca's guidelines). Usually such busts are decided by the ECN within the first 15 to 30 minutes of the trade.

Although those situations occur very rarely, they nevertheless may cause serious problems because they change the exposure and risk of the trading business. It is not nice, and can be very expensive, to suddenly find out that one leg of a pairs-trading strategy is not there any more, because the exchange decided to bust it. One now finds oneself in a naked position that needs to be dealt with immediately, by trading out of the other leg.

Hence a roll-back mechanism needs to be in place for the middle office database. And, most critically, a feedback mechanism from the middle office database back to the trading node database and process needs to be implemented.

It could be that, after a bust, the ECN sends a confirmation electronically (trade cancelled but not replaced), but it may not always be the case. Then this information needs to be input manually into the middle-office database and communicated back to the trading node.

The frustrating issue with this type of situation is that it is not the fault of the trading node nor a design flaw of the trading agent logic. The agent traded on legitimate information provided by the exchange. Even if one builds in specific stop-gaps to avoid aggressively trading on off-market prices, those situations may still occur because some resting orders got triggered.

From a practical point of view, the FSM representation of agents helps to deal with this situation at the primary logic level. Remember that the FSM representation is designed to provide logical closure, so that at any point in time and in any situation the agent knows what to do. If suddenly the agent finds itself in a naked position then either it will reduce its risk by itself or the swarm system will do it.

However, what is done is done, and the PL generated from the time the trade was initially accepted to the time it got rejected is simply not real.

Hence the negative of that PL needs to be saved into an error ledger that is independent of the trading node's swarm risk management system.

This of course does not mean that this error PL should be hidden; it is very real and has to be accounted for in the overall risk management layer by potentially updating exposure limits for the trading infrastructure. But this should not yield a recalculation of states of individual agents or swarm because the internal and external path-dependent logic had been resynchronized. It may yield an overall reduction of risk across the trading business, rather than unnaturally force the agents to change the logic of their states.

Of course not all busts are bad. Sometimes one is stopped out from a position at a loss. It feels very nice when that loss is reversed. Then the situation changes the other way. If after the loss the risk management layer reduced overall exposure, it may re-increase exposure when the stop-loss is busted and the error ledger is positive.

21.1.4 Give-Up Errors Causing Credit Line Problems

Give-up errors occur when the ECN or the broker sends trades to the wrong account, the wrong prime broker, or the wrong custodian.

Those are usually not business-critical unless the credit line of the prime broker that is supposed to receive the trade dries up because it fails to receive it. This may have consequences on being able to trade with that prime broker.

Assume for example that the trading node operates on aggregated FX price data from an ECN and from a bank's FX market-making platform. The bank also happens to be the prime broker for the trading business, and sets its exposure and credit limits. It will not allow the trading business to trade through its platform if the credit or exposure limit is seen to be breached.

Banks usually market-make in more currency pairs than ECNs, so there are pairs that the trading node can trade only through the bank but not the ECN. In this example we assume that the ECN primarily trades developed currencies through the ECN and emerging market crosses and NDFs through the bank.

Assume that at the prime broker account the trading node's position happens to be quite short USD against a whole bunch of other currencies and this short USD position is close to the bank's limit. However, the account happens also to be very long USDBRL at that point (short BRL and long USD).

Suppose now that the trading node gets short a large chunk of EURUSD via the ECN, hence it is short EUR and long USD. From the trading node's perspective, it has reduced its overall short USD risk. Assume, however, that the ECN mistakenly gives up the EURUSD trade to another account hence the bank does not see (or cannot confirm) that the USD short had been reduced.

Next trade, the trading node wants to reduce its short BRL exposure so is going short the USDBRL against the bank. This increases the USD short at the bank and breaches its credit limit. The trade is DK'd by the Bank and the trading node cannot reduce its short BRL risk, despite having reduced substantially its short USD risk via the ECN.

This is very dangerous because the trading node is put in a situation where it cannot risk manage its positions because of a give-up error. This situation is therefore equivalent to a disconnect from the bank's liquidity but not from the bank's pricing source.

21.1.5 Internal Systems Breakdown

A local server going down may or may not cause a problem for the trading node. If that server supports part of the cached memory or a database then the cached data is, by design, still on the network and can be retrieved by the processes. If the server supports part of the decision-making process then the problem is more acute.

One has to deal then with the recovery problem in a very similar way to the situation of a network disconnect and re-simulate the path-dependent state changes with historical data, as discussed above.

21.1.6 Planned Maintenance and Upgrades

Usually ECN planned maintenance and upgrades occur on weekends or holidays when markets are closed, and so should be the maintenance of the trading infrastructure. There is no recovery per se but just a restart. At restart, the physical database is reloaded into the memory cache in a way that the internal states and data of all the agents are the same as before the power-down. Then the trading infrastructure is connected to the ECNs, respecting the sequencing numbers and waiting for more fun processing the market updates.

21.2 A JAM OF LOGS IS BETTER THAN A LOGJAM OF ERRORS

Not all errors are caused by external sources or local hardware. It may be that the implementation of the trading infrastructure has bugs. Bugs happen to everyone, and sometimes cost a hell of a lot of money (and control), as Knight Capital found out in the summer of 2012.

It is very handy to keep generating logs, to be able to disentangle the sequence of events that caused the system to malfunction.

Logs can be generated and streamed to a compressed format asynchronously thanks to the memory caching architecture. Clearly, if faults do not occur, old logs can be erased periodically to free up disk space for new logs.

In general, it is important to create logs that are easily parsed via line-reading scripts based on Awk, Perl, or similar scripting languages.

Several logging applications are available, like Log4J in Java with its Chainsaw viewer from Apache.

Logs can also be used for data management. To save processing time or CPU load, it is sometimes handy to automatically log all the market event data received from the ECN and then asynchronously extract it into a physical database from the logs.

21.3 VIRTUAL MACHINE AND NETWORK MONITORING

One big factor in fault mangement is prevention. Of course, external breakdowns or hardware and communication failures cannot be predicted so efficient recovery mechanisms, as presented above, need to be in place and tested thoroughly.

However, other internal problems may occur and create bottlenecks and latency. For example, assume one of the servers supporting the memory cache breaks down. It is not a business-interruption situation because the trading node can keep operating on a lower permeation of the cache across the network. However, the load on the physical database writes will increase.

From an internal perspective, the problems that may occur, outside of bugs, are related to computational or communication bottlenecks.

Computational bottlenecks mostly occur when the GC is not tuned correctly. Chapter 19, "Principal Design Patterns," mentioned the importance of tuning and monitoring GC activity across processes. Java, for example, provides the Java Visual VM tool for this purpose.

Network bottlenecks can occur at the translation layer level and at the messaging bus level. Most commercial FIX engines provide a way to monitor the FIX traffic in and out of the trading business. Messaging buses also provide visual monitoring tools.

From my experience, the fine-tuning of the system takes time and is an evolutionary process in itself. It takes time and mistakes to learn. In general, the motto should be "When in doubt, get out!" This is a very well tested and good trading motto and extends to tuning the automated trading process. If for some reason tension appears on the computational or networking side, it is a good idea to reduce overall risk and exposure of the trading node.

This is where the human element comes in, and at the point in time that this book is being written, it is irreplaceable.

CHAPTER 22

Computational Efficiency

T he swarm systems studied in this book are composed of a sizable number of individual agents consuming data updates. Especially in the high-frequency world, where the data comes as bursts of ticks, the design of the individual agent and of the whole system needs to be computationally efficient. Otherwise, the system would not be able to consume and react to the data in a timely fashion.

The examples of the swarm systems presented thus far operated only on one data source. In reality, they are implemented on a series of markets. For example, in foreign exchange, there are almost a hundred liquid tradable pairs on which swarm systems can be implemented. In global equities, the number of could go easily to a thousand. The swarms discussed above contained up to 500 individuals so this could translate into half a million agents across all the markets.

Design patterns for the infrastructure necessary to sustain such scalability are based on a distributed computing architecture that is a set of concurrent trading nodes. Each trading node uses a parallel processing architecture at the level of the control layer to update the FSMs of each agent on a single market data or communication event.

22.1 CPU SPIKES

One of the main computational bottlenecks comes from the fact that computer CPUs operate in clock time, while data update events come in a random fashion. The impact of this difference is most visible in the high frequency domain. Clock time between tick arrivals varies greatly as a function of the activity of the market, and this is what creates the effect of volatility spikes: measures of volatility are computed in clock time. The strategies that are most appropriate for the high frequency domain are event driven, and the market volatility bursts translate directly into computational load bursts on the CPU.

To respond to such bursts, the system would either have to queue the data to process it at a later stage, or ignore all the data updates that come while the computational cycle is occurring.

The danger of queuing is that, by the time a computational cycle completes and sends the order to the OMS, the tick on which the OMS needs to act aggressively is already stale. An order rejection will result and the desired position will not be synchronized with the position in the market. The same can happen on the next cycle. Thus the system may be completely stalled for the whole period of increased market activity, unable to trade in or out of positions. Those periods are very often associated with large price moves, and they are exactly the periods when efficient repositioning and risk management ought to be applied.

Queuing can also be induced by garbage collection, and if the GC is not tuned properly, it risks being induced by a spike in market update events as discussed previously.

Another danger of ignoring data updates during a computational cycle is that one could lose the path dependency embedded in certain trading strategies. Designing each agent as an FSM helps to overcome this problem somewhat, as the strategy would know which state to transition to at the next update. But this transition may come with a large slippage cost.

Thus, it is of the utmost importance to ensure that swarm systems are designed to withstand such computational bursts. I have spent a fair amount of time optimizing the numeric and algorithmic aspects of this process, and the major results are presented here.

22.2 RECURSIVE COMPUTATION OF MODEL SIGNALS AND PERFORMANCE

One of the largest efficiency gains is to avoid loops while computing indicators and performance measures. Most indicators used in systematic trading are based on price history, and very often on a moving window of data. At each data update the newest element is added to the window, the oldest is dropped, and the indicator is recalculated. The CPU time needed to calculate the indicator in this fashion is proportional at least to the length of the window, but it could also grow as the square of the window length if the calculation includes standard deviations.

As an example, take a simple moving average

$$SMA(n, t) = (1/n) \sum_{i=0}^{n-1} x(t - i)$$

Calculating it involves a summation of n elements and one division. If at each step one saved the latest value of the SMA and the oldest element $x(t - n + 1)$ separately, then one could write

$$SMA(n, t + 1) = SMA(n, t) + (x(t + 1) - x(t - n + 1))/n$$

This calculation reduces to two summations and one division and becomes independent of the length n of the lookback period.

Even more efficient is to use an exponential moving average,

$$EMA(\alpha, t) = (1 - \alpha)EMA(\alpha, t - 1) + \alpha x(t)$$

because only its last value needs to be remembered. When $\alpha = 2/(n + 1)$ the EMA becomes very similar to the SMA in its smoothing and filtering properties so one can use it instead.

In general, a function that makes a call to itself with a different argument is called *recursive*. Suppose one pre-calculates $f(0)$ at step 0. If the calculation of f can be represented as $f(N) = G(f(N - 1), x)$ then, for step N, one only needs to remember the last value $f(N - 1)$ to calculate the next value $f(N)$ via a call to the function G. This sounds like not much, but representing calculations recursively is very efficient from a computational perspective. In fact, the theory of recursive functions is a precursor to modern computing and was initially called λ-calculus by its creator Alonzo Church in the 1930s. The computer language that naturally emerged from that research is LISP, which is being used throughout this book.

There is one particular style of writing recursive computational algorithms that gives the best time efficiency. It is called *tail-recursion*. The following is an example of a (non-tail) recursive function **ntrf** that calculates the sum of the consecutive **n** numbers:

```
(defun recsum (n)
       (cond ((zerop n) 0)
             (t (+ n (recsum (- n 1)))))))
```

A tail-recursive version of it is written as follows:

```
(defun trecsum (n & optional (counter 0))
       (cond ((zerop n) counter)
             (t (trecsum (- n 1) (+ counter n))))))
```

Here notice that at each iteration, the tail-recursive version calls itself last and by this is effectively storing, within itself, the previously calculated value. The reason why tail-recursion is faster is because the function needs to descend only n levels to 0 for the result to be calculated instead of $2n$

in the other case. Here is an example of the difference in CPU times for a summation of the first two million numbers (under CMU LISP):

```
* (time (recsum 2000000))

; Evaluation took:
;    1.52 seconds of real time
;    1.398788 seconds of user run time
;    0.085987 seconds of system run time
;    2,261,131,656 CPU cycles
;    [Run times include 0.59 seconds GC run time]
;    0 page faults and
;    47,213,832 bytes consed.

2000001000000

* (time (trecsum 2000000))

; Evaluation took:
;    0.93 seconds of real time
;    0.829874 seconds of user run time
;    0.077988 seconds of system run time
;    1,398,247,564 CPU cycles
;    [Run times include 0.05 seconds GC run time]
;    0 page faults and
;    47,993,808 bytes consed.

2000001000000

*
```

If all the FSM calculations for the swarm agents are designed to be recursive in the above sense, the whole swarm can be recalculated in one synchronized cycle. The effect of this computational efficiency can be quantified and demonstrated. For example, Figure 22.1 shows the comparative statistics on CPU time for the calculations of two swarms of 400 moving-average crossover models.

$$SAS_1 = \{S(a, b)|a, b \in \{3, 4, \ldots, 22\}\}$$

based on SMAs with lookback periods a and b, compared to

$$SAS_2 = \{E(\alpha, \beta)|\alpha, \beta \in \{2/(3 + 1), 2/(4 + 1), \ldots, 2/(22 + 1)\}\}$$

Additive Swarm Calculation Comparison		
	SMA	**AMA**
Indicators: Additions per tick	10,000	400
Indicators: Multiplications per tick	400	800
Fitnesses (NAVMOM(20)): Additions per tick	16,000	800
Fitnesses (NAVMOM(20)): Multiplications per tick	400	1,600
Swarm Agent Aggregation: Additions per tick	400	400
Total Calculations per Tick	27,200	4,000
Time Per Calculation (sec)	4.65E-07	4.65E-07
Total Time per tick (sec)	0.012648	0.00186
Total time (sec)	1,264.80	186.00
Total time (min)	21.08	3.10
Recursion Efficiency		6.8

FIGURE 22.1 Recursion and Computational Efficiency

based on EMAs with equivalent sensitivities as per the preceding formula. The $AMA(2/(n+1))$ can be seen as a tail-recursive version of an $SMA(n)$ where instead of n additions and one division, the system performs one addition and two multiplications. The additive swarm uses the $NAVMOM(20)$ fitness functions on 20 past observations for each agent. 100,000 ticks are taken to produce the statistics on full calculation time as well as average time per tick.

22.3 NUMERIC EFFICIENCY

Another important element is the way data is presented for computations. As a general rule, floating point operations (FLOPs) are more CPU time-consuming than the integer (or long integer) operations unless the processor is designed specifically for floating point manipulations. In the markets, the prices are by definition discrete. Only a handful of markets are quoted with more than three digits after the decimal, like the Natural Gas and Silver futures with three digits, most currencies with either two, four, or five digits, and US Fixed Income with at most with five digits (1/32).

The author found that programming the strategies so as to calculate all the indicators with long integers produces a run and simulation time gain on the order of 20 percent relative to the simpler but naive approach of using double-precision floating point representation. This is significant both for simulations and for optimizing the overall latency of the trading node. For example, here are two routines that add a series of random integer and floating point numbers. Their time and memory statistics for a run on 1 million numbers follow.

```
(defun inttest (n)
  (let ((result 1)
        (op 0))
    (dotimes (i n)
      (setf op (random 2))
      (if (zerop op)
          (setf result (+ result (+ 1 (random 10))))
          (setf result (- result (+ 1 (random 10))))))
    result))

(defun floattest (n)
  (let ((result 1.0)
        (op 0))
    (dotimes (i n)
      (setf op (random 2))
      (if (zerop op)
          (setf result (+ result (+ 1 (coerce (random 10) 'double-
float))))
          (setf result (- result (+ 1 (coerce (random 10) 'double-
float))))))
    result))

* (time (inttest 1000000))
; Evaluation took:
;    18.74 seconds of real time
;    18.308216 seconds of user run time
;    0.287956 seconds of system run time
;    28,035,164,804 CPU cycles
;    [Run times include 0.19 seconds GC run time]
;    0 page faults and
;    140,042,304 bytes consed.

-2254

* (time (floattest 1000000))

; Evaluation took:
;    23.96 seconds of real time
;    23.341452 seconds of user run time
;    0.436934 seconds of system run time
;    35,838,935,444 CPU cycles
;    [Run times include 0.25 seconds GC run time]
;    0 page faults and
;    204,041,704 bytes consed.

456.0d0

*
```

In order to implement a representation of the agents using long integers, one has to perform a "quantization" of all the relevant calculations for indicators and, desirably, for the fitness measures. The FSM representation also needs to be potentially modified to accommodate such a change as seen in the following example.

To see how such a "quantization" should be performed on a concrete model, consider a SWMR swing mean-reversion strategy as introduced in Part One. This model exhibits counter-trading swings of a certain threshold that are scaled by a rolling measure of volatility. It depends on four parameters, integers N and M, and floats α and β. Figure 7.9 of Part One is the full FSM state-transition matrix in traditional floating-point representation.

When the model starts from the *INIT* state the indicators are initialized by receiving a time period $N * M$ of prices that is an integer multiple of a 24-hour trading period (so as to remove intraday seasonality of volatility across time zones). The data is sliced into M-minute bars and the percent average range is computed via the formula

$$PAR(0) = (2/N) \sum_{i=1}^{N} (H_i - L_i)/(H_i + L_i)$$

where H_i and L_i are respective high and low traded prices in bar i. This *PAR* is recalculated every M minutes and a new value is stored for indicator calculations when the model transitions states.

At the end of the $N * M$ period, the model transitions to the *START* state and the first traded price P_0 defines the upper and lower trigger prices

$$S = P_0(1 + 0.5\alpha PAR(0)), \ L = P_0(1 - 0.5\alpha PAR(0))$$

The model remains in that state until the price breaches this channel. Here, the situation when the price breaches the lower channel is described in detail. The opposite situation is symmetric, and the reader would be able to follow the transitions from the FSM matrix.

In the situation where $P < L$, the model transitions into the *LONG* state and sends a buy order to the OMS at L or better. The following indicators are calculated

$$S = L(1 + \alpha PAR(1)) \ and \ SL = L(1 - \beta PAR(1))$$

and are the respective short reversal and stop from long levels and $PAR(1)$ is the latest *PAR* calculated before the state transition.

If the price keeps falling below L, S would ratchet down with it and be recalculated on every tick down:

$$S = P_{min}(1 + \alpha PAR(1))$$

whereas the SL remains the same. If then at a subsequent stage, the price trend reverses and $P > S > SL$, then the model transitions to the $SHORT$ state and sends an order to the OMS to reverse the position at S or better. The following indicators are then calculated

$$L = S(1 - \alpha PAR(2)) \; and \; SS = S(1 + \beta PAR(2))$$

where $PAR(2)$ is the latest PAR before this transition.

If, on the other hand, the price keeps falling and ticks below SL, then the OMS is ordered to sell stop at market, the position is flattened, and the model transitions to the $STOP - FROM - LONG$ state. At that stage, only short positions are permitted at a trigger level

$$S = SL * (1 + \alpha * PAR(2))$$

that ratchets down when the price keeps falling

$$S = P_{min}(1 + \alpha PAR(2))$$

If subsequently $P > S$, then the OMS triggers a sale at S or better and the model transitions to the $SHORT$ state.

Thus, the following four calculations are performed on every tick:

1. The current ith bar updates H_i and L_i by storing previous values and comparing to the current tick. At the end of the M-minute period the value $0.5(H_i - L_i)/(H_i + L_i)$ is stored in an array and the PAR is recalculated as an average of that array.
2. Depending on the state, either the L or the S level is updated by the above formula.
3. The comparisons $P < L$, $P < SL$, $P > S$, or $P > SS$ are performed, depending on the state.
4. If the tick entails a state transition, then additionally either the SS or the SL levels are calculated until the next state transition.

The quantization method replaces the inequalities that trigger the state transitions by equivalent inequalities on long integers. For this, first of all, one will multiply all prices by the necessary power of 10 so as to make them integer. Thus if Natural Gas futures are received as $P = 4.135$ by the translation layer, then they will be at the source transformed into $P^* = 4135$ for processing by the trading node.

The next step is to represent all the float numbers f as fractions f_n/f_d up to a certain precision p where $|f_d| < 10^p$. For example, if $p = 2$ and

SFL<L<S<SFS	SWMR Strategy: Swing Mean Reversion in LONG representation						
	P = Pn/Pd and L = Ln/Ld and S = Sn/Sd and SFL=SFLn/SFLd and SFS=SFSn/SFSd						
	Profit states are never attained						
	SFL, SFS are constants defined at the time of a transition from Init, Stop, Profit to Long or to Short						
	Init	Long	StopFromLong	ProfitFromLong	Short	StopFromShort	ProfitFromShort
Init	Ln*Pd*Sd<Ld*Pn*Sd<Ld*Pd*Sn	NIL	NIL	NIL	NIL	NIL	NIL
Long	SFLn*Pd*Sd<SFLd*Pn*Ld<SFLd*Pd*Ln	SFLn*Pd*Sd<SFLd*Pn*Sd<SFLd*Pd*Sn	Pn*Sd<Pd*Sn	NIL	SFLn*Pd*Ld<SFLn*Pn*Ld<SFLd*Pd*Ln	SFLn*Pd*Ld<SFLd*Pn*Ld<SFLd*Pd*Ln	NIL
StopFromLong	Pn*SFLd<=Pd*SFLn	Pn*SFLd<=Pd*SFLn	NIL	NIL	Pn*SFLd<=Pd*SFLn	Pn*SFLd<=Pd*SFLn	NIL
ProfitFromLong	NIL	NIL	NIL	NIL	NIL	NIL	NIL
Short	Sn*Pd*SFSd<Sd*Pn*SFSd<Sd*Pd*SFSn	Sn*Pd*SFSd<Sd*Pn*SFSd<Sd*Pd*SFSn	Ln*Pd*SFSd<Ld*Pn*SFSd<Ld*Pd*SFSn	NIL	Sn*Pd*SFSd<Sd*Pn*SFSd<Sd*Pd*SFSn	Ln*Pd*SFSd<Ld*Pn*SFSd<Ld*Pd*SFSn	NIL
StopFromShort	Pn*SFSd>Pd*SFSn	Pn*SFSd>Pd*SFSn	Pn*SFSd>Pd*SFSn	NIL	Pn*SFSd>Pd*SFSn	Pn*Ld>Pd*Ln	NIL
ProfitFromShort	NIL	NIL	NIL	NIL	NIL	NIL	NIL

FIGURE 22.2 FSM for SWMR Using Longs

$\alpha = 1.125$ then one can represent it as $\alpha = 1125/1000 = 9/8$. Then, for example, the comparison $P > S$ becomes

$$P^*\alpha_d PAR_d > P^*_{min}(\alpha_d PAR_d + \alpha_n PAR_n)$$

and so on and so forth for all the other inequalities that comprise the FSM transition matrix. The new FSM representation using longs is shown in Figure 22.2.

The updating of the PAR is happens only every M minutes and should be done in a separate thread. It could be optimized further by replacing the N-bar moving average by the corresponding recursive EMA, as discussed in the last section. It is then passed to the FSM as two long components of the approximating fraction PAR_n/PAR_d with precision p.

In order to implement the quantization of the FSM, one needs to ensure that no major loss of computational precision occurs. The maximal allowable precision p is a function of (1) the maximal long integer representation given by the compiler and (2) the complexity of the FSM calculations. Currently, under Java and C++, an 8-byte positive long integer is bound by

$$I_{max} = 18,446,744,073,709,551,615 = 2^{64} - 1 = 1.8 * 10^{19}$$

The quantized FSM inequalities above all contain terms that are multiplications of three integers. Thus to be safe, each of those integers should be less than $I_{max}^{1/3} = 2,642,245 = 2 * 10^6$. Hence the allowable precision is $p = 6$ and any floats above 0.000001 can be represented without loss of precision.

The approach presented here is usually more than sufficient for a very wide variety of strategies.

CHAPTER 23

Connectivity to Electronic
Commerce Networks

The external world of the trading infrastructure consists of the collection of electronic trading venues to which it is connected. Each electronic commerce network (ECN) has specific requirements and subtleties that need to be taken into account when building the connections.

These subtleties are ironed out during the certification phase that all ECNs require. Many of them also give access to simulated environments where no real trading may ever occur, but order placement, cancellation, disconnects, and all other features can be tested with no risk of losing money.

This chapter focuses on the situation where a certification phase has been completed and no issues remain as far as the raw connectivity to an ECN is concerned. The ECN can receive orders, send confirmations, cancellations, and fills, and, potentially through another channel, send price and order book updates.

23.1 ADAPTORS

It is important to realize that often the connectivity to the price source of the ECN and the order placement conduit are two different matters, and may require two different adaptors.

The adaptor manages the connectivity and maintains the heartbeat with the ECN. It listens to the heartbeat and emits one as well. If the connection is lost, both the trading infrastructure and the ECN will be aware of the disconnect.

To reconnect properly, the adaptor keeps track of the sequence number that the ECN emits with each message and that pertains to this particular connection. When the adapter requests a reconnection, it sends its own stale sequence number to the ECN, which compares it with its current one. It will then reconnect and resend all the messages (fills, order cancellations, etc.) to the adaptor since that stale number. Hence no information is lost and the adaptor can now resume sending orders to the ECN.

23.2 THE TRANSLATION LAYER

Given the good functioning of the set of adaptors, the information is passed on to the translation layer. This layer's top-level architecture is shown in Figure 23.1.

23.2.1 Orders: FIX

Most ECNs currently support a version of the FIX protocol for passing order and fill updates, and many use it for price updates as well.

A typical FIX message contains all the necessary fields to unambiguously identify the transaction. It is a series of (field number, field value) pairs and only the pairs with non-null values are transmitted for parsimony.

A FIX engine translates the message into an object in the domain model of the trading node. It also translates particular objects back into FIX messages to be sent to the specific adaptor that relays it to the ECN for which that message is intended.

There are several high-performance commercial and open source FIX engines, and there really is no point in reinventing the wheel in that domain.

The translation from FIX to the domain model is achieved in two stages. The FIX engine usually comes with a Java, C++, or .NET wrapper that has its own domain model. This consists of a set of basic classes representing orders,

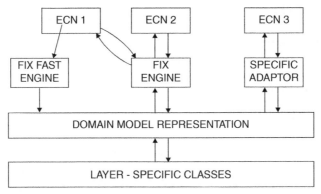

FIGURE 23.1 Translation Layer Architecture

fills, and prices and gives the first step toward representing the information in one of the trading infrastructure's languages. The translation layer, however, transforms those basic classes into its own domain model and potentially translates it into an altogether different language from the one provided by the FIX engine (e.g., Java to LISP).

23.2.2 Specific ECNs

Some ECNs have their own specific adaptors that use a proprietary protocol for data transmission. For example, in FX and fixed income, many banks provide connectivity to their market-making desks without using FIX. These ECNs provide Java, C++, or .NET adaptors to their streams, and those support, in one application, the communications pertaining to order routing and price updates.

From a maintenance perspective, it is more efficient to connect to such specific trading venues also via FIX, if and when supported. The FIX engines discussed above are designed for aggregating the connections to several ECNs at once, hence giving a plug-and-play scalability.

23.2.3 Price Sources: FAST

FIX is unfortunately very verbose and quite cumbersome, especially for transmission of basic data. Cracking FIX messages takes time and can impede the operation of the trading node in situations of market stress and large message throughput.

Some major ECNs use the ITCH protocol that is adapted to carry very lean messages for price and order book updates, but it is only a one-way direct data-feed protocol that does not support order passing.

The FAST protocol, which stands for FIX adapted for streaming, is a much lighter and more efficient data representation and compression mechanism than FIX. It achieves compression rates of 90 percent relative to either the original FIX messages or the native proprietary protocols that some ECNs use.

FAST is particularly adapted for streaming price and order book data, and decreases the effective latency (which includes the whole roundtrip ECN→trading node→ECN). Thanks to the higher compression rate, it uses much less bandwidth.

FAST has been compared and stress-tested against the proprietary ITCH protocol that is used by some major ECNs (see [fixglobal ITCH-FAST]). The results are that the bandwidth utilization of FAST is half that of ITCH, and that the speed of decoding and encoding is the same at roughly 100ns/message.

23.3 DEALING WITH LATENCY

There are several sources of latency, some that are within the control of the designer of the trading architecture and some that are not. The following are the two main sources:

1. External: Once the message has been sent by the adaptor, it leaves the trading infrastructure and potentially goes over a wire to a pipe (T1 line), gets processed by the ECN, comes back from the ECN on the T1, and then on the wire.
2. Internal: Once the message is received by the adaptor, it gets translated by the translation layer, then processed by the aggregator/disaggregator layer, by the OMS, and then by the control layer. A decision is potentially made that goes back to the OMS, aggregator/disaggregator layer, and back to the translation layer, then finally the adaptor.

23.3.1 External Constraints and Co-Location

The external constraints can be divided into hardware and ECN response time. Hardware constraints can be solved, but of course at a high cost. They are minimized by either installing dedicated pipes (T1 or multiple T1 lines), or even better, going the co-location route.

In the situation of installing dedicated pipes and avoiding any wires in between, the latency becomes purely a function of the physical length L of the fiber-optic pipe, hence the communications latency will be $2L/c$ where c is the speed of light. So for example, if one were to connect from Wellington, New Zealand, to the Eurex in Frankfurt, via a T1 line that would go around half the Earth, the latency would be on the order of $2*20,000/300,000 = 132$ ms. Of course, no one is going to lay a T1 all the way from the Antipodes, so a satellite would be used, and the latency would become much larger (to the order of a second), as the telecom satellites are usually on high orbits.

The co-location option reduces the communications latency to almost zero. It is a costly exercise and comes with a certain amount of constraints on the data that can be handled by the server.

Usually the ECNs are guarding the price updates very close to their chest. It is a big money business selling prices and ticks, and the exchanges make money on it. So the exchanges prohibit re-broadcasting of ticks outside of the trading node, unless there are specific licenses in place signed with end-users (e.g., customers using bank trading platforms).

In a co-location scenario, usually part of the trading node sits physically at the exchange (or the co-location site that is near). The latency-critical

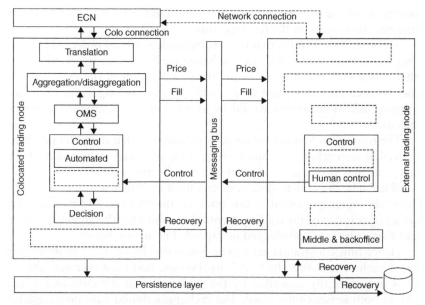

FIGURE 23.2 Architecture for Co-Location

translation, aggregation/disaggregation, OMS, and control layers would be running on machines sitting in the racks of the exchange. However, the physical elements of the persistence layer would not be, as well as the middle office, which would be based in the trading business's offices. Also the human control layer would be remote as well.

The flexible architecture for the trading infrastructure described in this book involves the use of memory cache and messaging bus technologies. As the information has to leave the exchange via those media back to home base, it is very important that an agreement and thorough understanding is in place with the exchange as to the nature and function of the data involved. In my experience dealing with a co-location project, this openness was very welcomed by the exchange officials, who originally were very uneasy about allowing the outbound communication of any data that was not directly related to orders and fills. Figure 23.2. shows an architecture of a co-located trading node.

23.3.2 Avoid Being Short the Latency Option

Whether a trading node is co-located or not, it is still short an option as far as the relationship with the ECN is concerned. Namely, the ECN puts constraints on the response-time of the client, but the client cannot put such stringent constraints on the response-time of the ECN.

Suppose, for example, that the trading node sends an order, and the latency happens at the level of the exchange itself (systems overload or any other problem that is specific to the timely operation of the matching engine). This can be discovered very quickly because as long as the exchange is connected, its heartbeat would be visible, and the timestamps remain objective.

The trading node waits for an acknowledgment that the order had been received by the exchange. While waiting, the market moves on, and the trading agents may no longer want that order in the market.

What state does the trading node find itself in, if such a situation occurs? The OMS design presented in this book is conservative, and would block further operations of the trading agents that submitted the aggregate order, until that order is acknowledged or cancelled by the exchange.

Hence time constraints need to be negotiated by the ECN to make sure that if such time is breached, and no response had been received, the order is automatically cancelled by the exchange and the customer is not held, in both senses of the word. The exchanges should have no excuse for making customers wait longer than necessary, given that they have developed the most sophisticated infrastructures. Hence the management of the trading business should strive to minimize as much as possible being short the operational latency option of any trading venue used.

23.3.3 Synchronization under Constraints

Connecting to several ECNs at once comes with its own subtleties, especially if one wants to implement trading strategies that consume synchronous collections of market update events.

Assume that one is interested in a pair-trading strategy between exchanges ECN_A and ECN_B and assume that the one-way communication latencies to the trading node are respectively L_A and L_B. The ECNs give clients maximal times T_A and T_B to react to a quote (before it is changed). Assume that the trading node receives a quote from A at time t. Any quotes from B received before $t - (T_B - 2L_B)$ are already stale. Any quotes received after $t + (T_A - 2L_A)$ will not be useful for trading against the original quote from A. Hence for any quote received from B in between those times, the trading node can implement the pairs strategy, sending respective buy and sell orders to the two exchanges at the same time.

The above is, of course, a very simple example of a situation that is quite complicated. Some companies specializing in ECN connectivity and client trading platforms have set up various relay nodes across the world to facilitate such synchronization between exchanges.

23.3.4 Improving Internal Latency

The internal latency constraints fall into three categories, namely translation, normal processing, and processing bottlenecks.

Translation has been dealt with above, and the conclusion is, at the time of the writing of this book, that FAST seems to be the most efficient protocol. It is efficient both in the cracking of messages at below 100ns/message, and in the reduced bandwidth usage, thanks to the compactness of its format.

The architecture presented in this book has been designed with the goal of minimizing the processing time of a translated message (order, fill, or market update event). It involves the distributed computing paradigm for running trading nodes concurrently, parallel processing of the FSMs of a collection of agents, and numeric efficiency stemming from the representation of data by long integers, where possible.

Processing bottlenecks can be reduced by a careful tuning of the GC process (or careful memory management and explicit destruction of unwanted instances of objects). The importance of tuning GC correctly cannot be overemphasized.

There are some further improvements that can be made from the computing hardware side, namely using FPGAs for FAST coding/encoding and GPUs for parallel processing of the agents' FSMs, especially in the context of supporting a swarm system.

CHAPTER 24

The Aggregation and Disaggregation Layer

The aggregation/disaggregation layer (ADL) provides an important element of efficiency when the trading node is composed of multiple trading agents per security. Its function is to aggregate orders coming from the OMS to be sent to the ECNs and disaggregate between the agents the resulting incoming fills from the ECNs.

The layer also provides the filtering and aggregation of multiple price sources for one security, as is often the case in FX and fixed income and equity dark pools.

Its top-level structure is described in Figure 24.1. It is composed of the synthetic book aggregator (SBA), order aggregator/disaggregator (OAD), and fills disaggregator (FD).

It is important to note that in some implementations, the ADL is an integral part of the OMS layer. Here it is discussed separately for more generality, but the reader should keep in mind that this layer is effectively the order management system for the resulting aggregate agent as defined in Part One.

The ensuing discussion about the OMS in the next chapter focuses on the control and feedback mechanisms between the OMS and the control layers, rather than on the specifics of the aggregation of agents' orders or price quotes.

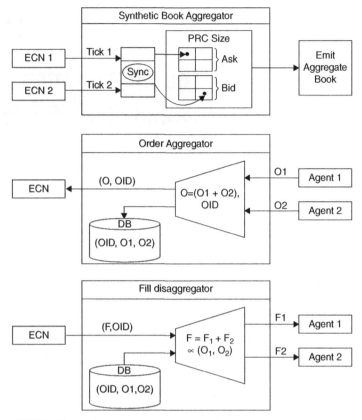

FIGURE 24.1 Aggregation-Disaggregation Layer

24.1 QUOTES FILTERING AND BOOK AGGREGATION

For the purpose of relaying market update events to the trading node's control layer, the aggregation/disaggregation layer acts as the primary filter and sometimes as an aggregator.

24.1.1 Filtering Quotes

The types of market update events that come from ECNs vary, and are dealt with by the translation layer. For example, exchanges send order book updates while banks' FX market-making desks send a two-way bid-offer stream with either an implicit or explicit size.

Sometimes there are errors in the quotes (false spikes or the wrong big figure printed), sometimes the quotes are too wide to be tradable, and sometimes they are not tradable at all (grayed out). Sometimes they are just stale, as happened during the Flash Crash of 2010.

The first step is to decide what quotes to relay to the control layer, and a price filter needs to be implemented by the price aggregator. The filter needs to monitor the following, at a minimum:

- Price relative to a band around the recent history
- Bid-ask spread relative to a rolling history and the expected average spread at that time of day
- Timestamp relative to the Universal Time adjusted by the average communications latency for the given ECN

24.1.2 Synthetic Order Book

Individual filtered quotes and order book updates from various ECNs for one security can be assembled into a synchronous synthetic order book.

The order book will change with the arrival of any new information, unless for all price levels, the aggregate size across ECNs is unchanged. The ADL keeps track of the constituents of the synthetic order book, because when an aggressive order is given, the execution algo needs to know which ECNs the order should be routed to, and how it should be split between them.

Latency was touched on in the previous chapter, especially in regard to connectivity to various ECNs. In the design and management of the synthetic order book, care should be taken to automatically remove stale quotes (quotes that would not be tradable because of communications latency).

24.2 ORDERS AGGREGATION AND FILLS DISAGGREGATION

For the purpose of relaying order status and fill update events to the trading node's OMS, the aggregation/disaggregation layer acts as a disaggregator. It acts as an aggregator on the way out from the trading node to the translation layer and on to the ECN.

24.2.1 Aggregating Positions and Orders

Assume the set of trading agents $A = \{a_1, \ldots, a_N\}$ consumes a particular market update event e. Each agent re-computes its desired market position in the security from which the event came from (it could be from an aggregated order book from various ECNs). Those computations are done concurrently and are synchronized and collected into the list $P(e) = \{p_1, \ldots, p_N\}$ by the OMS. Additionally, the OMS collects all the desired orders $O(e) = \{O_1(e), \ldots, O_N(e)\}$ where $O_i(e) = \{o_{ij}\}$ the individual set of orders emitted by agent i. It then compares the individual desired market positions to the actual ones, $M = \{m_1, \ldots, m_N\}$ and computes the vector $D = \{d_i\} = \{p_i - m_i\}$ of individual differences per agent.

The OMS sends these lists to the OAD. The OAD proceeds by aggregating the desired changes in market positions by summing up $AD(e) = \sum d_i$. In the case that the security is only traded in one trading venue, the OAD immediately sends to that trading venue the aggressive order that corresponds to $AD(e)$ (via, of course, the translation layer and the specific ECN adaptor). The aggressive order may or may not be routed to an algo, or would simply cross the bid-offer spread, like the **AGRESSOR** algo that was discussed in Part One.

The set of individual agent's orders lists $O(e)$ is treated in a similar fashion. Those, to be clear, are lists of limit orders (as all others are worked via algos, such as stop-losses or time stops). This means that it is a collection of bids below the market and offers above the market. The OAD module aggregates, if possible, limit orders by limit price. This way, when they are sent to the ECN, the FIFO principle would apply and there is no risk that two agents desiring the same price level for their limit would be in two different places in the ECN queue. Hence the $AO(e) = \{ao_k\}$ is sent to the ECN.

In the case that the security is traded across several trading venues, the aggressive trade order $AD(e)$, as well as the list of passive orders $AO(e)$, can be split across those venues according to an algorithm (e.g., gauging the different bid-ask spreads and volumes on those ECNs). This situation presents further complications, but the idea is the same as for one ECN. This is why this module is called the order aggregator/disaggregator, the disaggregation here is between ECNs.

To be clear, in the computational cycle of processing the market update event e, the OAD needs to wait for the OMS to communicate to it the result of the **consume** cycle for all the agents. The results of the potentially parallel processing of all the FSMs at once are funnelled into the D and O lists at the OMS level, which passes this information to the OAD, along with the choice of the algo to use.

While this is happening, the arrival of new fills and market update events are blocked (queued), until the OAD receives acknowledgment that all aggressive orders have been placed. If an order rejection is received then the

OMS would attempt to replace the rejected order. The logic of dealing with those situations is deferred to the OMS discussion in the next chapter.

In the LISP implementation, the aggregation performed by the OAD can be represented by the **AGGREGATEAGENT** class discussed in Part One. The OAD itself becomes the order management system that pertains to this aggregate agent. The fills disaggregator presented below is the feedback that fairly allocates partial fills among the aggregate agent's members.

24.2.2 Fills Disaggregation

When a fill comes from a particular aggregated order, be it $AD(e)$ or any of the ao_k's, it needs to be allocated back to the set of agents who participated in the aggregate order. Very often only partial fills come and need to be allocated proportionally between agents. Suppose, instead of $AD(e)$, the ECN only sends $\mu AD(e)$ where $0 < \mu < 1$. Then the allocation across agents should be $P = \mu D = \{\mu d_1, \ldots, \mu d_N\}$, with of course the appropriate logic of rounding fractions down to integers and making sure that the excess from rounding is allocated correctly. The same would apply to any partial fill on a resting order $ao_k(e)$.

In the case when the security is traded across several ECNs, it does not make sense to aggregate the fills. Any fill that comes from any ECN is disaggregated according to the above discussion. The FD keeps track of the change in the individual security position across agents so as to treat the arrival of partials correctly.

The arrival of a fill would block (queue) the arrival of a new market update, until all agents are allocated that fill.

24.2.3 Book Transfers and Middle Office

It is important to point out that in some situations, no market access is needed whatsoever when agents change their states. For example, if agent A goes from a position of 1 to 0 while agent 2, on the contrary, wants to go from 0 to 1, no net trade results $(D = 0)$ and no $AD(e)$ order is sent out. From the accounting perspective, the aggregation/disaggregation level just performs a book transfer, at the mid-price of the market update event e, between the two agents' accounts.

In the implementation of the trading architecture, the ECN's, brokers, and custodians do not see the allocations or the positions of the individual agents. The ECNs only see the trades done and orders outstanding, the brokers whatever they need to give-up, and the custodian and administrator the aggregated trades and positions.

However, the trading node needs to keep all the information at the individual agent level, in order to track performance and fitness of various trading strategies. Hence a middle office database needs to be maintained that reflects exactly the data contained in the agents' classes. Memory caching helps to operate that database concurrently without inducing bottlenecks on the core computational process.

CHAPTER 25

The OMS Layer

I n the present chapter it is assumed, for simplicity, that the control layer contains only one trading agent and that there is only one ECN to which the trading node is connected.

The goal is to discuss the possible degrees of interlinkage between the agent (i.e., the control layer) and the order management system.

The function of the OMS is to ensure that the desired market position and limit orders of the agent are reflected at the ECN, namely that they agree with the agent's market position and orders outstanding.

25.1 ORDER MANAGEMENT AS A RECURSIVE CONTROLLER

It is best to see the OMS as a recursive controller that has an explicit goal of making the external exposure state of the agent equal to its desired exposure state. Here *exposure state* means the agent's position in the security and the limit orders outstanding at the ECN. The external exposure state is what the ECN and the custodian see, and represents the legal exposure of the agent, as far as trading counterparties are concerned. The top-level design of the OMS is presented in Figure 25.1.

The design of the OMS feedback loop for the management of the agent's position and resting orders is described separately, and it is useful to consider two extreme types of control mechanism that agents may exhibit.

At one extreme, the aggressive agent (AA) identifies completely its state with the position it has in the market. When certain indicators trigger, the agent will change position at or near the prevailing price. The agent needs to be in the desired position, otherwise the logic of its operation is thrown, and it is in an undefined state and cannot process the next market update. By doing so, the agent accepts that it will incur a certain amount of price slippage.

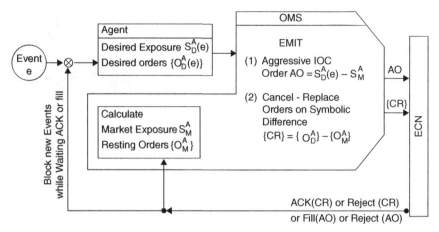

FIGURE 25.1   OMS

Examples of such agents are the trend-following and breakout strategies discussed in Part One.

At the other extreme, the passive agent (PA) worries about buying cheaper and selling more expensive every single unit of the security. It does not care how much stock it carries, as long as each time it buys a unit at P it aims at selling it above P. So the state of the agent is identified with its orders outstanding in the market. When the mid-price moves, the agent adjusts its resting bids and offers accordingly, trying to capture the oscillations of the market induced by waves of buyers and sellers who need instant liquidity and are ready to pay for it. In a sense, it is more appropriate to call this agent a patient agent rather than a passive agent. Example of such strategies are pure market-making strategies and limit-order–driven mean-reversion strategies.

The difference between the nature of the two agents needs to be emphasized here. The passive agent is not relaxed about price at the expense of uncertainty in its position, whereas the aggressive agent is not relaxed about its position at the expense of the uncertainty in price.

Unfortunately, akin to the Uncertainty Principle in physics, there is no way to be not relaxed about price and quantity at the same time, because it is inherently limited by the available liquidity.

This means that the design of a strategy needs to reflect the optionality of the position in the passive case, or the optionality of the execution price in the aggressive case. The nature of the coupling between the OMS and the agent is driven by this difference.

25.1.1   Management of Positions

In the aggressive case, the OMS and the agent are de-coupled. The OMS is basically an executor of the agent's change in its `positions`.

Assume that after consuming event e, the AA's desired position is P_0 but its position in the market is M_0. This means that there are no other orders outstanding (residuals or nearby resting orders) that can change the agent's market position in the immediate future. The OMS emits an immediate or cancel (IOC) aggressive order for $P_0 - M_0$ at the current best price or worse. While it waits for the acknowledgment, the agent cannot process any other market updates. The acknowledgment comes for a partial fill $|F_1| < |P_0 - M_0|$. The OMS then communicates the new position to the agent, and opens the agent to the consumption of the next market update.

After consumption of the event, the agent determines that now it needs to have position P_1. Its market position is $M_0 + F_1$, so the OMS will emit an aggressive order for $P_1 - (M_0 + F_1)$.

When the OMS acts in the aggressive capacity, it is of utmost importance to receive the fill information (none, partial, or full) before unlocking the agent to any further market update event, and that the residual order is cancelled. This is why an IOC order should be used.

If the ECN does not support IOCs, such logic should be implemented by the OMS directly, by cancelling the residual immediately after receiving the partial. However, due to communication latency, such a home-based approach would not be as good as a native IOC execution. The designer could also use the fill-or-kill orders (all or none) with no partial fills, if available.

In general, one needs to design the aggressive agents so that the average time between the agent-generated repositioning signals are more than $G = H + L + K + L + H$ where L is the one-way communications latency, H is the home-based complete computational cycle time, and K is the expected pessimistic response frequency of the ECN. K is an estimate of how long it takes for the ECN to acknowledge and accept or reject an order, before sending it back to the trading node.

It is safer to design the aggressive trading strategy so that the potential changes in desired position are a multiple of the minimal granularity G. This helps to de-couple the agent from the OMS as much as possible.

25.1.2   Management of Resting Orders

In the passive case, the OMS and the agent are completely coupled. In a way the agent *is* an OMS endowed with specific logic.

Assume for the sake of illustration that the agent is short inventory I and is waiting to buy it back at price P. After consuming an event e, the PA's desired resting order changes. It may either widen to $P_1 < P$ or improve to $P_2 > P$.

The OMS emits a cancel-replace order to change the limit price and the size, but does not lock the agent from processing any market updates or fills.

While the OMS waits for an acknowledgment of the cancel-replace, the agent is not allowed to emit any other order changes.

Assume an acknowledgment is received and the OMS managed to perform the cancel-replace. Then the agent is allowed to change it again on the next event update.

Assume now that instead, a rejection is received. This, with high probability, means that the original order was being partially filled when the OMS tried cancel-replacing it (at least this is the rule in the FIX protocol specification). In either event the inventory is either the same, or most probably had been reduced, so that the agent carries less risk.

At that point the agent-OMS couple may have various strategies. One is to do nothing until the earliest of the following information is received:

- Either a partial or full fill, which means that the market was hitting the agent's bid, while the price updates are all at its bid P.
- A tick up which means that the agent has been partially filled but has not yet received the fill information.
- A tick down which means that the agent has to be done on its full size.

It is important to note that the price information sometimes comes faster than the fill information.

In the third case the agent does not need to wait for the fill confirmation and would recalculate its state with the certainty that its order was filled. In the first case there is still uncertainty as to what the fill size is because even if the first partial has been received, the rest may still be queued by the ECN.

So the second and first cases are similar, and require being relaxed about time. The conservative approach is to wait until all fills are received and the price ticked up. Then the remainder of the order can be cancel-replaced when the market moves away. The fact is that the agent is first in the queue at price P in the first two cases (however, as discussed in Chapter 8 on market-making, the LMMs may still have precedence over the agent in certain exchanges).

25.1.3 Algorithmic Orders

When an agent emits an algorithmic order, be it internal to the trading node, or external and worked via a broker's platform, it implicitly assumes that this order will take a substantial amount of time. Here *substantial* means relative to frequency of arrival of the market update events.

In other words, the strategy of the agent or its willingness to amend the order is unlikely to change while the order is in force. For example, institutional investors working TWAP for large stock orders are not likely to be interested in the tick-by-tick fluctuations of the tape.

Most algo orders are hiding the full order size to the market, and selectively choose when to trade small clips either at market or with limit orders. Those clips can be pulled out of the market with very low consequences on slippage, hence that agent would know almost immediately what its residual unfilled size is. The strategies that use algos should not be sensitive to those relatively small uncertainties, and the concerns regarding immediacy of knowledge that were presented for the AAs and PAs should not apply to the same extent here.

25.2 CONTROL UNDER STRESS

The previous section dealt with the normal OMS-agent operation in the context of the lack of immediate responses or order cancellations from the ECN. Those issues happen all the time and the logic of dealing with them needs to be built in both at the OMS and the agent level. During normal operations, the OMS-agent system achieves coherence between the internal and the external exposure states within a time frame that is acceptable by the agent's strategy.

Because of potential internal and external problems, inclusive of power-downs, disconnects, and computational bottlenecks, it is not always obvious that the external and internal exposure states of the trading agent are the same. Those are not normal situations and great care needs to be taken in dealing with them exhaustively. Chapter 21 on recovery mechanisms already pointed out avenues to minimize the P&L impact in such unpleasant situations, from a global architectural standpoint.

The OMS also needs to be designed so that it always knows how to recover its external state in order to service the agent correctly. After a reconnect, the external state needs to be known as soon as possible, before any further processing by the agent can happen.

The OMS needs to have a built-in mechanism to automatically request the full list of outstanding orders from the ECN, as well as the history of fills since disconnect (by comparing sequence numbers).

After reconnection, a recovery period may ensue when the agent replays the history of fills and market updates to regain the correct FSM state. During that replay, the OMS-agent system acts as a simulator. At the time when the recovery simulation run catches up with the real-time market updates, the agent-OMS system is switched back on and starts performing its recursive differentiator function again as per normal.

In my practical experience it is always better to side with caution when designing the operation of the OMS. The degree of its interaction (coupling) with the agent is a function of the agent's strategy and this coupling presents an operational constraint that needs to be respected. The design of an efficient recovery mechanism needs to take into account the specific interaction between the OMS and the agent.

25.3 DESIGNING A FLEXIBLE OMS

The discussion above clearly points out the different levels of coupling between the OMS and the agent. The OMS is a service to the agent, and in its task to optimize that service it may sometimes requires a design where it literally morphs into the agent.

In my experience, to balance flexibility with efficiency, it is better to design the aggressive and the passive OMS separately and treat them as two separate but concurrent services for an agent.

A mostly passive agent may need from time to time the aggressive OMS to stop itself out of excess inventory. A mostly aggressive agent may use the passive OMS to place profit-taking orders. It is also sometimes useful to disaggregate a mixed agent into a set of aggressive and passive communicating agents that use the respective OMSs.

It is not necessarily optimal to have a one-size-fits-all OMS, and the reader needs to assess the business needs first, before either designing one or shopping for off-the-shelf solutions.

CHAPTER 26

The Human Control Layer

I t is of paramount importance to endow the trading infrastructure with an extensive set of monitoring tools and manual control mechanisms. The design of the trading node is complex, and complexity does not usually come error-free. Even without errors, the era of completely automated systems is still the stuff of science fiction, and whatever the degree of autonomy achieved, human control should still take precedence.

The role of the human control layer (HCL) is to provide some invasive control tools and some noninvasive monitoring tools ranging from the individual trading agents to the collection of trading nodes across securities. The HCL also contains the human-controlled component of the risk management layer that is discussed in the next chapter.

The components of the HCL are distributed and use the messaging bus to communicate with the rest of the trading infrastructure. They do not consume any of the core layer resources and should preferably be run on different servers altogether. The architecture and components of the HCL are shown in Figure 26.1.

26.1 DASHBOARD AND SMART SCHEDULER

The dashboard is a manual interface that allows the (re)setting of the agent's parameters and states, parameters of the swarm, position limits, and so on.

The smart scheduler helps to manage periodic de-riskings before shutdowns (e.g., into weekends and holidays).

26.1.1 Parameter Control

This module of the dashboard can directly set or modify the agents' classes with new parameters (be they numeric or functional, such as fitness functions and agents' algos). It provides the finest grain of monitoring and control over the whole set of individual agents. An example of it is shown in Figure 26.2.

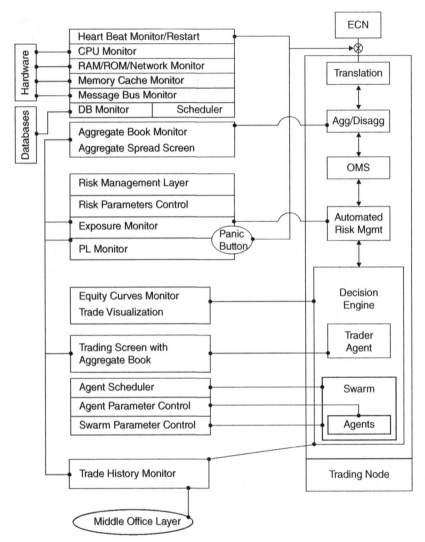

FIGURE 26.1 Components of the Human Control Layer

26.1.2 Scheduled Flattening of Exposure

The smart scheduler allows the trading node to gracefully exit out of positions ahead of scheduled events. It could be ahead of the weekend or ahead of the non-farm payrolls release. The scheduler is to disallow strategies that are flat from going into new positions, if the average trade duration is longer than the time left before the event. Also, strategies that flip positions ahead

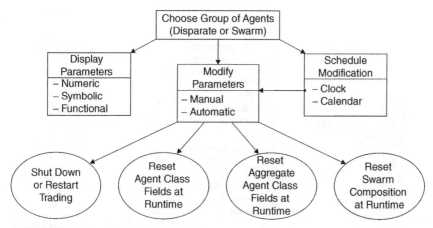

FIGURE 26.2   Trading Node Dashboard

of the event would be flattened instead. The set of agents that are still in position coming into the scheduled flattening would be exited at the net aggregate exposure.

26.2   MANUAL ORDERS AGGREGATOR

The functionality of the trading infrastructure extends naturally to handle a desk of human traders who would be internally represented by simple agents that take instructions from a trading screen application.

26.2.1   Representing a Trader by an Agent

A human trader is represented by a series of simple agents, each for a particular security and a particular strategy that the trader executes. For example, a good visual pattern trader would use the trading screen to execute, and each time would select a strategy switch (i.e., daily triangle breakout or weekly head and shoulders, etc.). The code representation of such a manually traded strategy would be an **AGENT** class (not an FSM agent), and the **update** method would simply read the position that the human trader has executed via the trading screen. The agent class contains the **positions** and **orders** fields and would automatically be calculating all the trade statistics and PL, which in turn would be reflected in the position and P&L monitor.

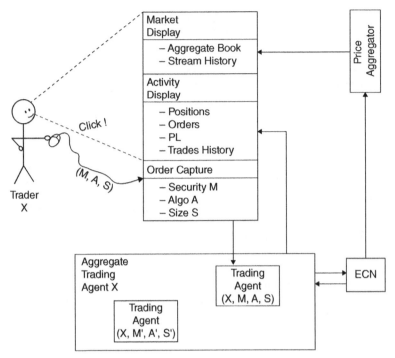

FIGURE 26.3 Trading Screen

26.2.2 Writing a Trading Screen

An example of a trading screen with a strategy switch is given in Figure 26.3. The actual screen displays the synthetic aggregated book with color-coding of the ECNs at each price level.

26.2.3 Monitoring Aggregated Streams

Another tool that helps to see liquidity on various markets visually is to plot the synthetic aggregated book in time. See Figure 26.4.

26.3 POSITION AND P & L MONITOR

Monitoring positions and P&Ls can be done for every single agent but also for any aggregation thereof. Swarm monitoring is provided by this module as well, showing the subset SFS of active agents, the aggregate size, and P&L.

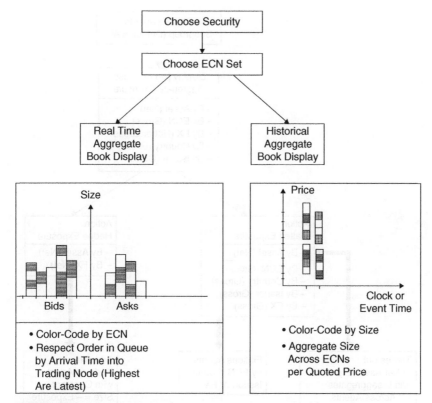

FIGURE 26.4 Stream Viewer

26.3.1 Real-Time Exposure Monitor

This module is designed for visual monitoring and for manual control. It is discussed in the next chapter constituting an important element of the risk management layer. It is shown in Figure 26.5.

26.3.2 Displaying Equity Curves

The individual agents contain the histories of their P&Ls and can be displayed on an individual or aggregate basis as shown in Figure 26.6.

26.3.3 Online Trade Statistics and Fitnesses

This module is important for understanding the performance of individual agents as well as for monitoring the swarm in real time. See Figure 26.7.

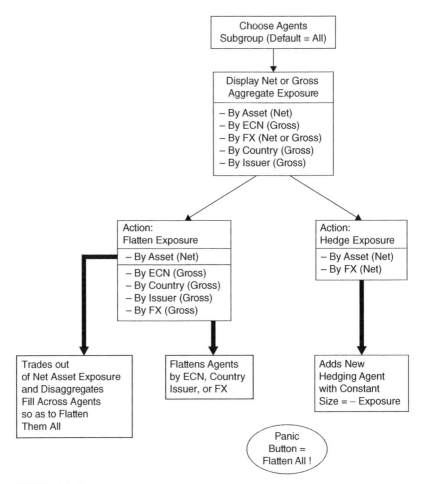

FIGURE 26.5 Exposure Monitor

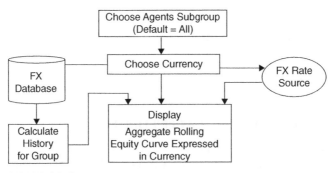

FIGURE 26.6 P & L Monitor

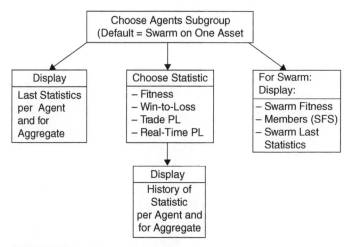

FIGURE 26.7   Fitness Monitor

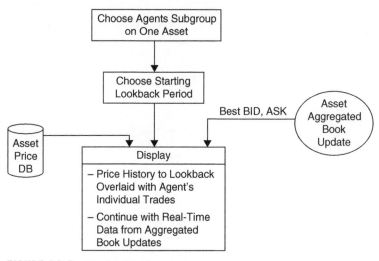

FIGURE 26.8   Trades Monitor

26.3.4 Trades Visualization Module

Trades from either individual or aggregated agents can be visualized in real time as seen in Figure 26.8.

CHAPTER 27

The Risk Management Layer

R isk management is the essence of self-preservation. In the trading world, self-preservation is akin to P&L preservation. Risks of losing money in an automated trading context are numerous, and losses come fast.

27.1 RISKY BUSINESS

The six major risks and ways in which they can be addressed are enumerated here:

1. Market Risk for Individual Agent. The strategy should be designed with money management and stop-loss mechanisms to prevent tail-event losses.
2. Model Risk. Strategies go in and out of favor as a function of the regime of the market. The adaptation embedded in the design of the swarm allows it to mitigate such situations.
3. Correlation Shocks. When strategies are deployed on several markets, sudden increases in the correlation of assets may create clusters of losses. This happens despite the fact that every single model has money management and participates in a swarm mechanism. A global aggregate PL monitor and associated money management need to be implemented.
4. Disconnects. It is always good to keep independent data sources, communication channels, and liquidity access. Good old brokers over copper phone lines and paper trade tickets can help save the day, basically.
5. Bottlenecks. Memory, computational, and communications bottlenecks need to be monitored by systems experts in order to control the infrastructure to reduce the particular resource load. Automatic price update throttling is sometimes a solution.

6. Race Conditions and Other Bugs. Those are the nastiest ones because they can lead to over-trading and disastrous losses. Thorough testing needs to be performed before launch. Red flags should go off when too many orders are generated by the system per unit of time, position sizes are breached, and so forth. Work needs to be done in cooperation with the sponsoring broker or the ECN itself to automatically short-circuit excess traffic.

Some risks are mitigated by the design of the trading logic, some need automated feedback mechanisms at the whole portfolio level, and some need human intervention.

27.2 AUTOMATED RISK MANAGEMENT

Here it is assumed that individual market risks are already addressed by the logic of the models and the risk of individual model performances by the design of the adaptive swarm. Therefore, the next risk is at the level of a porfolio of models across different assets.

Correlation shocks across assets can only be mitigated when the PL on the full portfolio is computed in real time, and a feedback mechanism exists between that PL and the aggregate positioning. This feedback mechanism is called the portfolio risk manager (PRM) and its top-level logic is described in Figure 27.1.

If the whole portfolio starts suddenly losing money, caused by a subset of agents, that subset will have its sizing cut down aggressively by the PRM. Overall, the size would be cut down when the winning agents' performance starts turning.

So instead of cutting positions across all agents proportionally, the PRM cuts the losers first and lets the winners run, in line with the old trading adage.

The real-time exposure monitor is endowed with an exposure dial-down control and would conservatively override the automated PRM (meaning that the manual intervention would only be allowed in the direction of risk reduction).

27.3 MANUAL RISK CONTROL
AND THE PANIC BUTTON

It is very hard to automate responses to risk that are not market-driven, like disconnects, bottlenecks, and race conditions.

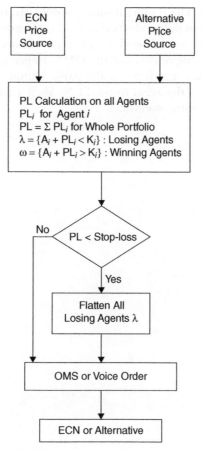

FIGURE 27.1   Risk Management Layer

To deal with disconnects from ECNs, at whatever level they happen, it is key to have access to an external data source in order to keep monitoring the P&L and risk levels in real time. This data source (like Bloomberg or Reuters) would bridge the disconnected ECN and keep the various HCL modules running. The data collected during a disconnect may also be used for replaying the events during the recovery phase.

In the stress situation when risk needs to be reduced but cannot be done via the ECN as the connection is down, the trading business would need to rely on the ability to reduce or hedge the position through a different (e.g., voice) channel. The trading business should always maintain various broker relationships in the products that the ECN trades.

Race conditions are altogether different because they may block transaction-critical components like the OMS. Hence dealing with them is not easy, and the only way is to hit the panic button that shuts down all communications from the agent to the ECN. Such a panic button appears on the real-time exposure monitor.

CHAPTER 28

The Core Engine Layer

The core engine layer consist of the set of trading agents and is the ultimate decision maker for the whole trading node. The central function of this innermost layer is to implement the consume method for each agent. Parts One through Three have been dedicated to the discussion of the implementation of individual agents, and this chapter presents some architectural guidelines.

28.1 ARCHITECTURE

The top-level diagram of the architecture of the core layer is shown in Figure 28.1. In the most general setting, the core layer is divided into the lists agents, ffc-agents, and aggregateagents that may or may not trade.

The members of the agents list fall into the following six categories:

1. Individual autonomous agents
2. Trader agents manually controlled via a trading screen
3. Hedge agents automatically invoked by the risk management system
4. Non-trading agents that are part of a trading aggregate agent
5. Non-trading agents that are FFC-controlled members of a swarm
6. Non-trading agents that emit events for the benefit of other agents or applications (e.g., bar generators)

There are various possible ways to implement the core layer. The simplest is to have all the agents run on the same CPU. In a multi-asset environment, however, this presents serious bottlenecks, so multithreading should be used in the following two ways:

1. Asynchronous threads: Market update events from different securities can be forked into individual asynchronous threads, as long as the

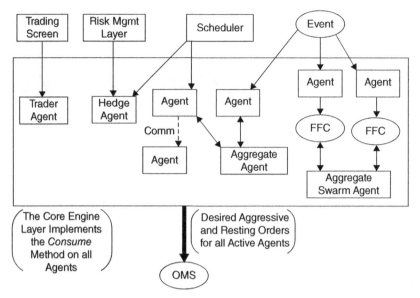

FIGURE 28.1   Core Engine Layer

agents do not require information on synchronized pairs or portfolios of assets. These threads invoke their own instances of the OMS and the aggregation-disaggregation layer.

2. Synchronized threads: For a particular market update thread, at the level of the aggregate agents and swarms operating on that asset, a synchronized forking can be implemented for the calculation of the individual agent's positioning and fitness. These synchronized threads join before entering the aggregate agent calculation.

If some subset of agents requires synchronized information on a set of quotes (pairs or portfolio trading), then the top-level asynchronous thread will be made to carry information on such a synchronized set of market update events. As discussed in a previous chapter, this architecture can also be implemented on a set of distributed hardware components. This helps to reduce the individual CPU overheads, memory usage, and IO bottlenecks. The best architecture ultimately is to have dedicated hardware for self-contained clusters of agents. Those consume different subsets of market events and do not communicate between clusters. The clusters may also be composed of different strategy styles. For example, it is always better to separate different hardware components' market-making activities from trading agents operating on a lower frequency.

28.2   SIMULATION AND RECOVERY

The importance of a robust architecture for the trading node cannot be overemphasized, and in this respect the core engine layer needs to be architected so as to avoid being the weakest link. It is clearly the layer that contains the most complexity and usually results from a hefty time and money investment in research and development. This engine, however, can be derailed by the malfunctioning of the other parts of the trading node, as discussed in the chapter on fault tolerance and recovery.

The best way, in my experience, to ensure recoverability is to endow the core engine layer with a dual purpose of simulator and real-time operation. This means that in the case of a market data disconnect, the recovery is made by replaying the recovered historical data in paper trading mode until such time as the history catches up with the real-time stream. This of course implies that the core engine layer should always operate at a fraction of its full capacity in the real-time trading mode versus simulated replay mode. The replay speed needs to be at least an order of magnitude faster than the real-time operation mode. In simple terms the replay mode should be capable of processing 10 times the amount of ticks per second as compared to the usual real-time throughput. During such a simulation replay no orders are being sent to the market. As soon as the replay catches up with the real-time data stream, the OMS is turned "live" and works out the difference between desired positions and orders at that time and the positions and orders that are actually live in the market. It then works to reduce those differences to zero and the state of the whole system falls in line with its historically desired state. It has been also emphasized that sometimes human intervention is inevitable, and hence it is always wise to keep good market access via voice brokers.

Another important aspect of the design of the core engine layer as both a real-time and simulation mechanism is that this approach ensures the closest possible fit between system development and trading. Often researchers develop trading models in one language or setting and they are then reimplemented in another language and a very different setting for the real-time implementation. Many tests need to be performed during such a translation phase and it most often wastes valuable time and resources. Access, however, to a development platform that has the same behavior in simulation as in real-time trading is very valuable and efficient. The approach taken by the author of being language-agnostic, in the sense that different ideas are best expressed in different languages, is not contradictory to this stance. Indeed, the various language interfaces, domain models, and foreign functions discussed earlier serve exactly the purpose of bridging the gap between efficient idea development and efficient implementation in the real world.

The ultimate design of the core engine is left to the reader's discretion. This is where the crux of the matter lies for ensuring the long-term profitability of the trading business. The author hopes that this book will help put the reader on the right path to achieve that ultimate goal.

CHAPTER 29

Some Practical
Implementation Aspects

This chapter gathers some further miscellaneous ideas and tips for what one will encounter during the implementation of the low latency trading architecture. It concludes by discussing the optimization of the design with specific modern hardware solutions.

29.1 ARCHITECTURE FOR BUILD AND PATCH RELEASES

The software behind the trading architecture is an evolving beast and even after several consecutive implementations, it is not necessarily possible to come up with a version that will remain static. However hard one tries to get everything spotless, there will always be some chopping and changing along the way. New ECNs and markets come online, hardware gets upgraded, and businesses change locations. Hence a degree of resilience needs to be built into the software to ensure smooth rollouts and, if needed, rollbacks.

29.1.1 Testing of Code before a Release

It is of paramount importance to test the new version of the code before releasing it into a production environment. The almost half-a-billion-dollar error that recently occured at a major brokerage house was probably due to inadequate testing.

The type of testing involved is a function of the layer of the infrastructure where the change in code is made. The deepest level occurs at the agent logic. When new agents are introduced into the swarm, their FSM logic should be tested first by simulating paths of realistic data with realistic slippage.

As was previously mentioned, it is very difficult to do this for strategies driven by limit orders, like the conditional market-making discussed in

Part One, because of the fundamental nonlinear nature of the market. The subtle feedbacks created by the sheer presence of a new strategy are not easy to model or predict. Hence, sometimes one needs to bite the bullet and release the new strategy with minimal possible absolute risk exposure, once connectivity and order-passing have been tested.

Most ECNs and direct market access vendors provide test environments for their specific connectivity and order management, and those should be used at all times before any new release.

Creating a realistic testing environment is difficult and cumbersome. It entails reproducing the set of glitches that can occur along with simulating normal behavior. An in-house testing environment should be built by integrating various ECN test environments with a simulation of faults occuring at each layer level. This is especially important in the case of a modular architecture where different layers are compiled separately and may reside on multiple hardware.

29.1.2 Versioning of Code and Builds

Once new code had been thoroughly tested, it is ready for production release. Prior to that it needs to be versioned so that all the changes can be recorded relative to the previous version.

In a multiple developer situation it is important to disaggregate the problem in such a way that there are no conflicts while a version of the code is being modified. The traditional code versioning systems like SVN operate like a non-recombining tree unless various parallel versions are merged into one by the group leader. The leader ought to keep track of the parallel versions and make sure they are tested in their own right.

When the branches are merged back by the head developer, the full testing will have to occur again. Only then can a new build be released into the wild, as shown in Figure 29.1.

29.1.3 Persistence of State during Version Releases

Some languages, like C++, require a full recompilation when changes occur. Some languages do not, and new pieces of code can be injected into either the Java Virtual Machine or the multithreaded LISP environment to be compiled on the fly.

However it is safer to stop the system completely and flatten the aggregate position on the shorter-term models altogether while releasing a new build.

If the new build contains changes to the agent classes or to any classes that are persisted in the cache, it is wiser to do a complete cache flush before

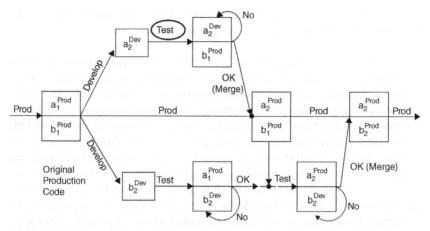

FIGURE 29.1   Releasing Code into Production

restart. The distributed memory cache architecture allows the state of the trading node to be preserved under the assumption that the structure of the persisted classes will not change at restart.

As a function of the adopted architecture, the restart would be performed according to one of the recovery procedures discussed previously. In general, it is wiser to perform such releases on the weekend when markets are closed.

29.2   HARDWARE CONSIDERATIONS

So far in this book, the models, algorithms, and software design patterns have been discussed independent of the hardware on which they run. A lot of emphasis has been given to the efficiency and resilience of the software implementation of the trading node.

The hardware aspect is an important component of the optimization of the whole process and should be considered carefully before the implementation. Given the fast evolution of the communications and computing technology, it is better to discuss the more general principles behind the analysis of the correct hardware architecture.

29.2.1   Bottleneck Analysis

Before choosing the hardware implementation, it is wise to perform a bottleneck analysis of the full flow of data, from events generated by an ECN to the orders being transmitted back to the ECN by the decision layer. The five principal bottlenecks and potential solutions are:

1. *Transmission Latency:* This is usually the largest contributor to the inefficiency and several techniques are used to mitigate it. The best but most expensive one is the co-location of the servers with the ECN. Co-location helps reduce the communication latency to microseconds from milliseconds (a factor of 1,000). Co-location is essential for successfully running market-making algorithms. The second solution is to use a series of dedicated fiber-optic communication lines (e.g., T-lines) from the ECNs to the server. This does not solve the problem of latency of communication along that line, which is directly proportional to its length.

2. *Computational Load:* In order to reduce the computational bottlenecks, parallel processing should be implemented wherever possible. For example, if the trading node runs independent strategies in a series of assets, it might make sense to distribute each asset computation onto separate hardware. New chip technologies discussed below could substantially contribute to the efficiency.

3. *Memory Load:* The memory bottleneck is related to the amount and size of objects needed at any point in time for the computational environment. The memory usage and its peaks depend on the software implementation. In Java the size of the virtual machine is settable and the garbage collection will be a function of that. As prices of RAM continue to go down, it becomes easier to expand the sizes of the computational environments. In an ideal situation one would like as much RAM as possible in order to avoid any garbage collection or object destruction, and flush the memory only at times when the markets are closed.

4. *Input-Output Load:* Some possible IO bottlenecks are related to communications between layers, between hardware components, and memory to processor. Some of them can be solved by software solutions, like the distributed memory caching that enables writing into physical storage an asynchronous process. Fast switches are used for optimizing communications between hardware components.

5. *Physical Storage Load:* The storage and processing of tick data creates serious demands on disk space. Although still very expensive, the solid-state disk technology is helping to reduce the IO time. For data used for off-line research and analysis, it is increasingly wise to use cloud computing solutions discussed below.

29.2.2 The Edge of Technology

Hardware is constantly evolving and improving and any particular detail and focus can become obsolete quite quickly. Not only is the traditional sequential Von Neumann computer architecture benefiting from the super-exponential Moore's Law but new computing paradigms are emerging. Such new paradigms involve their own hardware and will coevolve with it. The so-far elusive quantum computing uses detection of elementary particle states (like spin). The DNA computing uses wetware in the form of a test tube full of floating DNA molecules. The very promising advances in systemic computing use reconfigurable chips (FPGAs).

To further increase the efficiency and reduce the latency for automated electronic trading, the edge of hardware technology is an exciting avenue to explore and to exploit.

Cloud Computing   The cloud has essentially been floating around since the advent of ArpaNet, the defense precursor of the Internet. It is only recently that cloud computing (actually mostly storage) capabilities have been accessible to the larger public. The increasing amount of data, useful or useless, being generated by the digitization of almost everything has lead to the necessity of using an outsourced distributed memory cache, which is the cloud.

Per its design, cloud computing is useful for at least two activities underpinning automated trading: data storage and research. It is not necessary any more to buy petabytes of disk space to store tick data nor a supercomputer to analyze them. One could use a cloud to store it and run simulations on it remotely and in parallel.

Access to the cloud is performed via the network and is subject to the corresponding latency that one cannot control. Theoretically any non–latency-sensitive layer of the trading node could be outsourced to the cloud. However, issues remain about security, privacy, and potential loss of data for clouds operated by third parties. Hence it is better to avoid using public clouds for storing or processing proprietary information.

Massive Parallelism and GPUs   The advent of graphics processing units was spurred by the increasing need for three-dimensional image rendering in the computer gaming industry. GPUs were introduced to recalculate every pixel in parallel on the screen so that very high quality video with life-like motions, shading, and reflections could be achieved.

Since then, general purpose GPUs have been used for other massively parallel computations. Many problems in a variety of fields ranging from fluid dynamics to artificial life are amenable to natural parallelization.

The usual architecture of a GPU-endowed computer is simply a normal computer that has a CPU and an additional GPU processor. APIs are designed to broker between the CPU and the GPU in such a way that blocks of code that are marked as parallel are automatically channelled to the GPU.

Swarm systems introduced in this book are a very natural example of massively parallel processes. The action of event consumption can be parallelized between each member of the swarm.

FPGAs and Programmable Hardware   Field programmable gate arrays are chips that have a large amount of standard binary logic gates (AND, NAND, OR, XOR) that are all a priori interconnected. There is essentially a potential wire or an unobstructed path between each component. Any algorithm can be represented by a combination of memory storage and a series of logical binary operations.

An FPGA allows physical representation of an algorithm by connecting the relevant wires between relevant logic gates. This technology replaces the sequential program where the CPU would call the different logical functions turn by turn by a specialized hardware solution that embodies the algorithm. The resulting speed acceleration could be up to 500 times faster on the modern commercial FPGA chips.

Once the chip is burned for a particular algorithm, it can be subsequently modified to another algorithm if needed. However, the modification process is very slow compared to the execution time of the algorithm. Hence it is better to use FPGAs for algorithms that are not changing from one usage to another. By this it is meant that the logical (or tree) structure of the algorithm remains the same but numeric or symbolic parameters could change. The underlying language used to design the FPGA chip configuration is called Hardware Definition Language (HDL) and there are various APIs available for standard programming languages like C++, Java, and LISP.

FPGAs have been entering the finance arena for the last few years and I expect the trend to continue. For example, they are used for fast (almost real-time) Monte Carlo simulations of options and other derivative pricing.

For the automated trading architecture presented in this book, FPGAs have at least two natural places: the FIX and specific ECN translation can be coded into the FPGA. Hence the whole translation layer can be replaced by an FPGA purpose-made chip. That chip will have to be reconfigured each time a new ECN connection that uses a different protocol is needed. The decision engine, and in particular the swarm system, can be also burned to a specific FPGA. In the swarm, the collection of nonadaptive agents that represent the set of potential behaviors does not change often, so the chip does not need to be reconfigured unless new members are added.

I am currently researching the exciting avenues of GPUs and FPGAs for designing conditional market-making strategies that change behavior using a swarm of lower-frequency signaling strategies.

Auxiliary LISP Functions

This appendix describes auxiliary functions that were used in the various functions, generic functions and class definitions in the book. All the other functions used are the standard ANSI Common LISP functions and come embedded in any open source (e.g. CMUCL, SBCL etc.) or privately developed (AllegroCL, LispWorks etc.) common LISP environment.

Summation of a list where optionally one can transform each element by the transformer-function

```
(proclaim '(inline sum-list))
(defun sum-list (lst &optional (transformer-
function #'(lambda (x) x)))
  (if (null lst)
     0
   (reduce #'+ (mapcar transformer-function lst)))))
```

Averaging of a list where optionally one can transform each element by the transformer-function

```
(proclaim '(inline avg-list))
(defun avg-list (lst &optional (transformer-
function #'(lambda (x) x)))
  (if (null lst)
     0
   (/ (sum-list lst transformer-function) (length lst)))))
```

General append macro L,e -> L := (L e)

```
(defmacro list-append (L e)
  '(setf ,L (append ,L (list ,e))))
```

for macro and its auxiliary form

```
(defmacro for-aux (index-name from-index to-index &rest body)
 '(let ((sign (if (>= ,to-index ,from-index) 1 -1)))
    (dotimes (counter (+ (abs(- ,to-index ,from-index)) 1))
      (let ((,index-name (+ (* counter sign) ,from-index)))
           ,@body))))
(defmacro for (index-defs-list &rest body)
 '(for-aux ,(first ',index-defs-list) ,(second ',index-defs-list)
,(third ',index-defs-list) ,@body))
```

Sublist function (start-index and end-index are inclusive)

```
(defun sub-list (lst start-index end-index)
 (if (< end-index start-index)
    NIL
  (let ((result NIL)
        (L (length lst)))
    (when (< start-index L)
      (for (i start-index (min end-index (- L 1)))
           (list-append result (nth i lst))))
    result)))
```

case macro with test "equal" instead of standard with test "eq":

```
(defmacro case-equal (exp &body clauses)
 (let ((temp (gensym)))
  '(let ((,temp ,exp))
    (cond ,@(mapcar #'(lambda (clause)
            (destructuring-bind (keys . clause-forms) clause
                              (cond ((eq keys 'otherwise)
                                     '(t ,@clause-forms))
                                    (t
                                    (if (atom keys) (setq keys
                                        (list keys)))
                                    '((member ,temp ',keys
                                      :test #'equal)
                                      ,@clause-forms)))))
            clauses)))))
```

Julian Date Utilities and transformation between human-readable time stamps and Julian Dates.

```
(defun date-components (YYYYMMDD)
 (multiple-value-bind (YYYY MMDD)
```

```
    (truncate YYYYMMDD 10000)
  (multiple-value-bind (MM DD)
          (truncate MMDD 100)
    (values YYYY MM DD)))))
```

Julian date calculator (days from 01-Jan-1900)

```
(let ((days-in-months '(31 28 31 30 31 30 31 31 30 31 30 31)))
  (defun julian-day (YYYYMMDD)
    (multiple-value-bind (YYYY MM DD)
          (date-components YYYYMMDD)
      (let ((num-years-since-1900 (- YYYY 1900)))
          (multiple-value-bind (division-int division-rest)
              (truncate num-years-since-1900 4)
              (let* ((this-year-leap-p (zerop division-rest))
                      (num-leap-years-since-1900 (if this-year-leap-p
division-int (+ division-int 1)))
                      (num-days-since-year-began (+ DD
                                                (sum-list (sub-list
days-in-months 0 (- MM 2)))
                                                (if (and this-year-
leap-p (> MM 2)) 1 0))))
                (values (+ num-days-since-year-began
                            num-leap-years-since-1900
                            (* 365 num-years-since-1900))
                        num-days-since-year-began
                        num-leap-years-since-1900
                        num-years-since-1900)))))))
```

Fraction-of-day since midnight

```
(defun f-h-m (HHNN)
  (multiple-value-bind (HH NN)
    (truncate HHNN 100)
    (/ (+ (* HH 60) NN) (* 24 60))))
```

Universal timestamp using julian date and fraction of day after midnight

```
(defun u-d-h-m (YYYYMMDDHHNN)
  (multiple-value-bind (YYYYMMDD HHNN)
    (truncate YYYYMMDDHHNN 10000)
  (coerce (+ (julian-day YYYYMMDD) (f-h-m HHNN)) 'double-float)))
```

Trade Statistics calculations

Trade data structure

```lisp
(defstruct TRADE
 timestamp
 price
 quantity
 description)

(defun aggregate-trades (trades-list)
 (let* ((trades-list-sorted (sort trades-list #'(lambda (x y)
                                                 (>= (trade-timestamp x)
(trade-timestamp y)))))
      (agg-timestamp (trade-timestamp (first trades-list-sorted)))
      (agg-quantity (sum-list trades-list-sorted #'trade-quantity))
      (agg-description (concatenate 'string
                          "AGG_"
                          (flatten-list-to-string
                          (mapcar #'trade-description
trades-list-sorted))))
      (agg-price (/ (sum-list trades-list-sorted #'(lambda (x)
(* (trade-price x)
                                                 (trade-quantity x))))
                  agg-quantity)))
  (make-trade
   :timestamp agg-timestamp
   :price agg-price
   :quantity agg-quantity
   :description agg-description)))
```

Trade Stats structure (all cumulative numbers)

```lisp
(defstruct TRADESTAT
 percent-profitable
 win-to-loss
 average-logret
 tot-pl
 average-duration
 pos-pl
 neg-pl
 profit-factor)
```

Integrates a vector in a reverse-chronological order.

```lisp
(defun rc-integrate (rc-vector)
 (let ((L (length rc-vector))
          (integral 0)
```

```
                     (result NIL))
      (for (i (- L 1) 0)
                 (incf integral (nth i rc-vector))
                 (push integral result))
      result))
```

Routine that calculates trade statistics from a list of trades given either in reverse-chronological or chronological list. Splits trades by adding dummy trades so as to keep exact groups. Assumes initial position is zero.

```
(defun compute-tradestats (trds-list &key (rc T))
(let* ((trades-list (if rc (reverse trds-list) trds-list))
        (L (length trades-list))
        (num-trades-groups 0)
        (trades-groups-list NIL)
        (trades-groups-stats-list NIL)
        (current-group NIL)
        (new-position 0)
        (old-position 0)
        (ts NIL))
(for (i 0 (- L 1))
          (let ((new-trade (nth i trades-list))
                (dummy-trade-1 NIL)
                (dummy-trade-2 NIL))
           (setf new-position (+ old-position (trade-quantity
new-trade)))
           (if(zerop new-position)
              (progn
                  (list-append current-group new-trade)
                  (list-append trades-groups-list current-group)
                  (setf current-group NIL))
            (if (< (* old-position new-position) 0)
                   (progn
                     (setf dummy-trade-1 (make-trade :timestamp
(trade-timestamp new-trade)
                                       :quantity (- old-position)
                                       :price (trade-price new-trade)
                                       :description "Dummy1"))
                     (setf dummy-trade-2 (make-trade :timestamp
(trade-timestamp new-trade)
                                       :quantity new-position
                                       :price (trade-price new-trade)
                                       :description "Dummy2"))
                     (list-append current-group dummy-trade-1)
                     (list-append trades-groups-list current-group)
                     (setf current-group (list dummy-trade-2)))
               (if (= i (- L 1))
                     (progn
```

```lisp
                          (setf dummy-trade-2 (make-trade :timestamp
(trade-timestamp new-trade)
                                           :quantity (- new-position)
                                           :price (trade-price new-trade)
                                           :description "Dummy2"))
                    (list-append current-group new-trade)
                    (list-append current-group dummy-trade-2)
                    (list-append trades-groups-list current-group))
                  (list-append current-group new-trade))))
       (setf old-position new-position)))
(setf num-trades-groups (length trades-groups-list))
(for (i 0  (- num-trades-groups 1))
    (let* ((trades-group (nth i trades-groups-list))
           (buys (remove-if #'(lambda (x) (< (trade-
quantity x) 0)) trades-group))
           (sells (remove-if #'(lambda (x)
(> (trade-quantity x) 0)) trades-group))
           (avg-buy-price (avg-list buys #'(lambda (x) (trade-price x))))
           (avg-sell-price (avg-list sells  #'(lambda (x)
(trade-price x))))
           (avg-buy-index (avg-list buys  #'(lambda (x)
(trade-timestamp x))))
           (avg-sell-index (avg-list sells #'(lambda (x)
(trade-timestamp x))))
           (trade-length (abs (- avg-buy-index avg-sell-index)))
           (trade-logret (log (if (equal avg-buy-price 0) 1
(/ avg-sell-price avg-buy-price))))
           (trade-pl (sum-list trades-group  #'(lambda (x)
(- (* (trade-price x) (trade-quantity x)))))))
    (format T "TRDS GRP 'A : 'A '%" i trades-group)
    (list-append trades-groups-stats-list (list trade-length
trade-logret trade-pl))
    (format T "'A 'A 'A'%" trade-length trade-logret trade-pl)))
(labels ((positive-p (x)
           (if (>= (third x) 0) 1 0))
         (positivepl (x)
           (if (>= (third x) 0) (third x) 0))
         (negativepl (x)
           (if (< (third x) 0) (- (third x)) 0)))
(let* ((percent-profitable (avg-list trades-groups-stats-
list #'positive-p))
       (pos-pl (sum-list trades-groups-stats-list #'positivepl))
       (neg-pl (sum-list trades-groups-stats-list #'negativepl))
       (win-to-loss (if (<= neg-pl EPSILON) 100 (/ pos-pl neg-pl)))
       (average-logret (avg-list trades-groups-stats-list #'second))
       (tot-pl (sum-list trades-groups-stats-list #'third))
       (average-duration (avg-list trades-groups-stats-list #'first))
       (profit-factor (if (<= (+ pos-pl neg-pl) EPSILON) 0
(/ (- pos-pl neg-pl) (+ pos-pl neg-pl)))))
    (setf ts (make-TRADESTAT :percent-profitable percent-profitable
```

```
                    :win-to-loss win-to-loss
                    :average-logret average-logret
                    :tot-pl tot-pl
                    :average-duration average-duration
                    :pos-pl pos-pl
                    :neg-pl neg-pl
                    :profit-factor profit-factor))
    (format T "new tradestat 'S'%" ts)
    ts))))
```

Finally the ts-plot function is implementation dependent and results in plotting a time series graph on a GUI. It can be written directly in AllegroCL or SBCL using the graphic classes. In CMUCL one can output data to a flat file then use a script invoking GnuPlot, the open source graphics package.

Bibliography

Abell, Howard. *The Day Trader's Advantage*. Chicago: Dearborn, 2000.

Abelson, Harold, Gerald J. Sussman, and Julie Sussman. *Structure and Interpretation of Computer Programs*. Cambridge, MA: MIT Press, 1996.

Adamatzky, Andrew, and Macej Komosinski. Eds. *Artificial Life Models in Software*. New York: Springer, 2005.

Ainsworth, Ralph. *Profitable Grain Trading*. Greenville, SC: Traders Press, 1980.

Aldridge, Irene. *High Frequency Trading*. New York: John John Wiley & Sons & Sons, 2010.

Aleksander, Igor. *How to build a Mind*. New York: Columbia University Press, 2001.

Alesina, Alberto, and Enrico Spolaore. *The Size of Nations*. Cambridge, MA: MIT Press, 2005.

Alpaydin, Ethen. *Introduction to Machine Learning*. Cambridge, MA: MIT Press, 2004.

Anderson, Juel. *Trading, Sex and Dying*. New York: John John Wiley & Sons & Sons, 1998.

Ansbacher, Max. *The New Options Market*. New York: John John Wiley & Sons & Sons, 2000.

Artus, Patrick. *Anomalies sur les Marches Financiers*. Paris: Economica, 1995.

Astrom, Karl. *Introduction to Stochastic Control Theory*. New York: Dover, 1970.

Axelrod, Robert. *The Evolution of Cooperation*. New York: Perseus Books, 1984.

Babcock, Bruce. *The Four Cardinal Principles of Trading*. New York: McGraw-Hill, 1996.

Bagehot, Walter. *Lombard Street*. New York: John John Wiley & Sons & Sons, 1999.

Beckey, George, Henrik Christensen, Edmund Durfee, David Kortenkamp, and Michael Wooldridge. *Autonomous Bidding Agents*. Cambridge, MA: MIT Press, 2007.

Bellman, Richard. *Dynamic Programming*. New York: Dover, 2003.

Bent, Russell, and Pascal van Hentenryck. *Online Stochastic Combinatorial Optimization*. Cambridge, MA: MIT Press, 2006.

Bentley, Peter. *Evolutionary Design by Computers*. San Francisco: Morgan Kauffmann Inc., 1999.

Bishop, Christopher. *Neural Networks for Pattern Recognition*. Oxford: Oxford University Press, 1995.

Bonnabeau, Eric, Marco Dorigo, and Guy Theraulaz. *Swarm Intelligence*. New York: Oxford University Press, 1999.

Borsellino, Lewis. *The Day Trader*. New York: John Wiley & Sons, 1999.

Borsellino, Lewis. *The Day Trader's Course*. New York: John Wiley & Sons, 2001.

Bouchaud, Jean-Philippe, and Marc Potters. *Theorie des Risques Financiers*. Paris: Alea Saclay, 1997.

Brabazon, Anthony, and Michael O'Neill. *Biologically Inspired Algorithms for Financial Modelling*. New York: Springer, 1998.

Brockman, John. *The Next Fifty Years*. London: Phoenix, 2003.

Brockman, John. *Life, What a Concept!* New York: Edge, 2007.

Brooks, John. *The Go-Go Years*. New York: John Wiley & Sons, 1973.

Brooks, Rodney. *Cambrian Intelligence*. Cambridge, MA: MIT Press, 1999.

Brown, Julian. *Minds, Machines and the Multiverse*. New York: Simon and Schuster, 2000.

Bubnicki, Z. *Modern Control Theory*. New York: Springer, 2005.

Butz, Martin, and Olivier Sigaudand Pierre Gerard. Eds. *Anticipatory Behavior in Adaptive Learning Systems*. New York: Springer, 2003.

Camazine, Scott, Jean-Louis Deneubourg, Nigel R. Franks, James Snade, Guy Theraulaz, and Eric Bonabeau. *Self-Organization in Biological Systems*. Princeton: Princeton University Press, 2001.

Caplan, David. *The New Options Advantage*. New York: McGraw-Hill, 1995.

Carroll, Terry. *NLP For Traders and Investors*. London: TTL, 2000.

Chande, Tushar. *Beyond Technical Analysis*. New York: John Wiley & Sons, 2001.

Charniak, Eugene. *Statistical Language Learning*. Cambridge, MA: MIT Press, 1993.

Collins, Art. *Market Rap*. Greenville, SC: Traders Press, 2000.

Collins, Art. *When Supertraders meet Kryptonite*. Greenville, SC: Traders Press, 2002.

Colman, Andrew. *Game Theory and its Applications*. Butterworth-Heinemann, London, 1999.

Connors, Laurence, and Linda Bradford Rashke. *Street Smarts*. Los Angeles: M Gordon Publishing Group, 1995.

Conway, Mark, and Aaron Behle. *Professional Stock Trading*. Waltham, MA: Acme Trader LLC, 2003.

Covel, Michael. *Trend Following*. London: Prentice Hall, 2004.

Coveney, Peter, and Roger Highfield. *Frontiers of Complexity*. New York: Ballantine, 1999.

Crabbe, Paddy. *Metals Trading Handbook*. Boca Raton, FL: CRC Press, 1999.

Cragg, Richard. *The Demographic Investor*. London: FT-Pitman Publishing, 1998.

Cristianini, Nello, and John Shalle-Taylor. *Support Vector Machines*. Cambridge: Cambridge University Press, 2000.

Davalo, Eric, and Patrick Naim. *Des Resaux de Neurones*. Paris: Eyrolles, 1989.

David, F.N. *Games, Gods and Gambling*. New York: Dover, 1998.

Davis, Morton. *Game Theory*. New York: Dover, 1997.

Dawkins, Richard. *The Selfish Gene*. Oxford: Oxford University Press, 1976.

DeMark, Thomas. *The New Science of Technical Analysis*. New York: John Wiley & Sons, 1994.

DeMark, Thomas. *New Market Timing Techniques*. New York: John Wiley & Sons, 1997.

DeMark, Thomas, and Thomas DeMark Jr. *DeMark on Day Trading Options*. New York: McGraw-Hill, 1999.

Distin, Kate. *The Selfish Meme*. Cambridge: Cambridge University Press, 2005.

Dorigo, Marco, and Marco Colombetti. *Robot Shaping*. Cambridge, MA: MIT Press, 1998.

Doya, Kenji, Shin Ishii, Alexandre Pouget, and Rajesh P.N. Rao. *Bayesian Brain*. Cambridge, MA: MIT Press, 2007.

Dreman, David. *Contrarian Investment Strategies*. New York: Simon and Schuster, 1998.

Drew, Garfield. *New Methods for Profit in the Stock Market*. Burlington, VT: Fraser Publishing, 1966.

Drobny, Steven. *Inside the House of Money*. New York: John Wiley & Sons, 2006.

Duffie, Darrell. *Security Markets: Stochastic Models*. London: Academic Press, 1988.

Duffie, Darrell. *Dynamic Asset Pricing Theory*. Princeton: Princeton University Press, 1992.

Dunbar, Nicholas. *Inventing Money*. New York: John Wiley & Sons, 2000.

Dyson, Freeman. *Origins of Life*. Cambridge: Cambridge University Press, 1999.

Ehlers, John. *Rocket Science for Traders*. New York: John Wiley & Sons, 2001.

Ehlers, John. *MESA and trading Market Cycles*. New York: John Wiley & Sons, 2002.

Ehlers, John. *Cybernetic Analysis of Stocks and Futures*. New York: John Wiley & Sons, 2004.

Eiben, A.E., and J.E. Smith. *Introduction to Evolutionary Computing*. New York: Springer, 2003.

Ekbia, Hammond. *Artificial Dreams*. Cambridge: Cambridge University Press, 2008.

Elder, Alexander. *Trading for a Living*. New York: John Wiley & Sons, 1993.

Elder, Alexander. *Trading For a Living: Study Guide*. New York: John Wiley & Sons, 1994.

Eliasmith, Chris, and Charles H. Anderson. *Neural Engineering*. Cambridge, MA: MIT Press, 2003.

Ellis, Charles, and James Vertin. *Wall Street People* (2 volumes). Hoboken, NJ: John Wiley & Sons, 2003.

Eng, William. *Trading Rules*. Chicago: Dearborn, 1990.

Eng, William. *The Day Trader's Manual*. New York: John Wiley & Sons, 1993.

Eng, William. *Trading Rules II*. Chicago: Dearborn, 1996.

Engelbrecht, Andries. *Computational Intelligence*. Hoboken, NJ: John Wiley & Sons, 2007.

Epstein, Joshua, and Robert Axtell. *Growing Artificial Societies*. Cambridge, MA: MIT Press, 1996.

Demange, Gabrielle, and Jean-Charles Rochet. *Methodes Mathematiques de la Finance*. Paris: Economica, 1997.

Falloon, William. *Charlie D, The Story of the Legendary Bond Trader*. New York: John Wiley & Sons, 1997.

Farmer, Roger. *Macroeconomics of Self-Fulfilling Prophecies*. Cambridge, MA: MIT Press, 1993.

Farrell, Christopher. *Day-Trade Online*. New York: John Wiley & Sons, 1999.

Feldman, David. *The Ups and Downs*. Burlington, VT: Fraser Publishing, 1997.

Ferguson, Brian, and G.C. Lim. *Dynamic Economic Models*. Manchester: Manchester University Press, 1998.

Fisher, Mark. *The Logical Trader*. Hoboken, NJ: John Wiley & Sons, 2002.

Flake, Gary-William. *The Computational Beauty of Nature*. Cambridge, MA: MIT Press, 1998.

Forbes, Nancy. *Imitation of Life*. Cambridge, MA: MIT Press, 2005.

Forbus, Kenneth, and Johann de Kleer. *Building Problem Solvers*. Cambridge, MA: MIT Press, 1993.

Ford, Kenneth, Clark Glymour, and Patrick J. Hayes. *Thinking about Android Epistemology*. Cambridge, MA: MIT Press, 2006.

Fraser, James. *Crises and Panics*. Burlington, VT: Fraser Publishing, 1965.

Frost, A.J., and Robert Prechter. *Elliott Wave Principle*. New York: John Wiley & Sons, 1998.

Galbraith, John-Kenneth. *The Great Crash 1929*. London: Penguin, 1992.

Gallacher, William. *Winner Take All*. New York: McGraw-Hill, 1994.

Gallea, Anthony. *Bulls Make Money, Bears Make Money, Pigs Get Slaughtered*. New York: New York Institute of Finance, 2002.

Gann, William. *45 Years in Wall Street*. Pomeroy, WA: Lambert-Gann, 1976.

Gann, William. *Truth of the Stock Tape*. Pomeroy, WA: Lambert-Gann, 1977.

Geisst, Richard. *Wheels of Fortune*. Hoboken, NJ: John Wiley & Sons, 2002.

Glasserman, Paul. *Monte Carlo Methods in Financial Engineering*. New York: Springer, 2004.

Glimcher, Paul. *Decisions, Uncertainty and the Brain*. Cambridge, MA: MIT Press, 2004.

Gold, Gerald. *Modern Commodity Futures Trading*. New York: Commodity Research Bureau, 1975.

Graham, Paul. *On LISP*. New York: Prentice Hall, 1993.

Graham, Paul. *ANSI Common LISP*. New York: Prentice Hall, 1996.

Graham, Paul. *Hackers and Painters*. Sebastopol, CA: O'Reilly, 2004.

Graifer, Vadym, and Christopher Schumacher. *Techniques of Tape Reading*. New York: McGraw-Hill, 2004.

Grant, James. *The Trouble with Prosperity*. New York: John Wiley & Sons, 1996.

Grauwe, Paul De, and Marianna Grimaldi. *Exchange Rates in a Behavioral Finance Framework*. Princeton: Princeton University Press, 2006.

Greene, Robert. *48 Laws of Power*. London: Penguin, 1998.

Greene, Robert. *The Art of Seduction*. London: Penguin, 2003.

Greene, Robert. *The 33 Strategies of War*. London: Penguin, 2006.

Gross, William. *Bill Gross on Investing*. New York: John Wiley & Sons, 1998.

Guillot, Agnes, and Jean-Arcady Meyer. *How to Catch a Robot Rat*. Cambridge, MA: MIT Press, 2010.

Gyllenram, Carl. *Trading with Crowd Psychology*. New York: John Wiley & Sons, 2001.

Hall, J. Storrs. *Beyond AI*. New York: Prometheus Books, 2007.

Hamilton, William-Peter. *The Stock Market Barometer*. New York: John Wiley & Sons, 1998.

Hastie, Trevor, Robert Tibsherani, and Jerome Friedman. *The Elements of Statistical Learning*. New York: Springer, 2001.

Haug, Espen-Gaarder. *Derivatives: Models on Models*. New York: John Wiley & Sons, 2007.

Hecht-Nielsen, Robert. *Confabulation Theory*. New York: Springer, 2007.

Heilbronner, Robert. *The Worldly Philosophers*. New York: Simon and Schuster, 1992.

Helweg, Mark, and David Stendahl. *Dynamic Trading Indicators*. Hoboken, NJ: John Wiley & Sons, 2002.

Herbst, Anthony. *Analysing and Forecasting Futures Prices*. Lincoln, NE: Authors Guild, 2000.

Hill, John, George Pruitt, and Lundy Hill. *The Ultimate Trading Guide*. New York: John Wiley & Sons, 2000.

Hirshleifer, Jack, and John G. Riley. *The Analytics of Uncertainty and Information*. Cambridge: Cambridge University Press, 1992.

Hoffman, Michael, and Gerald Baccetti. *Pit Trading: Do You Have the Right Stuff?* Greenville, SC: Traders Press, 1999.

Holland, John. *Emergence*. Oxford: Oxford University Press, 1998.

Holzner, Steve. *Design Pattern for Dummies*. Hoboken, NJ: John Wiley & Sons, 2006.

Homer, Sydney, and Richard Sylla. *A History of Interest Rates*. New Brunswick, NJ: Rutgers University Press, 1996.

Huang, Chi-Fu, and Robert Litzenberger. *Foundations for Financial Economics*. Englewood Cliffs, NJ: Prentice Hall, 1988.

Hull, John. *Options, Futures and other Derivative Securities*. London: Prentice Hall, 1997.

Ilinski, Kirill. *Physics of Finance*. Hoboken, NJ: John Wiley & Sons, 2001.

Jablonka, Eva, and Marion J. Lamb. *Evolution in Four Dimensions*. Cambridge, MA: MIT Press, 2006.

Jenks, Philip, and Stephen Eckett. *Investing Rules*. London: Global Investor, 2001.

Johnston, John. *The Allure of Machinic Life*. Cambridge, MA: MIT Press, 2008.

Jones, Ryan. *The Trading Game*. New York: John Wiley & Sons, 1999.

Steele Jr., Guy. *Common LISP*. New York: Digital Press, 1990.

Wilder Jr., Welles. *New Concepts in Technical Trading Systems*. North Carolina: Hunter Publishing Co, 1978.

Kaeppel, Jay. *The Four Biggest Mistakes in Furtures Trading*. Ellicott City, MD: Marketplace Books, 2000.

Katz, Jeffrey-Owen, and Donna McCormick. *The Encyclopedia of Trading Strategies*. New York: McGraw-Hill, 2000.

Kauffman, Stuart. *Investigations*. Oxford: Oxford University Press, 2000.

Kaufman, Perry. *Smarter Trading*. New York: McGraw-Hill, 1995.

Kaufman, Perry. *Trading Systems and Methods*. New York: John Wiley & Sons, 1998.

Kempf, Hubert, and William Marois. *Monnaie, Taux d'Interet et Anticipations.* Paris: Economica, 1992.

Kestner, Lars. *Quantitative Trading Strategies.* New York: McGraw-Hill, 2003.

Khinchin, A.I. *Mathematical Foundations of Information Theory.* New York: Dover, 1957.

Kiev, Ari. *Trading to Win.* New York: John Wiley & Sons, 1998.

Kiev, Ari. *Trading in The Zone.* Hoboken, NJ: John Wiley & Sons, 2001.

Kiev, Ari. *The Psychology of Risk.* Hoboken, NJ: John Wiley & Sons, 2002.

Kindelberger, Charles. *Manias, Panics and Crashes.* New York: John Wiley & Sons, 1996.

Kleinfeld, Sonny. *The Traders.* Greenville, SC: Traders Press, 1983.

Koppel, Robert, and Howard Abell. *The Inner Game of Trading.* New York: McGraw-Hill, 1994.

Koppel, Robert, and Howard Abell. *The Outer Game of Trading.* Chicago: Probus Publishing, 1995.

Korb, Kevin, and Ann E. Nicholson. *Bayesian Artificial Intelligence.* New York: Chapman and Hall CRC, 2004.

Koza, John. *Genetic Programming.* Cambridge, MA: MIT Press, 1992.

Koza, John. *Genetic Programming II.* Cambridge, MA: MIT Press, 1994.

Koza, John, Forrest Bennett III, David Andre, and Martin Keene. *Genetic Programming III.* San Francisco: Morgan Kauffmann Inc., 1999.

Koza, John, Martin Keene, Matthew Streeter, William Mydlowec, Jessen Yu, and Guido Lanza. *Genetic Programming IV.* New York: Springer, 2003.

Kreps, David. *Game Theory and Economic Modelling.* Oxford: Oxford University Press, 1990.

Krohs, Ulrich, and Peter Kroes. *Functions in Biological and Artificial Worlds.* Cambridge, MA: MIT Press, 2009.

Kroll, Stanley. *The Professional Commodity Trader.* Greenville, SC: Traders Press, 1974.

Kroll, Stanley. *Kroll on Futures Trading Strategy.* Homewood, IL: Dow Jones-Irwin, 1988.

Krugman, Paul. *Currencies and Crises.* Cambridge, MA: MIT Press, 1995.

Krustinger, Joe. *Trading Systems.* New York: McGraw-Hill, 1997.

Kurzweil, Ray. *The Age of Spiritual Machines.* London: Penguin, 1999.

Kurzweil, Ray. *The Singularity is Near.* London: Penguin, 2005.

Langdon, William, and Ricardo Poli. *Foundations of Genetic Programming.* New York: Springer, 2002.

LeBon, Gustave. *The Psychology of Revolution.* Burlington, VT: Fraser Publishing, 1989.

Lee, Tim. *Economics for Professional Investors.* New York: Prentice Hall, 1998.

Lefevre, Edwin. *Reminiscences of a Stock Operator.* New York: John Wiley & Sons, 1994.

Leinweber, David. *Nerds on Wall Street.* Hoboken, NJ: John Wiley & Sons, 2009.

Levitt, Steven, and Steven Dubner. *Freakonomics.* New York: HarperCollins, 2005.

Li, Deyi, and Yi Du. *Artificial Intelligence with Uncertainty.* New York: Chapman and Hall CRC, 2008.

Lifson, Lawrence, and Richard Geist. *The Psychology of Investing.* New York: John Wiley & Sons, 1999.

Livermore, Jesse, and Richard Smitten. *How to Trade in Stocks.* Greenville, SC: Traders Press, 2001.

Longstreet, Roy. *Viewpoints of a Commodity Trader.* Greenville, SC: Traders Press, 1967.

Lowenstein, Roger. *When Genious Failed.* London: Fourth Estate, 2001.

Josh Lukeman. *The Market Maker's Edge.* New York: McGraw-Hill, 2000.

Mackay, Charles. *Extraordinary Popular Delusions and the Madness of Crowds.* London: Wordsworth, 1995.

MacKay, David. *Information Theory, Inference and Learning Algorithms.* New York: Cambridge University Press, 2003.

Maes, Patti, Maja J. Mataric, Jean-Arcady Meyer, Jordan Pollack, and Stuart Wilson. Eds. *From Animals to Animats 4.* Cambridge, MA: MIT Press, 1996.

Magee, Jeff, and Jeff Kramer. *Concurrency.* Hoboken, NJ: John Wiley & Sons, 2007.

Mak, Don. *Mathematical Techniques in Financial Market Trading.* Singapore: World Scientific, 2006.

Malvergne, Yannick, and Didier Sornette. *Extreme Financial Risks.* New York: Springer, 2006.

Mamon, Rogemar, and Robert J. Elliott. *Hidden Markov Models in Finance.* New York: Springer, 2007.

Mandelbrot, Benoit, and Richard L. Hudson. *The (Mis)-Behavior of Markets.* London: Profile Books, 2005.

Mangot, Mickael. *50 Psychological Experiments for Investors.* Hoboken, NJ: John Wiley & Sons, 2007.

Masover, Hal. *Value Investing in Commodity Futures.* Hoboken, NJ: John Wiley & Sons, 2001.

Mataric, Maja. *The Robotocs Primer.* Cambridge, MA: MIT Press, 2007.

Mathis, Jean. *Finance Internationale.* Paris: ESKA, 1991.

Mayer, Martin. *Markets.* New York: Norton, 1988.

McCall, Richard. *The Way of the Warrior Trader.* New York: McGraw-Hill, 1997.

Meadows, Donella. *Thinking in Systems.* White River Junction, VT: Chelsea Green, 2008.

Medio, Alfredo. *Chaotic Dynamics.* Cambridge: Cambridge University Press, 1992.

Melamed, Leo. *Leo Melamed on The Markets.* New York: John Wiley & Sons, 1993.

Melamed, Leo, and Bob Tamarkin. *Escape to the Futures.* New York: John Wiley & Sons, 1996.

Menchel, Robert. *Markets, Mobs and Mayhem.* Hoboken, NJ: John Wiley & Sons, 2002.

Menzell, Peter, and Faith d'Alusio. *Robo Sapiens.* Cambridge, MA: MIT Press, 2000.

Merton, Robert. *Continuous-Time Finance.* Cambridge, MA: Blackwell, 1992.

Meyer, Jean-Arcady, Herbert L. Roitblat, and Stuart W. Wilson. *From Animals to Animats 2.* Cambridge, MA: MIT Press, 1993.

Minsky, Marvin. *The Society of Mind*. New York: Simon and Schuster, 1985.

Minsky, Marvin. *The Emotion Machine*. New York: Simon and Schuster, 2006.

Mintz, Steven. *Five Eminent Contrarians*. Burlington, VT: Fraser Publishing, 1994.

Mitchell, Melanie. *An Introduction to Genetic Algorithms*. Cambridge, MA: MIT Press, 1996.

Mitchell, William. *ME++*. Cambridge, MA: MIT Press, 2003.

Montier, James. *Behavioural Finance*. Hoboken, NJ: John Wiley & Sons, 2002.

Moravcsik, Julius. *Meaning, Creativity and the Partial Inscrutability of the Human Mind*. Palo Alto, CA: CSLI Publications, 1998.

Moravec, Hans. *Mind Children*. Cambridge, MA: Harvard University Press, 1988.

Moravec, Hans. *Robot*. Oxford: Oxford University Press, 1999.

Murphy, John. *Technical Analysis of the Financial Markets*. New York: New York Institute of Finance, 1999.

Neill, Humphrey. *Tape Reading and Market Tactics*. Burlington, VT: Fraser Publishing, 2002.

Niemeyer, Patrick, and Jonathan Knudsen. *Learning JAVA*. Sebastopol, CA: O'Reilly2005.

Niemira, Michael, and Gerald Zukowski. *Trading the Fundamentals*. New York: McGraw-Hill, 1998.

Noble, Grant. *The Trader's Edge*. New York: McGraw-Hill, 1995.

Nolfi, Stefano, and Dario Florentino. *Evolutionary Robotics*. Cambridge, MA: MIT Press, 2000.

Norvig, Peter. *Artificial Intelligence Programming*. San Francisco: Morgan Kauffmann Inc., 1992.

Nowak, Martin. *Evolutionary Dynamics*. Cambridge, MA: Harvard University Press, 2006.

Padhy, N.P. *Artificial Intelligence and Intelligent Systems*. New York: Oxford University Press, 2005.

Pardo, Robert. *Design, Testing and Optimization of Trading Systems*. New York: John Wiley & Sons, 1992.

Paris, Alexander. *A Complete Guide to Trading Profits*. Greenville, SC: Traders Press, 1970.

Pierce, John. *An Introduction to Information Theory*. New York: Dover, 1980.

Plummer, Tony. *The Psychology of Technical Analysis*. New York: McGraw-Hill, 1993.

Prechter, Robert. *The Wave Principle of Human Social Behavior and the New Science of Socionomics*. Gainesville, GA: New Classics Library, 2002.

Pruitt, George, and John Hill. *Building Winning Trading Systems with TradeStation*. Hoboken, NJ: John Wiley & Sons, 2003.

Rapoport, Anatol. *2-Person Game Theory*. Dover, New York, 1996.

Rasmussen, Carl-Edward, and Christopher K.I. Williams. *Gaussian Processes for Machine Learning*. Cambridge, MA: MIT Press, 2006.

Redmond, George. *Stock Market Operators*. FT-London: Prentice Hall, 1999.

Resnick, Mitchell. *Turtles, Termites and Traffic Jams*. Cambridge, MA: MIT Press, 1997.

Rhea, Robert. *The Dow Theory*. Burlington, VT: Fraser Publishing, 2002.

Roehner, Bertrand. *Hidden Collective Factors in Speculative Trading.* New York: Springer, 2001.

Rosen, Robert. *Life Itself.* New York: Columbia University Press, 1991.

Rosen, Robert. *Essays on Life Itself.* New York: Columbia University Press, 2000.

Rotella, Robert. *The Elements of Successful Trading.* New York: New York Institute of Finance, 1992.

Sargent, Thomas. *Bounded Rationality in Macroeconomics.* Oxford: Clarendon Press, 1995.

Sasha, Dennis, and Cathy Lazere. *Natural Computing.* London: Norton, 2010.

Satchwell, Chris. *Pattern Recognition and Trading Decisions.* New York: McGraw-Hill, 2005.

Schenider, Eric, and Dorion Sagan. *Into the Cool.* Chicago: University of Chicago Press, 2005.

Schleifer, Andrei. *Inefficient Markets.* Oxford: Oxford University Press, 2000.

Schroedinger, Erwin. *What is Life.* Cambridge: Cambridge University Press, 1967.

Schultz, Harry, and Samson Coslow. *A Treasury of Wall Street Wisdom.* Greenville, SC: Traders Press, 1996.

Schwager, Jack. *Market Wizards.* New York: Harper Business, 1993.

Schwager, Jack. *The New Market Wizards.* New York: Harper Business, 1994.

Schwager, Jack. *Managed Trading, Myths and Truths.* New York: John Wiley & Sons, 1996.

Schwager, Jack. *Stock Market Wizards.* Hoboken, NJ: John Wiley & Sons, 2001.

Schwartz, Randall, and Tom Phoenix. *Learning Perl.* Sebastopol, CA: O'Reilly, 2001.

Seibel, Peter. *Practical Common LISP.* New York: Apress, 2005.

Shannon, Claude, and Warren Weaver. *The Mathematical Theory of Communication.* Chicago: University of Illinois Press, 1963.

Sharp, Robert. *The Lore and Legends of Wall Street.* Homewood, IL: Dow Jones-Irwin, 1989.

Shelton, Ronald. *Gaming The Market.* New York: John Wiley & Sons, 1997.

Smith, Edgar-Lawrence. *Tides in the Affairs of Men.* Burlington, VT: Fraser Publishing: 1989.

Smith, John Maynard, and Eros Szathmary. *The Origins of Life.* Oxford: Oxford University Press, 1999.

Smitten, Richard. *Jesse Livermore.* Hoboken, NJ: John Wiley & Sons, 2001.

Smitten, Richard. *Trade like Jesse Livermore.* Hoboken, NJ: John Wiley & Sons, 2005.

Sole, Rircard, and Brian Goodwin. *Signs of Life.* New York: Basic Books, 2000.

Sornette, Didier. *Why Stock Markets Crash.* Princeton: Princeton University Press, 2003.

Soros, George. *The Alchemy of Finance.* New York: John Wiley & Sons, 1994.

Soros, George. *The New Paradigm for Financial Markets.* London: Public Affairs, 2008.

Sperandeo, Victor. *Trader Vic—Methods of a Wall Street Master.* New York: John Wiley & Sons, 1991.

Sperandeo, Victor. *Trader Vic II—Methods of a Wall Street Master.* New York: John Wiley & Sons, 1994.

Steidelmayer, Peter. *Steidelmayer on Markets*. Hoboken, NJ: John Wiley & Sons, 2003.

Stigum, Marcia. *Money Market*. New York: McGraw-Hill, 2007.

Stridsman, Thomas. *Trading Systems that Work*. New York: McGraw-Hill, 2001.

Stridsman, Thomas. *Trading Systems and Money Management*. New York: McGraw-Hill, 2003.

Summa, John. *Trading Against the Crowd*. Hoboken, NJ: John Wiley & Sons, 2004.

Sutton, Richard, and Andrew Barto. *Reinforcement Learning*. Cambridge, MA: MIT Press, 1998.

Sweeney, John. *Maximum Adverse Excursion*. New York: John Wiley & Sons, 1997.

Nassim Taleb. *Dynamic Hedging*. New York: John Wiley & Sons, 1997.

Taylor, John. *Monetary Policy Rules*. Chicago: University of Chicago Press, 1999.

Thrun, Sebastan, Wolfram Burgard, and Dieter Fox. *Probabilistic Robotics*. Cambridge, MA: MIT Press, 2005.

Toghraie, Adrienne. *The Winning Edge 4*. Greenville, SC: Traders Press, 2001.

Train, John. *Famous Financial Fiascos*. Burlington, VT: Fraser Publishing, 1995.

Tvede, Lars. *The Psychology of Finance*. Hoboken, NJ: John Wiley & Sons, 2002.

Voit, Johannes. *The Statistical Mechanics of Financial Markets*. New York: Springer, 2003.

vonBertalanffy, Ludwig. *General System Theory*. New York: George Brazillier, 1969.

vonNeumann, John. *The Computer and the Brain*. New Haven: Yale University Press, 1958.

Ware, Jim. *The Psychology of Money*. Hoboken, NJ: John Wiley & Sons, 2001.

Watts, Dickson. *Speculation as a Fine Art*. Burlington, VT: Fraser Publishing, 1979.

Webb, Robert. *Macroeconomic Information and Financial Trading*. Oxford: Blackwell, 1994.

Wei, William. *Time Series Analysis*. New York: Addison Wesley, 1994.

Weintraub, Neal. *Tricks of the Floor Trader*. New York: McGraw-Hill, 1996.

Weintraub, Neal. *Trading Chicago Style*. New York: McGraw-Hill, 1999.

Wiener, Norbert. *Cybernetics*. Cambridge, MA: MIT Press, 1961.

Wiener, Norbert. *God and Golem, Inc*. Cambridge, MA: MIT Press, 1964.

Wiener, Norbert. *The Human Use of Human Beings*. London: FAB, 1989.

Williams, Larry. *The Definitive Guide to Futures Trading*, 2 Volumes. Brightwaters, NY: Windsor Books, 1988.

Williams, Larry. *Long-Term Secrets to Short-Term Trading*. New York: John Wiley & Sons, 1999.

Winograd, Terry, and Fernando Flores. *Understanding Computers and Cognition*. Boston: Addison Wesley, 1986.

Wooldridge, Michael. *Multi-Agent Systems*. Hoboken, NJ: John Wiley & Sons, 2002.

Wright, Russel. *Chronology of the Stock Market*. London: McFarland and Co, 2002.

X., Trader, Dancing with Lions. Novato, CA: Portal Publications, 1999.

Yuen, C.K. *Prallel LISP Systems*. London: Chapman and Hall, 1993.

Zaknich, A. *Principles of Adaptive Filters and Self-Learning Systems*. New York: Springer, 2005.

Zweig, Martin. *Winning on Wall Street*. New York: Warner Books, 1997.

Index

Printed and bound by CPI Group (UK) Ltd, Croydon, CR0 4YY

23/04/2025

14660919-0004